Faulkner and the Craft of Fiction

FAULKNER AND YOKNAPATAWPHA

1987

Faulkner
and the Craft of Fiction

FAULKNER AND YOKNAPATAWPHA, 1987

EDITED BY
DOREEN FOWLER
AND
ANN J. ABADIE

UNIVERSITY PRESS OF MISSISSIPPI
Jackson and London

*This book has been sponsored by the University of Mississippi's
Center for the Study of Southern Culture*

The paper in this book meets the guidelines for permanence and durability of the
Committee on Production Guidelines for Book Longevity of the Council on Library
Resources.

Library of Congress Cataloging-in-Publication Data

Faulkner and the craft of fiction : Faulkner and Yoknapatawpha, 1987 /
    edited by Doreen Fowler and Ann. J. Abadie.
        p.   cm.
    Essays originally presented at the 1987 Faulkner and Yoknapatawpha
Conference, the fourteenth in a series held at the Oxford campus of
the University of Mississippi.
    Includes bibliographical references and index.
    ISBN 0-87805-372-7 (alk. paper).—ISBN 0-87805-373-5 (pbk. :
alk. paper)
    1. Faulkner, William, 1897–1962—Technique—Congresses.
2. Yoknapatawpha County (Imaginary place)—Congresses.   3. Narration
(Rhetoric)—Congresses.   I. Fowler, Doreen.   II. Abadie, Ann J.
III. Faulkner and Yoknapatawpha Conference (14th : 1987 : University
of Mississippi)
PS3511.A86Z78321127   1988
813'.52—dc19   88-36904
                                                                            CIP

British Library Cataloguing-in-Publication data is available.

Contents

Introduction

In 1944 William Faulkner wrote to Malcolm Cowley, "I'm telling the same story over and over which is myself and the world. That's all a writer ever does, he tells his own biography in a thousand different terms."[1] With these words, Faulkner suggests that what changes in the course of his prolific novel-writing career is not so much the content but the style, the "different terms" of his fiction. With each successive novel, Faulkner strove to develop new "terms," new forms for his fictions. Thus, there is no single representative Faulknerian style. Rather, his technique is protean. Constantly experimenting, never satisfied, Faulkner quested throughout his fiction-writing career for the perfect form, "a vase," like the one an old Roman so loved that "he wore slowly [the rim] away with kissing it."[2] And as the shapes of the novels changed, so also did the meaning of his fictions. Technical experimentation constantly led Faulkner to ask new questions and to see his imagined world from new and different perspectives.

Faulkner never repeats himself. In 1929 American readers found themselves confronted with a novel unlike any they had ever known before as they opened *The Sound and the Fury* and read, "Through the fence, between the curling flower spaces, I could see them hitting." Immediately there followed *As I Lay Dying* (1930), a bizarre melding of comedy and tragedy, the story of a mother's passing and her family's grief, formulated in the manner of classical comedy. In his next novel, *Sanctuary* (1931), a feverishly pitched, intensely suspenseful drama, Faulkner manipulates the conventions of detective fiction; in *Light in August* (1932), he turns to a more leisurely storytelling mode, reminiscent of nineteenth-century writers like Balzac; in *Absalom, Ab-*

salom! (1936), Faulkner, eschewing all fictive models, fashions a novel that is itself an inquiry into knowing and telling; in *The Wild Palms* (1939), he creates a form "contrapuntal in integration,"[3] making a coherent whole of two seemingly unrelated narratives; in *The Hamlet* (1940), he experiments with the pastoral; and in *Go Down, Moses* (1942), with the folk tale. Relentlessly, in novel after novel, Faulkner explored one narrative possibility after another, testing and challenging traditional notions of storytelling and pushing the novel form to its limits. Throughout a career that produced some twenty novels, Faulkner, like Benjy, unceasingly kept "trying to say."

Various dimensions of Faulkner's rich narrative inventiveness are explored in the essays in this volume, which were originally presented by scholars at the 1987 Faulkner and Yoknapatawpha Conference, the fourteenth in a series of conferences held on the Oxford campus of the University of Mississippi.

Who better to open the volume than Cleanth Brooks, whose *William Faulkner: The Yoknapatawpha Country* (1963) influenced a generation of Faulkner scholars? Brooks's essay, which addresses the issue of perspective in Faulkner's works, begins by recalling that William Empson defined the essence of the pastoral as a matter of perspective: in the pastoral the reader stands at a higher, more sophisticated plane from that occupied by the unsophisticated people written about. Extending this claim in the opposite direction, Brooks asserts that "in the heroic mode the author turns his gaze upward and writes about beings that are extraordinary, larger than life, even heroic." Applying this definition to *The Unvanquished*, Brooks argues compellingly that in this novel Faulkner experiments with perspective and fuses the real with the ideal: Bayard Sartoris, for example, does not belong to an imagined, mythical realm; he does not consort with wood nymphs or fairies; nevertheless, he manages to achieve heroic status.

Perhaps the most important work of Faulkner criticism since Brooks's contribution is John T. Irwin's *Doubling and Incest/ Repetition and Revenge* (1976), a Freudian reading that identifies a pattern of repetition in Faulkner's fiction, with the son becoming the father, the victim becoming the victimizer. Building on Irwin's findings, two essayists, Donald Kartiganer and Richard Moreland, focus on Faulkner's use of repetition. In "Faulkner's Art of Repetition," Kartiganer first recalls Kierkegaard's distinction between a recollection—a duplication of the past without change—and a repetition forward—a revision of the past in a new key so that "the past is rewritten, becoming a part of a new narrative expanding into the future." Applying Kierkegaard's definition to Faulkner, Kartiganer maintains that nearly all of the novels, with the striking exception of *The Sound and the Fury*, can be characterized as repetitions forward. Selecting *As I Lay Dying* as a representative example, Kartiganer demonstrates how this novel can be read as a revisionary text. In a companion essay, "Compulsive and Revisionary Repetition: Faulkner's 'Barn Burning' and the Craft of Writing Difference," Richard Moreland, making a distinction similar to Kartiganer's using the terms compulsive and revisionary repetition, contends that "Barn Burning" represents the moment in Faulkner's career when he turned from one kind of repetition to the other. In "Barn Burning" Faulkner repeats with a difference the scene of social silencing and exclusion enacted in *Absalom, Absalom!*, when the young sharecropper, Thomas Sutpen, is barred from the planter's door. As it is written in *Absalom, Absalom!*, Thomas Sutpen compulsively repeats the act of exclusion, becoming the planter and barring the door to Charles Bon; but when Faulkner returns to this scene again in "Barn Burning," published three years after *Absalom*, the oppressive primal scene is reconceived. Unlike Thomas Sutpen, Ab Snopes refuses to be silenced or repressed and leaves his signature on the planter's rug, forcing the unwilling planter to recognize his humanity.

Moreland's discussion of a sharecropper's private revolt against an oppressive social system appropriately introduces the next three essays, which attempt to relate Faulkner's craft to the social and historical realities of his culture. Each of these essays addresses the question—to what extent is Faulkner's craft informed by social and cultural contexts? In "Faulkner's Narrative Frames," John Matthews argues that Faulkner typically uses a host of framing devices, like the narrator who relays another's story or narrative trappings such as appendices, notes, introductions, etc., "to introduce the social and historical contexts kept at bay by the narrative's longing for purity." Matthews analyzes Quentin Compson's position as frame narrator in three stories that succeed *The Sound and the Fury*,—"That Evening Sun," "A Justice," and "Lion"—and identifies a contradictory impulse inherent in Faulkner's use of frames. Even as the frame attempts to comprehend the historical background—the social order, racism, white superiority, social victimization—it also works to resist comprehension at the same time. "In Faulkner's texts, the frame often forecloses precisely what it promises to open." In a related essay, "A Trap Most Magnificently Sprung: The Last Chapter of *Light in August*," Chris Lalonde examines Faulkner's use of one particular framing device. In the closing chapter of *Light in August*, Faulkner, after having related twenty chapters through the eyes of an omniscient narrator, abruptly introduces a new narrator, a furniture salesman. To this new narrator, the proverbial travelling salesman, Lena represents a threat to masculine control "because of her denial of the power men receive from both intercourse and discourse." By means of this framing narrator, then, by trapping Lena within "the confines of the bantering, sexually ripe talk of the travelling salesman," Faulkner exposes the sexist, phallocentric culture within which Lena is locked. The last essay to deal with the impact of the author's culture on his craft is William Meyer's "Faulkner's Patriotic Failure: Southern Lyricism versus American Hypervision." Meyer provocatively contends that while American art tends to be intensely visual and vividly descriptive (Hemingway writes, "that which others hear I see"), Faulkner's art, like Southern literature in general and the tradition of old-world literature which it emulates, tends to "appeal not to the eye but to the ear." *The Sound and the Fury* is Faulkner's most lyric novel: Reverend Shegog's sermon, for example, is an extended illustration of the power of the word. Simultaneously, then, it is also Faulkner's "most splendid failure"[4] because he failed to achieve the American ideal of visual art. In *Light in August*, Meyer claims, Faulkner proposes to overcome his Southern rhetorical bias and write a patriotic novel, a novel that conforms to the American ocular norm; however, despite Faulkner's extended experimentation with an expanded descriptive technique in this novel, still the "thunder and music of prose" overshadows the power of the eye.

Closely related to Faulkner's artistic shaping of his historical and cultural heritage is the matter of the author's own personal experiences: how important to Faulkner's craft were the actual events of his life? Two paired essays offer varying, perhaps even contradictory answers to this question. In "'Drowsing Maidenhead Symbol's Self': Faulkner and the Fiction of Love," Judith Sensibar suggests that Faulkner's characteristic use of antithesis may owe a large debt to his real-life experiences, and, in particular, to his relationship with his wife of thirty-three years, Estelle Faulkner. Drawing on information gathered in recent and as-yet unpublished interviews with the author's daughter, Jill Faulkner Summers, Sensibar shows that love relationships in Faulkner's fiction seem accurately to reflect the sexual politics of his marriage. "Antithesis, tension, and conscious theatrics are love's essence," contends Sensibar, in both Faulkner's fiction and in his life. Taking quite the opposite point of view, Robert Hamblin's essay, "Carcassonne in Mississippi: Faulkner's Geography of the Imagination," argues that Faulkner's art owes little to the particulars of his real-life surroundings. Supporting his case with Faulkner quotations that illustrate the author's preference for invented as opposed to representational art, Hamblin maintains that many critics overemphasize the actual in Faulkner's work and fail sufficiently to credit the transforming powers of the writer's mythic imagination, the way in which he "sublimates the actual into the apocryphal."[5] For Faulkner, Hamblin concludes, the actual world, Oxford, was never more than "somewhere to start from."[6]

Hamblin's discussion of Faulkner's creative imagination is fol-

lowed by an inquiry into the nature of Faulknerian identity. In
"'Thinking I Was I Was Not Who Was Not Was Not Who': The
Vertigo of Faulknerian Identity," Philip Weinstein, drawing on
the theories of Althusser and Lacan, investigates the complex
relationship that exists between the self and society in Faulkner's
texts. By juxtaposing *Absalom, Absalom!* with Margaret
Mitchell's *Gone with the Wind,* Weinstein underscores a striking
contrast: whereas Mitchell's novel constantly reassures the
reader of his/her identity as a fixed, separate, and unchanging
essence, Faulkner's novel just as constantly reveals the self to be
penetrated by external social networks, which alter and reconstitute the self. Weinstein ends with this question, "Is it too
much to say that Faulknerian tragedy is generated precisely by
the civil war between these internalized social scripts and a
something within the self more primordial than social scripts?"

Finally, Faulkner is an international artist who belongs not
only to the South, nor even just to the United States, but to the
world. How do non-English-speaking readers perceive
Faulkner's craft? The concluding essay reaches beyond national
boundaries and includes foreign perspectives on Faulkner's art.
In "A Word without a Word: How the French Translations of
Faulkner's Texts Don't Always Fit What They're Trying to Say
At," Beth Biron focuses on the limitations of Maurice Coindreau's French translations of Faulkner's texts, namely "their
failure to reproduce accurately many aspects of Southern culture
so richly described in the original" and "their failure to capture
the symbolic and metaphysical implications of much of the language." Biron concludes that the French translations "reinvent"
Faulkner in the sense that the French texts "are passed through
a screen of translation and interpretation that often filters out
important elements essential to a full understanding of the
work."

Taken together, the essays in this volume once again affirm
Faulkner's secure status as one of America's most important
writers. In addition, these essays illustrate that the Mississippi
writer's greatness is not the product of his hauntingly evocative

themes alone, but the combination of these themes with his seemingly inexhaustible narrative power to reinvent, or, in Faulkner's words, the ability to tell "the same story over and over . . . in a thousand different terms."

Doreen Fowler
The University of Mississippi
Oxford, Mississippi

NOTES

1. *The Faulkner–Cowley File: Letters and Memories, 1944–1962*, ed. Malcolm Cowley (New York: Viking Press, 1966), 14.

2. "An Introduction to *The Sound and the Fury*," reprinted in *Faulkner: New Perspectives*, ed. Richard H. Brodhead (Englewood Cliffs, N.J.: Prentice Hall, 1983), 23.

3. *The Faulkner–Cowley File*, 116.

4. *Faulkner in the University: Class Conferences at the University of Virginia, 1957–1958* (Charlottesville: University of Virginia Press, 1959), 77.

5. *Lion in the Garden: Interviews with William Faulkner, 1926–1962*, ed. James B. Meriwether and Michael Millgate (New York: Random House, 1968), 255.

6. *Essays, Speeches, and Public Letters by William Faulkner*, ed. James B. Meriwether (New York: Random House, 1965), 8.

A Note on the Conference

Each year since 1974, in Oxford, Mississippi, home of William Faulkner, the University of Mississippi has sponsored a conference as a forum for Faulkner scholarship. While the principal activity of the 1987 conference, "Faulkner and the Craft of Fiction," was the delivery of the essays contained in this volume, the conference also featured a number of special events. Chief among these events was a ceremony at which a Faulkner commemorative stamp was issued by the U.S. Postal Service. Among the nearly 900 persons who attended the ceremony were the novelist's daughter, Jill Faulkner Summers, and 250 conference participants from thirty-four states and nine foreign countries. Speakers included author Eudora Welty, postal officials, and representatives of Oxford and the University. Their remarks are printed in this volume along with ten essays originally presented as lectures during the six–day conference.

At the opening session on Sunday, August 2, Eudora Welty read her classic story "Why I Live at the P.O." and responded to questions about her work and Faulkner's. The conference ended on the evening of Friday, August 7, with "Faulkner's Artistry and the Arts of Black America," a program of readings, music, and dance directed by Sister Thea Bowman of the Catholic Diocese of Jackson, Mississippi. Scheduled between the opening reading and the closing performance were lectures, discussion sessions, and numerous other events.

Actress Ruth Ford, whose friendship with William Faulkner and his family began while she was an Ole Miss coed in the 1930s, returned to the campus for two special appearances during the conference. She was featured in a reading of *Requiem for a Nun* and later in a question-and-answer session entitled "Remembrances." Faulkner wrote the stage version of *Requiem* for her, and she starred in the play's 1957 premiere in London and in a 1959 production in New York.

Four scholars from the A. M. Gorky Institute of World Literature in Moscow participated in the conference. Nicolai Anastasiev presented a paper on "Faulkner the Mythmaker," and Sergei Chakovsky discussed Faulkner's theories of composition. Both scholars joined Maya Koreneva and Tatiana Morozova as panelists for a session on "Soviet Perceptions of William Faulkner."

Maggie Brown, Marjorie Lewis, Minnie Ruth Little, and Bessie Sumners were featured in "Oxford Women Remember Faulkner," a panel discussion moderated by Chester A. McLarty. Howard Duvall and John Ramey served as panelists and M. C. Falkner as moderator for sessions on "William Faulkner of Oxford." Other conference events included a slide lecture by J. M. Faulkner and Jo Marshall, a program of slides and music by photographer Jane Rule Burdine and bluesman Walter Liniger, guided tours of North Mississippi, and a picnic at Faulkner's home, Rowan Oak.

The John Davis Williams Library mounted displays on William Faulkner, Ruth Ford, and Eudora Welty. The University Museums exhibited photographs Eudora Welty made while working as a publicist for the Works Progress Administration as well as photographs by Lafayette County artist Milly Moorhead. The campus television station aired Faulkner films throughout the week, and the University Press of Mississippi hosted an exhibit of Faulkner books published by various university presses throughout the United States.

The conference organizers are grateful to all the individuals and organizations that support Faulkner and Yoknapatawpha annually and offer special thanks to Dr. and Mrs. M. B. Howorth, Jr., Dr. and Mrs. C. E. Noyes, Mr. and Mrs. Guy N. Turnbow, Jr., Mr. Richard Howorth of Square Books, and the Yoknapatawpha Arts Council.

Faulkner and the Craft of Fiction
FAULKNER AND YOKNAPATAWPHA
1987

Faulkner: Master of the Heroic
and the Pastoral Modes

CLEANTH BROOKS

Some years ago that brilliant if sometimes eccentric British literary critic, the late William Empson, reformulated the concept of pastoral poetry. It was not essentially an affair of shepherds watching their flocks and singing love lays to pretty shepherdesses or bemoaning hopeless loves or celebrating the simple joys of their carefree life. The essence of the pastoral was a matter of perspective. In the pastoral, the poet and the readers for whom he wrote stood at a more sophisticated social and intellectual level from that occupied by the unsophisticated people written about. Our more complicated affairs were mirrored thus in a less complex world, and this shift in perspective could be refreshing and sometimes illuminating.

Empson's perception is itself illuminating. I decided long ago to extend it in the opposite direction. Instead of the author's writing for his own kind about more primitive and even unlettered folk, what if he turns his gaze upwards and writes about beings that are extraordinary, larger than life, even heroes? Homer did that in the *Iliad* and even makes his heroes special favorites of certain gods and goddesses, and occasionally actually shows them contending with gods physically. His heroes literally fear neither god nor man. Think of Achilles; think of Ulysses; think even of Virgil's Aeneas—a more temperate, even god-fearing hero, but even so, the true son of a goddess, no less than Venus herself.

Strangely enough, the worlds of the heroes and of the pastoral figures tend to resemble each other; the extremes do meet. Both

1

worlds are simpler, in some ways more noble than the everyday life in the typical city.

Indeed, in Milton's *Paradise Lost* we can think of Adam and Eve, perfect man and perfect woman, able to receive angels as ordinary guests; yet this perfect pair live a simple life in a garden with no household furniture of any kind, "innocent of fire" as the poet tells us, a circumstance that begets the most inept line in this magnificent poem. For Milton observes that among the advantages of the earthly paradise there was "no fear lest dinner cool."

To speak more seriously, in both the heroic world and the pastoral world the pettifogging little cares of the accustomed world are absent and the basic emotions are expressed more directly. Quotidian concerns melt away. There is little worry about respectability and with burnishing one's public image, though there may be a powerful concern for one's honor.

Indeed, the world of the *Iliad* and of the *Odyssey* is heroically simple. If my argument seems to be leaning too much on hifalutin examples, take a look at Synge's one-act play *Riders to the Sea*. The characters are people who lead a precarious life on the Aran Islands off the western coast of Ireland. They live by fishing.

I am not suggesting that only simple people can attain nobility any more than I am arguing that only the upper classes can act heroically. I am doing no more than pointing out some of the advantages for depicting intense emotions that the artist may gain by getting rid of some of the clutter of the usual everyday happenings of town and city life. Faulkner himself makes this point. He has one of his characters state the matter thus. Mr. Compson, in conversation with his son, Quentin (*Absalom, Absalom!*, Vintage Edition, 89), says that the men and women of the 1850s and '60s were "people too as we are, and victims too, as we are, but victims of a different circumstance, simpler, and therefore, integer for integer, larger, more heroic and the figures therefore more heroic too, not dwarfed and involved, but distinct, uncomplex." Yet the heroic and the pastoral modes, for all their advantages, are, however, tricky and for the inept writer dangerous. Pastoral scenes can become prettified and intolerably sentimental. Attempts at the heroic can become preposterously overblown and full of windy rhetoric.

So I am very much interested in looking at Faulkner's bold attempts to use, on occasion, not one but both difficult perspectives—and, to cap it all—sometimes to use both in the same novel.

The Hamlet is such a novel. In discussing that novel in an earlier book, I referred to Frenchman's Bend, where the action of the novel takes place, as Faulkner's "Savage Arcadia." For the Greeks, Arcadia was the landlocked interior of the Peloponesus, a mountainous country with few towns and cities, whose inhabitants led simple lives. In our ruder American terms it was countrified, backward, out in the sticks, a backwater of civilization. Naturally it was the home of pastoral poetry. Greek poets like Bion and Theocritus made a virtue of its simplicity and so did the Latin poets who followed them. And so did the English poets bred up on the classics as they were. Faulkner knew these English poets well. His own early poetry, much of it, is in the pastoral mode. When Faulkner wrote *The Hamlet*, however, he dropped any hint of falsifying prettinesses of the conventional kind. He made his Mississippi Arcadia of the earth, earthy. The early reviews thought the novel disgusting. For example, Faulkner provides his pastoral with a faun, a proper pastoral stage property, but instead of dressing him up properly in his conventional costume of a goat's hairy legs and horny hooves and equipped with horns peeping through his wild locks and letting us get glimpses of him in the twilight as he plays on his Pan's pipes or chases a properly clad (or properly unclad) nymph through the glade, we see an idiot dressed in faded overalls. He is the idiot, Ike Snopes, and I suppose that he does in a meaningful sense answer to the Greek conception of a faun, that is, a man who is really more animal than human. At any rate, Faulkner's Mississippi faun is indeed "close to nature," uninhibited, at the mercy of his animal impulses and quite beyond the ordinary bounds of good and evil. Faulkner has simply expressed realistically and logically the way in which his faun is bound to behave. But Faulkner is no Jonathan Swift, turning Ike into a monster, a vicious Yahoo. Ike risks the flames to rescue his inamorata, the cow he reveres, and happily eats her food along with her. Ike is not conscious of committing a crime against nature. He is at one with nature and his loved one for him *is* nature. Faulkner actually at one point describes her as a horned nature goddess. Indeed, in the sensitive reader Ike awakens a sense of profound pity, as he does in Ratliff. But Ike is not merely "natural." In his lack of avarice and greed and in his disinterested love, Ike puts to shame his mean-spirited cousin, Flem, and proves himself the more truly human of the two.

In short, I am claiming not that Ike is heroic but that he is a being who so stretches the limits of humanity that we can hardly deal with him in our usual terms. The Greeks symbolized his nature in the term *faun*. A faun was one of the retinue of Great Pan, the god of nature. The Christian Middle Ages might have called him "God's fool." Today, of course, we would make a more clinical diagnosis.

Yet, whatever we want to call him, Faulkner has been able to make him come credibly alive for us, and a main element in Faulkner's method is to set Ike free in a natural environment where we can see Ike's virtues and impulses at their best. Faulkner has endowed his account of the wanderings over the hills of Ike and his cow with some of the finest nature poetry of our time.

The term *heroic* in its literal meaning could almost be given to Labove, the schoolteacher of Frenchman's Bend. Labove's heroic stature is obscured for most readers by the utter simplicity and single-mindedness of this young man. We don't like to think of our heroes as absurd, and our impulse is to laugh at Labove rather than esteem him. That a young, full-blooded American believes that words are the most powerful things to be had and that this boy born and brought up on a hard-scrabble hill farm could eventually become Governor of Mississippi by dint of acquiring such an education will provoke from most of the present-day generation more guffaws than applause. I, myself, find much of the Labove section very funny, and I'm sure that Faulkner meant us to find it so.

You will remember that when Labove became a star on the Ole Miss football team he marvelled at the team's wonderful collection of shoes. That they were cleated shoes didn't matter much if most of one's family had no shoes at all. But Labove—who apparently made most of his team's touchdowns—occasionally picked up a pair of shoes to send home. He did so only when his team won. Then he evidently believed he had fairly earned a pair. So his old grandmother, sucking on her clay pipe, proudly clattered in cleated shoes over the rough puncheon cabin floor back in the hills. But we are told that she most enjoyed the nice clattering noise the shoes made when she rocked back and forth in her rocking chair.

Much of the Labove section is hilarious, though I can't remember ever hearing that this serious young scholar-schoolmaster ever laughed. He took his duties, his studies, and his mission too seriously for that. Yet, withal, he was simple, not puffed up with his own importance. He was just too hardworking, too much pressed for time to indulge in anything so frivolous as just kicking up his heels and having a good time. He is a true Spartan. Interestingly enough, he seemed to take no pride in being a football star. Apparently, he was a matchless running back, but had no muscles puffed up by steroids or a wallet stuffed with special emoluments. We are told that he did have his tuition paid, but he laid the morning fires for a half dozen faculty members, lived in the chilly unheated attic of another and fed and milked his cow, morning and evening. He told Varner that he didn't like football and simply accepted it as a job that he took to get an education. Labove simply tried to give solid satisfaction, and then there was the matter of free football shoes.

What days of innocence for college athletics, with Labove the most innocent of them all. Certainly, his adventures are funny,

but I also put him in the rank of heroes. If you don't agree, well
and good; but you will have to agree that he is an unusual man.
You won't find his like every day. I wish I could. In fifty years of
teaching, I've had only students who resembled him enough to
convince me that it is possible to find such a person. Faulkner
has made him seem completely convincing, but to find a living
example will not be as easy as locating four-leaf clovers.

The character in this novel, however, who is the farthest from
the ordinary, and who wears an almost mythical aura, is Eula
Varner. She seems quite unconscious of the magnitude of her
powers, though her presence in this little backwater community
amounts to that of a powerful goddess of fertility. She might be a
manifestation of Aphrodite, the Greek love goddess herself. But
Faulkner is too good an artist to make any direct presentation of
her physical appearance. Oh, yes, I have not forgotten that
marvelous purple patch of rhetoric that opens book 2 of the novel
and is entitled "Eula."

> When Flem Snopes came to clerk in her father's store, Eula Varner
> was not quite thirteen. She was the last of the sixteen children, the
> baby, though she had overtaken and passed her mother in height in
> her tenth year. Now, though not yet thirteen years old, she was
> already bigger than most grown women and even her breasts were
> no longer the little, hard, fiercely-pointed cones of puberty or even
> maidenhood. On the contrary, her entire appearance suggested
> some symbology out of the old Dionysic times—honey in sunlight
> and bursting grapes, the writhen bleeding of the crushed fecundated
> vine beneath the hard rapacious trampling goat-hoof. She seemed to
> be not a living integer of her contemporary scene, but rather to exist
> in a teeming vacuum in which her days followed one another as
> though behind sound-proof glass, where she seemed to listen in
> sullen bemusement, with a weary wisdom heired of all mammalian
> maturity, to the enlarging of her own organs. (*The Hamlet*, Vintage
> Edition, 95)

Yet even here the emphasis is not on pearly teeth, ruby lips, a
Grecian profile. We don't even learn the color of her hair. What
is described is her associations with the fertility of nature and the
way she affects other people and especially all males. Further-

more, we are allowed to laugh or at least smile at some of these disturbing effects as we listen to the complaints of her disgruntled brother. Faulkner himself, as author, makes a little joke about her precocious blooming into womanhood. He describes Mrs. Varner walking out with her child, Eula, being carried—she refuses to walk—in the arms of a black male servant of the Varners. It looks like a "chaperoned Sabine rape," the author remarks. In short, Faulkner does not overwhelm us with words of conventional praise of female beauty in order to persuade us that she is a love goddess. He is content to show how men react to her and particularly the austere young Labove—even his reserve crumbles before her. The levelheaded V. K. Ratliff is not smitten with her fatal power, but views her as a distant observer. Maybe for that very reason Faulkner allows him to refer to the beauty of Eula's face, but, since she has now been married off to the reptilian Flem Snopes, Ratliff uses, along with the adjective "beautiful," the adjective "damned." Ratliff is touched at the sheer waste that has occurred. Like a precious ointment poured out into the dust, this Helen of Troy is in effect bought by the man whose only interest is to buy up and "own" every desirable thing in sight.

It can be argued that Flem also comes close to being a mythical character, a man whose acquisitiveness is so absolute that it has smothered nearly every other emotion and left him so abstract that he is scarcely human. In fact, I have already argued this view, and since I can add nothing to what I have written earlier, I shall repeat only this: If Eula is a kind of nature goddess, then Flem is the enemy of nature. Faulkner was right in stating in a later book that Flem was impotent, but if Flem has worked himself almost out of the natural world, poor Ike is so deeply immersed in the world of nature that he only barely gets into the human world at all. But such a pattern is almost too neat: *The Hamlet* is a richly concrete novel and can be said to have a number of meanings. But Frenchman's Bend, though a simpler world than ours, can mirror the more complex world in which you and I live and may even give us a new perspective on

ourselves. I, for example, can see resemblances between some of
the characters in *The Hamlet* and some living people; but I shall
not name them. I don't want to be sued for libel.

Let me make one more point very briefly. When in *The Town*
Flem and Eula move into Jefferson, our perspective changes.
The nature goddess is now a small-town housewife—even if she
will soon involve herself in an extramarital affair, but it is scarcely
romantic. It is about as unromantic as an arranged adultery that
assuages certain physical needs for the two people involved. That
at least is the way the liaison is presented in *The Town*. I am
probably unfair to this second member of Faulkner's trilogy.

I don't want to see Eula humanized, to watch her dwindle
from a kind of fertility goddess—the very spirit and essence of
burgeoning nature—into a matron living, so far as the reader is
allowed to see, a rather routine small-town life. *Madame Bovary*
was one of Faulkner's favorite novels, but Faulkner does not
convert Eula into Flaubert's woman caught up in romantic
dreams and longings. On the contrary, Eula is wonderfully practical and even direct in her actions. Yet, whether we are to
regard *The Town* as one of Faulkner's achieved successes or give
it a lower estimate, the thesis I set forth at the beginning of this
lecture remains unshaken. Our perspective has been changed.
We have left the nymph-faun haunted countryside, which seems
at least hospitable to men and women of almost supernatural
character, for a more realistic world of more limited goals and
aims. To go back to my original figure, we are not looking up to
demigods but on something like the same level as ourselves,
quite human, indeed all too human. It is no accident therefore
that something like social comedy gets the main focus, as when
the bemused and idealistic Gavin Stevens is pathetically funny
when he gets into a fist fight to defend Eula's "honor," a virtue
which she didn't pretend to claim and was presumably amused
as well as annoyed to have him rather publicly defend.

In *The Unvanquished* Faulkner tried something perhaps more
difficult to bring off than his quasi-mythical world: the exploits of
flesh-and-blood heroes *in action*. Indeed, when *The Unvan-*

quished appeared, the reviewers gave it a rough ride. Faulkner was glorying in the exploits of his Confederate heroes, exhibiting them as accomplishing impossible deeds of derring-do, and serving up to his reader the old stale stereotypes: the dashing Confederate cavalry officer, the heroic white-haired matriarch, the bowing-and-scraping faithful black servant, and all the rest. It sounded like a true bill of indictment, and it was generally taken as such. In short, Faulkner was taking some of his *Saturday Evening Post* short stories and working them up into one of his episodic "novels." Yet this plausible dismissal won't stand up to analysis. The fact that certain materials have been worn down into stereotypes does not mean that these materials can never again be used effectively by a genuine artist. If it did, the possibilities of character and situation would be so impoverished that literature would have been brought to an end for lack of fresh things to write abut. The real question is whether Faulkner has made Colonel Sartoris sufficiently complex as to be credible.

If the Colonel is seen as hero through his thirteen-year-old son's worshipful eyes in the early episodes of the novel, a careful reader—not skimming pages to make the deadline for his review—will find plenty of evidence in the later chapters that the Colonel is an interesting and complicated human being. That same reader who is paying attention to his reading will have noted that the whole of *The Unvanquished* is reported to the reader by Bayard Sartoris and the novel as a whole is an account of his development from a boy of thirteen to a young man of twenty-six, who now with the death of his father and with his own crucial moral decision, has truly entered into the realm of full manhood. As we move through the book, we are tracing some of the stages of Bayard's growing up and of his maturing view of the world and of the members of his own family. A good reader will take Bayard's changing perspective into account as he makes his estimate of the reality of the characters and of Faulkner's ability to make them seem credible to the reader. Yet, before pursuing this line of argument any further, I want to take up a second point. I remarked that Faulkner was accused of making his heroes accomplish impossible deeds, but were they impossible? Did such things really happen in the War between the States? They did. There were daring cavalry men, heroic grandmothers, and all the rest. One can believe or almost believe the exploit of Aunt Jenny's brother who raided a Federal camp in order to get himself some anchovies. Yet, in the light of this episode one may well ask where does true bravery degenerate into mere foolhardiness? The question is proper but the answer is not easy. In this war, the two were sometimes hard to disentangle. Consider, for example, General W. T. Sherman's description of the dashing young Confederate cavalry man: Sherman wrote to General Halleck in 1863 of the "young bloods of the South" that "war suits them, and the rascals are brave, fine riders, bold to rashness, and dangerous in every sense. . . . They are splendid riders, first-rate shots, and utterly reckless."

As to their courage, Sherman's testimony bears great weight. As for some other aspects of his analysis (such as his belief that they had no concern for "land" or "past, present, or future") and as for Sherman's statement that these "men must all be killed or *employed by us* before we can hope for peace [italics supplied]" they are patently absurd. Did any of these "young bloods of the South" leave the Confederate service to be employed by the Federal forces?

In any case, the attentive reader of *The Unvanquished* will find that, for all the deeds of reckless bravery recounted, the novel finds its focus in a deed of resolved moral courage, and it should be clear that the reader is inevitably led to believe that in such an act the finest heroism is displayed.

Did Faulkner himself believe that the period of the War between the States was an Age of Heroes? Indeed, he did, and said so explicitly. In a letter to Lambert Davis, dated 25 July 1946, he wrote: "There are times when I believe that there has been little in this country good enough since 1860–1870, etc. to make literature. That since then we have become a nation of bragging sentimental and not too courageous liars." Faulkner's statement may seem to many far too extreme, but the issue here is not the soundness of Faulkner's judgment but what he believed about the mid-nineteenth century American.

In writing about this earlier period, Faulkner apparently truly believed that there were in the land genuine heroes to write about, and doubtless this belief gave conviction to him. But does it give conviction to his reader? Not necessarily. A poor writer may fervently believe in the truth of what he is saying but, as we know all too well, his work may nevertheless be empty rhetoric, full of clichés, overwrought similes, annoying ploys to excite emotion. Look into thy heart and write doesn't help very much if that is the ambitious author's sole resource. Even for love poetry it is never enough and for the heroic mode it is hopeless. Consider Miss Rosa Coldfield's odes to the Confederate soldiers. Had mere sincerity been enough, they might have amounted to truly deathless verse. Significantly, in *Absalom, Absalom!* Faulkner never quotes any of her verse.

All of which explains why, if one is to convince the doubter, one needs to show that Faulkner in this novel is still functioning as a competent literary artist and not merely humming "Dixie" while he waves the Stars and Bars.

The literary power of the novel, however, will scarcely avail with the reader who simply cannot credit such events as Faulkner relates, who is sure that they didn't happen because that sort of thing couldn't have happened and that therefore Faulkner is telling these yarns in an attempt to justify a discredited rebellion against the U. S. Government engaged in a holy cause. But bravery is bravery, even if exerted for what was to be a lost cause and may not cease to be an expression of some virtues even if the cause be later judged an unworthy cause.

It is for the benefit of such a reader that a little earlier I invoked the testimony of General Sherman, who can scarcely be impeached as being a Confederate sympathizer. There were deeds of bravery in those days, even of what some would call foolhardiness. There is such a story in my own family. One of my grandfathers, who served, by the way, under Faulkner's favorite general, Nathan Bedford Forrest, once volunteered to ride back

into West Tennessee to report on the strength and disposition of
the Federal forces around Jackson, Tennessee. His parents lived
near Jackson. He hoped to slip in and see them, and he did know
the countryside well. At first all went perfectly. He did see his
mother and father; and, later still, his sweetheart; but soon after,
he and a civilian friend, from whom he was to secure further
information, were picked up by a Federal patrol that had just
happened by. To make matters worse, my grandfather, though
dressed in Confederate uniform, had foolishly on this chilly
morning put on a civilian overcoat as if to conceal his uniform.
Three Union officers charged him with spying and proceeded to
examine him in proper court-martial style. But my grandfather
kept his head and took the only course that could possibly have
saved him: he decided to play the role of the ignorant, illiterate
country yokel. Apparently he did play it to perfection. He didn't
have any idea as to what the war was about. It did seem to be, as
he had been told, a rich man's war and a poor man's fight. When
he was accused of being a spy, he stoutly denied it. His name was
Billy Witherspoon. Everybody knows that. His ridiculous answers soon had the officers laughing, and the louder that they
laughed, the safer he felt himself to be. When the court-martial
finally sent him out of the room and recessed for a few minutes,
he told the friend captured with him what he had done so that he
could back up the fraudulent story when he was himself to be
examined. When Lieutenant Witherspoon was called back in to
hear the verdict, the Union officers told him that they would
indeed allow this poor ignorant boy to go back to his ma and pa,
their only child and sole support, since they were convinced that
he was tired of soldiering and wanted only to go home.

Any sensible man would have gone on his way rejoicing, but
my grandfather pressed his luck. Thus far his story illustrates no
more than his ready wit and plausible tongue, not any reckless
courage. But at this point he did become reckless. He begged
the officers to let him have his horse back. That steed had in the
telling been reduced from a Kentucky thoroughbred to "Old
Charlie," a plowhorse, the only horse the family owned. How
could he make a crop without a plowhorse? Furthermore, he

even begged that they grant an order for the return of his companion's horse. My grandfather had by this time become so proficient in his lying that he had invented a plausible excuse for even that. Curiously enough, he got a favorable answer to both requests.

His companion, however, was naturally worried. They surely had better forget the horses and get out of town. That's what I would have done, but not Lieutenant Witherspoon. After they had searched in vain for their mounts—after all, there were 20,000 Federal troops in Jackson—my grandfather actually returned to the officers of the court-martial to solicit their help in locating the patrol that had picked him up on the night before. The officers continued to be indulgent to this poor bewildered farm boy. Then wonders of wonders, my grandfather saw through the open door of the courthouse one of the men from the patrol that had captured him draw up to the well to water his horse. My grandfather eagerly pointed him out to the officers. The members of the patrol were called in, identified my grandfather and his civilian friend as the men they had captured, and the two were given their fair dismissal, horses and all. And so my grandfather rode back the seventy-five miles he had to travel to get back to Forrest in Mississippi. I don't quite know what I should conclude about my grandfather: that he could keep his wits under fire or that he was brave to the point of foolhardiness or that he was a truly accomplished liar. Maybe he had all three traits. But as I recently reread his account of this adventure, I was impressed with how he evidently hated to face *walking* seventy-five miles. If it had only been twenty, maybe he would have just hotfooted it home.

This little story allows us to view from a rather different angle Sherman's conception of the Confederate cavalryman, but it does affirm a quality of courage that sometimes seems to border on folly, and that may seem incredible to an age like ours that finds it hard to discover anything heroic in war.

My grandfather's story makes another point pertinent to *The Unvanquished:* I have in mind Faulkner's care in portraying the essential humanity of Federal officers and troops. Clearly the officers of the court-martial were not really eager to hang this young man of twenty-three. The point is never made explicitly, but it is there by implication, and after my grandfather was released, he and the men who captured him immediately went off to a bar to have a drink together.

In the first chapter of *The Unvanquished* when twelve-year-old Bayard Sartoris and his black playmate, Ringo, fire a musket at a mounted Yankee and kill the horse but not the rider, they rush for cover to the house, and when the house is searched, the only place in which they can be hidden is under Bayard's grandmother's crinoline skirt. Colonel Dick, who is in command of the force that searches the house, is perfectly aware of the fact that the boys are hidden under Miss Rosa's skirt, but he admires her spirit and refuses to press the issue. He also evidently has little liking for disturbance of the civilian population, and all the more intensely would he hate to be involved in a war on the civilian population. In still another way, *The Unvanquished* shows that it is not a simple glorification of the Southern cause and that it does not picture the slaves as docile, contented retainers. Some are, and some cannot easily change old attitudes and are hesitant at venturing into the new life that freedom offers. But Loosh longs to be set free: He dares to say to the boy, Bayard, things that he will not say to the adults, but take notice of what Faulkner allows Loosh to say when Miss Rosa rebukes him for showing the Yankees where she had buried the silver. Loosh ought to remember, though now free, as he claims, and though he no longer belongs to John Sartoris, that the silver belonged to Mr. Sartoris. Loosh had no right to give it away. Loosh's reply has force: "Let God ax John Sartoris who the man name that give me to him. Let the man that buried me in the black dark ax that of the man what dug me free" (Vintage Edition, 85).

Later on in the book there are the great scenes in which a multitude of the former slaves fill the roads as they make their way to the river—which they call "Jordan" and mean to cross over into freedom where the Federal army is camped on the other side.

Many of the slaveholders did indeed seem to have been honestly shocked when they found how much their servants had yearned all along to be free. In this matter also, Faulkner is reporting the historical situation quite accurately.

So, let me repeat, *The Unvanquished* is not, as has been claimed, a false and sentimentalized view of the old slave South at war. It is true that in some of the episodes Faulkner may seem to have fallen into the mode of "the tall tale" of the Old Southwest. For example, how can anyone have possibly garbled the names of the mules "Old Hundred" (doubtless named for the celebrated hymn tune) and "Tenney" into 110 mules. In part, the author is poking fun at the inefficiency *and* insane literalism of army red tape. But perhaps Faulkner is also relying on the tolerant humanity of Union officers like Colonel Nathaniel Dick.

Miss Rosa had appealed to him to recover her mules, her slaves, and her chest containing the family silver. As a matter of fact the Union armies in the South sought to disencumber themselves of the slaves who were flocking to them. They were not prepared to feed and house them, and the slaves got in the way of their military movements. General Sherman himself declared that his "first duty will be to clear the army of surplus negroes, mules and horses." So there is some historical justification for what may appear a farcical exaggeration. All in all, it was a remarkable war and all sorts of odd things happened.

Miss Rosa, for example, could not quite understand what was happening. She knew that Colonel Dick was a gentleman and since he was, she could appeal to him directly to get back her property. So she borrows a hat from Mrs. Compson, for as Andrew Lytle observed years ago, she sees herself as making a social call and no lady would go hatless to make such a call. Why does she not wear her own hat? Because Federal troops had a few days before burned her house and everything in it to the ground. Yet she is still unable to grasp the situation fully, and she resolutely retains her faith—and in this instance rightly—in Colonel Nathaniel Dick's qualities as a gentleman. And Colonel Dick seems as troubled about the situation as Miss Rosa is confused. At one point he bursts out with the exclamation:

"Damn this war." The war is too concrete, too inhumanly human, when the enemy includes gray-haired old ladies who speak the same language that you do and remind you of old ladies back home. Helping God trample out the vintage where the grapes of wrath are stored, in the actual process, can become an unpleasant task. War against a civilian population—however just the cause—can have some very unpleasant aspects, as we found out from our experience in World War II and in Viet Nam—even though these people did not speak our own language.

Young Bayard Sartoris, who tells the story, is obviously Southern to the core. Nevertheless, Faulkner sees to it that, on the whole, he gives an honest report; the Yankees are not merely devils, they are human beings: some are compassionate men.

Bayard naturally sees his father as a hero, but before the book has finished, he has come to see him for what he is: a passionate, ambitious man, more and more in love with power, a man who has a streak of ruthlessness, who is too quick with his pistol, as when he shoots the hillman who he thought was about to rob him, and merciless in jibing at his former business partner, Redmond, once he had broken with him. Bayard is also perfectly aware of what has happened to his kinswoman, Drusilla Hawk.

He is much attracted to this spirited woman, who by force of personality prevents the Yankee horsemen from taking her horse—she will shoot him rather than give him up. Drusilla also sees to it by skillful riding that the wagon on which Miss Rosa is traveling when she pays her "social call" on Colonel Dick gets safely across the river without tipping over. Later still, she persuades Bayard's father, Colonel Sartoris, to take her into his cavalry troop, where she rides as a uniformed soldier through the last two years of the war. Surely Faulkner is building her up into a glamorously romantic figure, a kind of Brunhilde or Maid of Orleans. But Faulkner makes her pay a price for her reckless gallantry.

Drusilla's conventional mother seems to have worried far less at the possibility of her daughter's being killed in battle than in losing her good name. Think of her lying there night after night in camp surrounded by all those men! Drusilla must marry Colonel John Sartoris, though neither of them seems to have the slightest romantic interest in the other. Finally, however, they are legally married, and Drusilla—whose true love was killed early in the war—finds herself in a loveless marriage, and Bayard finds himself with a beautiful stepmother, just eight years older than he.

Yet this dynamite-laden situation is not played out to what one might expect to be its natural conclusion in the wonderful concluding chapter of the novel. The struggle within Bayard is not the familiar contest between love and honor. Bayard is a man of honor, but it is far from clear that he is in love with Drusilla. Drusilla may have believed that she was in love with him and demands that he kiss her. He does but says that now he must tell his father what he has done, to which Drusilla readily assents. But his father is so preoccupied with his plans for the future that he does not take in what his son has just told him. His very abstraction speaks volumes. He literally cannot "hear" what Bayard has said. Very shortly after this, Bayard goes off to law school, and while he is there Ringo rides in to bring the news that the Colonel's former business partner, Redmond, has shot the Colonel down. Bayard prepares at once to leave for home.

This last magnificent section of the novel, which bears the title "An Odor of Verbena," has had so much commentary, including, I must confess, a good deal by myself that I think I need not go into it now in much detail. But the great scene with Drusilla, not clothed in widow's weeds but dressed in a yellow ballroom gown, is highly pertinent to the matter of her love for Bayard. What she seems really in love with is the masculine code of honor. Faulkner describes her as the priestess of a rite of "succinct and formal violence." In a high and silvery voice she gives Bayard the dueling pistols with which to avenge his father's death. Of course, she may well be sending this young man to his own death. But in this almost sacred circumstance his very death would be itself glorious. When some instinct tells her that

Bayard may not be willing to kill Redmond, she goes into hysterics. Apparently the community at large expects Bayard to call Redmond to account. Masculine honor requires it. The members of the Colonel's old troop offer to handle the matter for Bayard, but he thanks them and says he can handle the matter himself. Yet this kind of honor is a male prerogative, and the women take no part in it, though they expect observance of this code from their men. Women do not fight duels or serve in the army. This is why Drusilla's attitude is so special. Aunt Jenny takes what Faulkner evidently regards as the valued feminine role. She believes that the male code is foolishly boyish. She needs no further proof that Bayard loved his father or that he is no coward. She begs Bayard not to go to Redmond's office, but she recognizes his feelings and the pressures exerted on him.

The solution that Bayard found was to go into Redmond's office and thus vindicate his friend's belief in his courage, but he went unarmed and satisfied his conscience that having killed Grumby, the bushwhacker and murderer of Miss Rosa, he would never kill again. Needless to say, he went into Redmond's office expecting to be killed. Redmond was expecting him. Redmond's code of honor forbade him to run away. He would expect Bayard to be armed and to enter shooting. But as Bayard entered, he saw that the two shots fired by Redmond were deliberately aimed away from him. Redmond also had expected to die. He had killed the Colonel for what he evidently believed was a just reason. He had decided not to kill the son. Both men were lucky in that his opponent was a man of tender conscience. Redmond promptly left town. And the town? What did the town think of Bayard? After a few moments of incredulous shock, they praised Bayard for what he had done, and even George Wyatt, the sternest partisan that the Colonel had, told Bayard that maybe he was right, maybe there had been too much killing already.

So for those who sneer at the reckless hairbreadth exploits of Faulkner's Confederate cavalry men, here is a story of the moral hero: the man with a conscience who makes the difficult choice and risks his life to keep it. In fact, the heroism celebrated in *The*

Unvanquished culminates in an example of heroism of just this sort.

So how are we to judge this novel? It will hardly do to excerpt "An Odor of Verbena" and throw everything that precedes it away. Much that precedes the last section feeds into it and prepares for it. The fine chapter that tells how Bayard and Ringo, boys of sixteen, had to take matters into their own hands and hunt down and kill Grumby has much to do with Bayard's decision never to kill again. In the early chapters the view of Colonel Sartoris through the eyes of a hero-worshiping son of thirteen provides a useful marker to two different but related things: the change that occurred in Colonel Sartoris in a decade and the widening and deepening vision of Bayard as he grew up into adulthood. For we must not lose sight of the fact that *The Unvanquished* is not simply a collection of stories but a novel told by Bayard Sartoris and providing us with an account of his moral and intellectual development.

The happenings of this novel fall into the period that Faulkner regarded as a heroic age. Many of the characters seem to be larger than life and some of their deeds foolhardy. (One might argue that Bayard's walking into Redmond's office unarmed was just damned foolishness.)

Did other Southern authors attempt to deal with the heroic? Warren certainly did in some of his novels. Indeed, it was the "Cass Mastern" episode in *All the King's Men* that elicited the passage that I quoted earlier in Faulkner's letter to Lambert Davis. His long poem "Brother to Dragons" might also be cited. Some of Andrew Lytle's novels—*The Long Night*, for example— have larger-than-life characters. I would mention also Allen Tate's *The Fathers*. But with matters such as these we are obviously not dealing with hard and fast entities, but with tendencies and approximations. As we get further from the earlier periods of American history and especially from the Civil War, we may expect fewer direct attempts to deal with the heroic, and as we become more and more sophisticated, fewer and fewer attempts at the *genuine* pastoral. There is little point in lamenting this state of affairs. Writers can give us only what their circumstances allow them to give. To strain for the heroic is to court failure. I honestly believe that *The Unvanquished* is a much more successful novel than it is commonly held to be, but I concede that the problems that it raises for the modern reader are formidable even with Faulkner himself as author.

The pastoral, too, is not an easily accepted mode. It is difficult to keep the characters simple without making them seem stupid or allowing them powerful feelings without sentimentalizing them or—worse—giving them up to Dogpatch comedy.

It is small wonder that a number of our Southern authors now take for granted that their readers occupy about the same social level as themselves and dramatize for such readers the lives of people who live on much the same level as themselves. The last thing that I mean to say is that such work is dull and drab or that it deals with only one stratum of society. How could it be dull or uninteresting since one would place in this general category the work of Peter Taylor and Walker Percy, to name only two of its best exponents. It is a world that abounds in social comedy and ideas, slight and topical or serious and profound. It is a complex world, neither grand and heroic nor charmingly idyllic. It is in a very special sense our own world. At their best our Southern writers have provided us with genuine literature and one of which we can be thoroughly proud. Moreover, there has been no real break here, for the stance adopted is that of most writers through the ages. Faulkner, himself, uses it most of the time; so does Eudora Welty; so does Warren; so did Katherine Anne Porter. In spite of their occasional adventuring with the pastoral and the heroic, the staple mode has never been discontinued.

Faulkner's Art of Repetition

Donald M. Kartiganer

What does it mean to repeat something?

A great deal, if not the bulk, of modern thought and literature revolves around that question. Within the ranges of repetition we have discovered the way of our knowing as well as the impossibility of knowing; the name of our bondage to what has already been as well as the name of our release—indeed, an invitation, in the face of aimless recurrence, to will the world. Repetition is our disease, our compulsion to reenact endlessly old, forgotten desires, and our cure, compulsion redeemed into dialogue, in which we revise the past, retrieving new possibilities from determinate origins.

The fact of repetition seems to lie at the very center of Faulkner's fiction, as its art, its meaning, and the process of its formation. In a word, Faulkner's craft of fiction is to tell stories, and then tell them again. This is the strategy that animates each of the novels, and is implicit to the stories; moreover, it describes the dynamic space between the texts, the relation from one text to another. Repetition may also describe the strategy of the life—of what it meant to be Faulkner the eldest son of the fourth generation leading away from and back to his formidable great grandfather—as well as the strategy of the writer's historical position, of what it meant to be Faulkner the American postwar modernist leading away from and back to Joyce, Conrad, and James, Melville and Hawthorne. But these biographical and literary anxieties of inheritance are not my concern here. Rather it is the repetitions and revisions within, and occasionally between, Faulkner's texts alone that I wish to consider.

To repeat: he tells stories, then he tells them again. Within each of the novels he creates a series of voices that report, interpret, or perform a single event, circling it, like ripples in a pool surrounding the no longer visible stone of their occasion. Whether the voices are the silent consciousnesses of interior monologue, or the garrulous speakers of elaborate, hairsplitting commentary, or actors effecting deeds as well as words—they are always repeaters, performing what has been performed, meditating on the well-meditated. The families Compson or Bundren, reiterating the loss of sister or mother, the loss of a fullness glimpsed vaguely in the variously connected fragments of their mourning; or those obsessively text-bound critics, Rosa Coldfield, Mr. Compson, Quentin and Shreve, turning over and over again the old letters, the shreds of fact, gossip, and rumor, reproducing the Sutpen story that they suspect has somehow fathered them all; or Joe Christmas, Lena Grove, Gail Hightower, and Joanna Burden, duplicating each other's acts of alienation from the community, and each other's attempts to reestablish some vital, sustaining connection with the past— each of these characters, each of the fictional fragments they enact, participates in a drama wholly driven by repetition. Their lives are exponential, an unproblematic primary nowhere to be found. They cross each other's paths like mirrors moving in a funhouse, reflecting each other reflecting on similar events.

If retelling is the core of Faulkner's practice, there is also the curious fact of retelling as the complex route from one text to another. I refer here not only to his reuse of earlier written and often published material—the short stories that reappear in new guises in *The Unvanquished, Absalom, Absalom!, The Hamlet, Go Down, Moses, A Fable, The Town*, and *The Mansion*—but to his habit of rewriting whole novels or large sections of novels: the repetition of *The Sound and the Fury* as *As I Lay Dying, Sanctuary* as *Requiem for a Nun, Absalom, Absalom!* as *Go Down, Moses*, "Wild Palms" as "Old Man," the Mink section of "The Long Summer" in *The Hamlet* as "Mink" in *The Mansion*.

At issue here is the whole question of what it means that these fictions should come to dwell in repetition—that they should describe the essential human act, and the essential narrative act, as the compulsion and craft of duplication: the return to lives already lived, acts already performed, tales already told.

1

In its most ancient forms repetition is preeminently the way of knowing, the way of experiencing reality and significance. In his several studies of the archaic mind, Mircea Eliade has described in detail the discovery of reality as the profane object or event repeating itself as the sacred. The profane is above all the single, the unconnected, naked of past and paradigm. It may have practical value—an act such as cultivation or reproduction that sustains life—but to the archaic mind it does not truly *mean*, it is neither human nor real, until it achieves the status of the sacred by being recognized as the repetition of an earlier act. The epitome of this earlier act is the creation of the world itself: the building of a home reproduces the divine act of cosmic building, the appropriation of land reproduces the original "transformation of chaos into cosmos," the celebration of a festival "reactualizes" something that took place "in the beginning."[1]

The experience of this repetition comprises a kind of double perception, for the tension between profane and sacred is preserved even as the vacancy of insignificance is momentarily filled by recollection of a confirming priority. "By manifesting the sacred," Eliade writes, "any object becomes *something else*, yet it continues to remain *itself*, for it continues to participate in its surrounding cosmic milieu. A *sacred* stone remains a *stone*."[2] The man digging his field knows that the tool he uses has an archetypal phallic origin, that his seed is simultaneously semen. But he also knows that a spade *is* a spade, the seed, corn, and that his family will not survive on significance alone. "[L]ife," Eliade continues, "is lived on a twofold plane; it takes its course as human existence and, at the same time, shares in a trans-human life, that of the cosmos or the gods."[3]

Clearly, the emphasis of this ontology and epistemology is on the submission of the present to the past. A human life signifies as "the ceaseless repetition of gestures initiated by others."4 We know ourselves only doubled, as the imitators of the gods. Although the idea of relationship between the present individual and the ancestor persists, and the reality of that ancestor remains mythic rather than historical, the superior strength of the origin is unmistakable. Its power is not bestowed by the present but merely recognized by it. Rather the past verifies the present, provides the doubling context that rescues it from that singleness which, knowing only itself, knows nothing.

The passage from this archaic perception to the Judeo-Christian tradition is complex, involving, among other things, the shift from a theory of eternal return, in which events are important through their reproduction of prior events, to a theory of history, the replacement of cyclical time with what Eliade calls "one-way time": a linear, progressive development, with a beginning, middle, and end.5 This history begins at a particular moment and moves, if erratically, to a close, whether culminating in the Judaic vision of a world of justice on all God's holy mountain, or the Christian vision of a postworld paradise of the redeemed: when it shall be said, "the former things have passed away."

What links the archaic and the Judeo-Christian perceptions, however, is the continuing sense of repetition as a solidly grounded vehicle of knowing and identity. Although each moment in the life of the individual and in time is now a new moment, never to come again, it is yet a moment that resonates with a meaning rooted in the context of the whole—the whole history to be completed in the future, but whose intelligible pattern has been predicated in the past. Each new moment, then, takes its place within a pattern—exactly as each moment in the Aristotelian mode of narrative bends itself to the mythos ordained from the beginning—and receives its highest meaning only as a fulfillment, a repetition in real, actual time of that which has been foretold.6

It is obviously this notion of a solidly grounded repetition that begins to come undone under the assaults of the modern consciousness. Location of the origin of the modern can hardly withstand the modern questioning of the idea of origin itself; nevertheless, submitting to the current convention of the late eighteenth century as *a* time, if not *the* time of modernism, we discover there abundant evidence of resistance to the idea of knowing as a duplication of prior things, the idea that inherited station or social role are the necessary vehicles of identity, or that imitation is the vehicle of art. Instead, we see the signs of forgetting, what Paul de Man, perhaps our best theorist of the subject, claimed as the essence of the modern: "Modernity exists in the form of a desire to wipe out whatever came earlier, in the hope of reaching at last a point that could be called a true present, a point of origin that marks a new departure."[7]

Repetition as the reenactment of a given ground becomes, so the modernists contend, a way of knowing only that dimension of one's self and moment that is similar to what has already been, only that which *continues*. The modernist quest, replacing mythic memory with personal memory, is to establish the identity of a single solitary self, unlike all others that have ever been or will be. The quest, as Rousseau insisted, is itself without precedent, a desire to produce an unprecedented self, the mold broken at the making. This is a self no better than anyone else— the comparison is senseless—but is unquestionably different: it signifies because it is *unlike*. Such a glorification of unlikeness, from Eliade's point of view, is the destruction of the sacred on behalf of the profane, and therefore the destruction of meaning.

It is not destruction of the double perception, however, but only of its ground. The mind still understands in recurrence; the memory, as we see in Rousseau and Wordsworth, is very much the vehicle of knowledge—but now the connecting threads of those recurrences begin to unravel. Free of confirmation in mythic archetype, a completed history, the Forms of knowledge, repetition assumes new and ghostlier guises, establishes coherences whose conviction and validity are of a different and far more problematic nature. Partly out of will, the knowing defiance of all anteriority, partly out of loss, the sense that the past may be our invention after all, the modern mind plots and destroys its repetitions in dazzling and at times dizzying ways.

In the multiple repetitions and theories of repetition that emerge in the nineteenth and twentieth centuries, an opposition between grounded and ungrounded repetition is a necessary if unstable schematic. J. Hillis Miller conveniently summarizes much of the thinking about that opposition by distinguishing between a Platonic repetition and a Nietzschean one. In the Platonic—a late version of what Eliade identifies as the archaic sense of repetition—art and life fulfill themselves as "copies" of a "solid archetypal model." Their validity rests on mimesis: the "truth of correspondence to what . . . [they] cop[y]." Nietzschean repetition results not in "copies" but "phantasms": "each thing . . . is unique, intrinsically different from every other thing." Doublings are merely suggestive, tantalizing but ultimately illusory. Versions of a past event are only the "constructive, fictive, falsifying aspect" of an "affective 'memory' . . . a vast intricate network of lies, the memory of a world that never was." Such remembering is in fact "posited on the negative work of forgetting."[8]

This schematic, and similar versions of it, makes its own values clear enough. The truths that come forth from prior sources are like children still-born in the womb, already empty of any vitality that might distinguish them as something other than their origins; whereas the fictions of loosened utterance possess a new, boundless freedom of saying anything and everything. As Jacques Derrida argues in his now classic statement distinguishing Levi-Strauss and Nietzsche, Levi-Strauss finally reveals himself as an incomplete, self-mystifying modernist. Embedded in his work is "an ethic of nostalgia for origins, an ethic of archaic and natural innocence, of a purity of presence and self-presence in speech"; and it produces what Derrida calls the "sad, *negative,* nostalgic, guilty, Rousseauist facet of the thinking of free play." This abiding nostalgia is countered by the Nietzschean refusal of all ground—moreover, the refusal to consider this loss of ground *as* loss. Refusal takes the form of what Derrida terms "*affirmation*—the joyous affirmation of the free play of the world and without truth, without origin, offered to an active interpretation."9 The groundlessness of repetition, in other words, becomes in its Nietzschean extremity, a reason for joy rather than regret, becomes the opportunity of all our fictions—supreme by virtue of their fully acknowledged freedom, not from the past but from its originary power.

In effect, as I read Derrida and the deconstructionists generally, there really is no place in a modernist text for the solidly grounded fiction. The division they see in modern literature is really the division between nostalgia and gaiety: those texts that still yearn, however secretly, for a lost origin they can never regain, and those texts that celebrate the loss, exposing the fictiveness of their repetitions—if not with joy, then at least with candor. This division is seldom if ever pure; it is the interaction of the two possibilities that is the field of deconstructionist practice. The adequate reading of a text demonstrates the nostalgia with which the text asserts its gaiety or the gaiety with which it exposes its nostalgia. The upshot is undecidability. Texts know not what they are or want, but at their best they force that very fact to the front of their language. Lesser texts are guilty of a kind of pretense: they propose a freedom they cannot carry through—Rousseau's free play tries to conceal its nostalgia and guilt—or they prop themselves securely on a ground—any nineteenth-century novel will do—that is always being deferred.

Nietzsche provides the deconstructionists with a stance and style of celebration of the collapse of structure. He confronts repetition as an eternal recurrence, the universe as "a monster of energy, without beginning or end . . . a sea of forces storming and raging in itself, for ever changing, for ever rolling back over incalculable ages to recurrence . . . for ever blessing itself as something which recurs for all eternity." This thought is not to be denied or sublimated but to be transformed by "the transvaluation of all values. Pleasure no longer to be found in certainty but in uncertainty; no longer 'cause and effect,' but continual creativeness; no longer the will to self-preservation, but to power; no longer the modest expression 'it is all *only* subjective,' but 'it is all *our* work! let us be proud of it.'"[10]

But perhaps the text dearest to the deconstructionist cause is Freud's *Beyond the Pleasure Principle*, for it displays such open warfare between its drive to destroy structure and what remains of its nostalgia for the principles of development and an identifiable origin. Searching for origin, the ruling instinct, *Beyond the Pleasure Principle* performs a methodical exercise in investigative procedure, even as it dismantles such procedure as incapable of shedding conclusive light on the problem. The most notorious suggestion of the text is that the true origin of human behavior is the death instinct, and that the usual humanistic perception of life as Erös, as an urge to develop and progress, refers only to what Freud calls "detours"—masks of a more fundamental instinct to restore a primal state of nonbeing. But this origin is really a *parody* of origin—no origin at all: it is a void, a blank, a stark inanimacy that has been disturbed into an action that now reveals itself as a circuitous journey back to nothingness.

The structure of *Beyond the Pleasure Principle*—somewhat like the structure of such an experimental novel as *The Sound and the Fury*—unfolds as a series of "failed" disciplines, another set of "detours." Every avenue of approach available to Freud—ordinary and psychoanalytic observation, neurology, chemistry, biology, philosophy, myth—finally proves indecisive. The question of origin that inaugurates the text is never definitively answered. And this narrative undecidability becomes the strange equivalent of the death instinct itself (which cannot be established), as if the aimless and endless recurrence of the quest confirms the truth of its grimmest hypothesis: that our desire is our own demise, our absence, our unmeaning. The quest for ground empties into its own groundlessness.[11]

Between the poles of grounded and ungrounded repetition, or between a nostalgic or joyous response to the fact of the latter, lies another possibility, and, so it seems to me, the bulk of our major modern literature. This is a type of "middle ground" repetition in that it both empties the ground of its original power to determine future versions or fulfillments of itself, *and* restores it, reempowering it, so to speak, but according to the desires of the present. Middle ground repetition effects a design that is neither locked within its center, restricted to the performance of variations on a given theme, nor completely uprooted, merely making and unmaking itself as a display of artful turns above the abyss. Repetition, in other words, becomes a mode of meaning in language and consciousness that invests the past with a new, yet correspondent power that, in turn, constitutes the "source" of a new design or narrative.

This is the possibility that Kierkegaard explores in his small volume *Repetition*, published in 1843. Kierkegaard makes an important distinction there between what he calls "recollection" and "repetition": "Repetition and recollection are the same movement, except in opposite directions, for what is recollected has been, is repeated backward, whereas genuine repetition is recollected forward. Repetition, therefore, if it is possible, makes a person happy, whereas recollection makes him unhappy."[12] What Kierkegaard calls "recollection" is the notion of remembering or actively duplicating, without change, the pattern of a completed past. This is what Miller means by a Platonic, grounded repetition, as the mind secures itself within the parameters of its apparent origins, never going beyond the imitation of what have been its generating assumptions. Kierkegaard's second type of repetition, a modern existentialist view, yet different from Miller's, emphasizes the potential for reexperiencing the past in a new key—revising its initial meanings so as to signal an individual growth within repetition. This is what Kierkegaard calls a "repetition forward," in that the past is rewritten, becoming part of a new narrative expanding into the future. Recollection, as one commentator has put it, "is the immediate recoil of the then upon the now"; repetition "is the reflective reinterpretation of that immediacy."[13]

This second form of repetition has been linked by some critics with Heidegger's notion of repetition, which, according to his English translators, "does not mean either a mere mechanical repetition or an attempt to reconstitute the physical past; it means rather an attempt to go back to the past and retrieve former *possibilities*."[14] Kierkegaard's "repetition forward" is a synthesis of grounded and ungrounded repetitions—a synthesis that recovers new possibilities in repetition and yet avoids the alternative of the utter abandonment of meaning or some clarity of value. This new repetition is at once grounded and un-grounded. It loosens the control of the archetype—that which can only be the product of what Kierkegaard calls "recollection," what Heidegger calls "foreconception"—and yet it resists the condition of utterly free fictions, broken from all origin and unable to reconnect in a formation of meaning. As a "repetition forward," a mind, a character, a text can release itself from its enabling origins into the adventure of time; and yet it can also claim a continuity within an expanding intention, a possibility of adequate, demonstrable meaning that is not merely what Miller calls the "memory of a world that never was." Repetition be-comes the fulfillment of possibilities only latent in the past, the completion of what only the present can awaken.[15]

A striking illustration of such a repetition forward lies in what is probably Kierkegaard's most famous text, *Fear and Trembling*, published the same day as *Repetition*. Kierkegaard's task as an existentialist theologian, embodied in the persona of *Fear and Trembling*, Johannes de Silentio, begins as a deconstruction, an ungrounding of the past, for it is a too solidly grounded Chris-tianity that the good citizens of Copenhagen, according to Johannes, are sleeping through each Sunday morning. Ground has become merely complacency, a substitute for genuine faith. The story of the near-sacrifice of Isaac by Abraham has become, in fact, the supreme image of such a complacently grounded faith. As we read the story within the Judeo-Christian tradition, Abraham's act is replete with justification and intelligibility at its outset. We follow it as a narrative already fulfilling a great paradigm, as if it were the beneficiary of the tradition rather than its source. In this way, Johannes claims, we miss precisely what makes Abraham Abraham. The deconstructive effort of Johannes is to empty the tale of its authorization, and to gaze fully on the visible Abraham: the strange and silent man who looks for all the world like a prospective infanticide. This Knight of Faith, the exemplar of submission to God, reveals himself to the deconstructive eye as the madman, ready to murder—for no stated reason—his son. Moreover, according to Johannes, the end result of the attempt at murder has nothing to do with Abraham. Certainly it does not "explain" him. God may or may not supply rams at a convenient moment, but Abraham is still the madman.

Having emptied this crucial act of faith of its traditional way of meaning—this act that completely typifies all acts of faith to follow, including the crucifixion—Johannes then refills that act, reestablishes meaning from his position in the present. He decides that Abraham is surely the Knight of Faith, not a madman at all, but solely because Johannes, the present believer, has faith that Abraham *is* such a Knight. As Kierkegaard puts it elsewhere, Johannes becomes "contemporary" with that past he is trying to understand. This act of contemporaneity is for Kierkegaard the only way in which one can truly be a Christian. Abraham remains an archetype, a source, not in the traditional sense, but only as Johannes first *subverts* that source—sees the act for the madness and meaninglessness that it is—and then *reempowers* it from a new vantage point. Johannes's faith reproduces Abraham's faith but not in the form of a fully grounded repetition. The reproduction involves a leap, and the gap Johannes leaps is his own ungrounding of his goal. Johannes's interpretation, however, is not a completely groundless repetition, a deconstructionist free playfulness, any more than the Jesus of Kierkegaard's existential Christianity is a fictional being. Abraham's act generates *Fear and Trembling;* it is a powerful and potentially sustaining act whose identity is continuous with the present, a prior armature and imagery that the present believer has revised but not invented. There is a structure here of interac-

tion and exchange, a dependency whose result is neither meaninglessness nor old meaning but new meaning, meaning
renewed, created now, for the millionth time and the first. [16]

2

My argument is that nearly all of Faulkner's major texts can be
read as versions of a repetition forward. The striking exception in
the canon—as it remained exceptional in a number of ways for
Faulkner—is *The Sound and the Fury*. Inescapable as a kind of
"origin" of the books to follow—in the sense of being reworked
and revised—it is, taken in itself, as close to the ungrounded text
as anything Faulkner would ever write. Constantly unmaking
itself, refusing its own fictional coherences even as it describes
the failing coherences of its four narrative consciousnesses, *The
Sound and the Fury* combines a sense of extraordinary creative
vitality with a sense of nostalgia or loss, touching on despair. We
find a similar combination in such texts as *Beyond the Pleasure
Principle*, *The Trial*, *Nostromo*, and *The Waste Land*. They seem
to drive toward a pure freedom of expression, ridding themselves of referentiality, even as they sustain their own lingering
nostalgia for what is lost in the form of aimless repetitions. They
name a source in actions and language that not only defer it but
question its existence.

Rather than propose a reading of *The Sound and the Fury*, I
want only to comment on Faulkner's two most famous statements
about the writing of it, for they provide an excellent gloss on its
dynamic of vitality and loss. In one he described the writing as a
series of failures to tell the story that lies hidden beneath an
image: "It began with the picture of the little girl's muddy
drawers, climbing that tree . . . I tried first to tell it with one
brother, and that wasn't enough. That was Section One. I tried
with another brother, and that wasn't enough. That was Section
Two. I tried the third brother . . . And that failed and I tried
myself—the fourth section—to tell what happened, and I still
failed." [17] In the other comment, however, Faulkner described

the writing of *The Sound and the Fury* as an unforgettable, and unrepeatable, experience of freedom: "One day I seemed to shut a door between me and all publishers' addresses and booklists. I said to myself, Now I can write." And that writing was a feeling of "ecstasy . . . eager and joyous faith and anticipation of surprise . . . without any accompanying feeling of drive or effort, or any following feeling of exhaustion or relief or distaste."[18]

Both statements are about loss—but one seems, in Derrida's terms, to affirm that loss as *other* than loss: as opportunity to write; while the other mourns the loss, the protracted inability to exhaust an image. The statements are not really separable, just as the text of *The Sound and the Fury* is the seamless coexistence of the mental conditions they indicate. On the one hand, there is the writing as exuberant denial, defiance of controlling center, a kind of insatiable creative hunger that urges the text through the temptations of its centering, refusing to allow Caddy or any other potential origin to emerge in clear or complex resolution. On the other hand, there is the language of that creative drive. The voices that actually constitute the words written down are the "failures" to tell: the voices of Benjy, Quentin, Jason, and "Faulkner," repeating-as-loss the centers that fail to materialize—like the writer perpetually in quest of the image that has inspired his powers beyond the sufficiency to articulate it. Together these two statements about the freedom of writing, about the writing of failure, reverberate in the novel as the drive and the "detours" that finally open it to its radical statement of unmeaning.[19]

The Sound and the Fury is not a novel to be repeated, but it may be said that Faulkner builds a career out of revising it—that is, revising the sense of ungrounding that it so brilliantly invokes. As a series of repetitions-forward, the texts following *The Sound and the Fury* trace an action of creative duplication, performing the imperfectly realized possibilities of a deconstructed ground. And as that tracing, they transform a characteristically fragmentary and discontinuous narrative into a structure that is neither the "copy" of a determinate pattern nor an "intricate network of lies." Instead, there is an achievement of difficult design that survives even the imminence of its own collapse.

Within this mode Faulkner's range and inventiveness, as in most aspects of his art, is extraordinary. Each of the relevant texts is truly of its own distinctive kind, and attempts to lump them together cannot help but distort. There is, for example, a comic repetition forward, most notably in *As I Lay Dying*, a text whose action is to revise the controlling ground of Addie Bundren's desire, reproducing a narrative of interment as a narrative of survival. I will examine this text at greater length below.

There is also a tragic repetition forward—different from the irony and absurdity of *The Sound and the Fury*, which is a tragedy of the perpetual deferral of meaning, and therefore, generically speaking, not tragedy at all. In *Light in August* and *Absalom, Absalom!* we have modern tragedies that describe the amazing capacities of consciousness, however trapped it may be in pasts that will not disclose their meaning, and yet whose culminations are already fixed. Both Quentin Compson and Joe Christmas confront an ambiguous inheritance, one that threatens a catastrophic narrative for any attempt to "know" it. The tragic triumph of these texts is that, however intact the outcome—as inevitable as the narrative line at work in classical tragedy—consciousness *remakes* its past, empowers it with new significance. Joe Christmas revises his unverified mulatto identity from the essence of nonself—" 'you dont know what you are. And more than that, you wont never know' "—into a tortured but palpable process of *full* self, incorporating into his existence the presumably opposed poles of being—black and white, mind and body, female and male, ego and id, life and death. From a blankness of being, belonging to no segment of the community or the narrative compelled to divide him along the rigid lines of language, Christmas achieves the status of modern icon—the image that, borrowing its beginnings from the past, in this case the Christ narrative, comes to "mean" beyond any determination or interpretation: "the man seemed to rise soaring into their memories forever and ever. They are not to lose it . . . it will be there . . . of itself alone serene, of itself alone triumphant."[20]

In *Absalom, Absalom!* Quentin Compson returns once more to the moral enigma of his Southern past, its violence and racism. Instead of passively receiving that past, however—"his very body was an empty hall echoing with sonorous defeated names"—Quentin revises it into new, if still destructive, significance.[21] His explanation of Sutpen's fall and Henry's murder of Charles Bon as the consequence of Bon's hitherto unknown blackness is his creative entrance into history, telling what the past has refused to know of itself. Quentin's end in suicide remains the controlling context of his explanation, but his repetition forward of the past has altered his identity from that of victim to that of tragic creator.

In *Go Down, Moses*—in many ways the representative text of Faulkner's last phase—there is a modification of the repetition forward, with its implicit displacement of origin, toward a more traditional repetition verging on the religious. Ike McCaslin bases the act of relinquishing his property on his assumption of a center to the world: a complete history from fall to redemption, given and presided over by God, that the McCaslin family and the South have been unconsciously implementing. To everyone but Ike, it seems, that history is one of continuous, unchanging violation—repetition as Nietzsche's eternal recurrence: violation of the blacks, of the wilderness, especially of the black kinswoman. These violations continue into Ike's old age, long after his relinquishment; and certainly one of the effects of this continuation is to secure the modernity of *Go Down, Moses*, problematizing the coherent history of eventual salvation that Ike claims to see.

Nevertheless, Ike's vision gathers all the phases of McCaslin violation within its comprehensive pattern. History remains the will of God: "'And Grandfather did own the land nevertheless and notwithstanding because He permitted it, not impotent and not condoning and not blind because He ordered and watched it. . . . Maybe He saw that only by voiding the land for a time of Ikkemotubbe's blood and substituting for it another blood, could He accomplish His purpose. Maybe He knew already what that other blood would be . . . Maybe He chose Grandfather out of all of them He might have picked. . . .'"

History contains and redeems its sins, just as the rituals of the hunt—the scene of Ike's moral instruction—redeem the killings it engenders: the buck Ike has killed "still and forever leaped, the shaking gunbarrels coming constantly and forever steady at last, crashing, and still out of his instant of immortality the buck sprang, forever immortal."[22] Reasoning from the lessons of the hunt to history, Ike constructs his faith that the future freedom of the blacks is implicit in their oppression, that redemption for the whites is already enfolded in their violations.

Like Quentin and Joe Christmas, Ike is retrieving, repeating forward possibilities subverted elsewhere in the text. Yet his vision has a weight that theirs lacks—and does not want—if only because he has "reinvented" the West's most traditional, enduring pattern.[23]

3

The status of *As I Lay Dying* as a revisionary text is evident at the outset in its relationship to *The Sound and the Fury*. For the later novel may be said to repeat the earlier one forward, echoing the aristocratic Compsons with the hill-farmer Bundrens, retrieving the novel of obsessive and therefore futile remembering as the novel of strategic and effective forgetting, the narrative of paralysis and the deferral of meaning as the narrative of a strange yet unmistakable completion of action and signification.

Within the text of *As I Lay Dying*, repetition is the relationship of the various members of the surviving Bundren family to the mother, Addie, who is dying through one part of the novel and dead through the other—although the distinction is not always clear. Addie is the obvious source, the ground of the novel. Her request to be buried in Jefferson, first made at the time of Darl's birth nearly thirty years before, initiates the subsequent journey and the fifty-nine monologues that enact it—for all these monologues refer back, implicitly or explicitly, to the death and the exacted promise that are its center.

But that center, as things turn out, has unexpected ambiguities. For we can read the relationship between the Bundrens and Addie as either Platonic, traditional repetition, or as Nietzschean, modern repetition—that is, as either grounded or ungrounded. Nearly every modern text, as I have suggested earlier in my discussion of Kierkegaard, will at some point present itself as either one or the other, and very likely both. We can thus read *As I Lay Dying* as a grounded novel whose plot unfolds like a doom, everything implicit from the beginning, each of its stages "recollecting" or fulfilling some segment of a predetermined structure. From this perspective the story is that of a grieving family carrying out the wish of its deceased mother, in the course of which they repeat the most basic of narrative actions—the journey, the quest, the interment. The story concludes with a respectful if horribly belated burial. But of course we can also read *As I Lay Dying* as ungrounded, with its performances of Addie's desire almost completely fictional: duplication as the self-empowering, self-serving illusions for which Addie Bundren is merely an excuse. From this perspective, the story is of a group of thoroughly alienated individuals with the same surname, each of whom conducts a journey of his or her own private purpose. They are all linked to a single source—but it is one which is already decomposing in their wagon, vanishing *as source* literally and figuratively. The chain of their connection to that source is like the dotted roads on maps—signs of hypocrisy or imagination—floating free of any referent.

As a middle-ground repetition, a repetition forward, *As I Lay Dying* implies *both* of these possibilities, the Platonic and the Nietzschean. It deconstructs the one *and* regrounds the other; it establishes a dependency of modes, of traditional and modern, past and present. The result is a signification comprised of the burial of the deceased mother in Jefferson in the place of her desire, and the adaptation of that act to the different, autonomous desires of the remaining Bundrens.

In the specific terms of the text the Bundren's revision of their assignment consists of the tension between their fidelity to Addie's wishes and their own private motives and obsessions. That these private motives require the same narrative as their fidelity, like a fresh pencil line tracing an already existent, if fading pattern, is the nature of a repetition forward. And yet this repetition produces an effect distinguishable from either a wholly grounded or ungrounded repetition.

The fidelity has a solidity of its own. The grief of Jewel, Cash, Dewey Dell, and Vardaman is easily documentable, and so for that matter is Anse's: fumbling with the quilt on Addie's dead body; reiterating, like a litany he finally may begin to believe: " 'I give my promise. . . . She is counting on it' "; or reminiscing in this late passage, just on the verge of becoming engaged to the second "Mrs. Bundren": " 'You all dont know. . . . The some-body you was young with and you growed old in her and she growed old in you, seeing the old coming on.' "[24] Real as grief or affection may be, however, they fulfill a static, already completed and death-filled narrative. And thus, out of that grief, the Bundrens contrive a new narrative of present, not past desires. Each of these desires, as a number of critics have noted, revolves around a physical object, what psychologists call a "transitionary object"—the coffin itself, the set of false teeth, the foetus, the fish, the tools, the toy train, the graphophone—which enables a passage from grief to recovery. These desires, and their various objects, become the means by which the Bundrens simulta-neously fulfill the originating narrative and revise its signifi-cance, transforming a procession of the dead into a progress of the living.

Even Jewel possesses such an object in his horse, another vehicle of transition—despite the fact that he is the one member of the family without ulterior motive. In fact, he represents a traditional repetition in that his desire is absolutely at one with Addie's. Appropriately, he has only one of the fifty-nine monologues: he is *all deed,* an almost grotesque figure of stasis and singlemindedness. And yet, ironically, his actions—clearly the most effective in accomplishing the task of getting Addie to Jefferson—support the larger, revisionary action of the family as a whole. The climax of that action is to displace the very source of authority, as Anse buries Addie on one day and takes a new wife on the next. The journey turns from the fulfillment of a dead wife's request to a quest for a new wife. The "Mrs. Bundren" of the novel's last sentence becomes retroactively the propelling force, a second "source" of the narrative. The long dying, and the suffering it has imposed, metamorphoses into the unlikely language of a prothalamion.

The tensions of the Bundrens' repetition are the tensions of Addie Bundren herself. The revision that her family has performed on the bones of her authority is actually modeled—such are the complexities of revision—on the struggle of her own life between the poles of past and present. As Addie makes clear in her monologue, she too has been bound to a powerful source: her father's statement (it is all we ever learn about him) that "the reason for living was to get ready to stay dead a long time" (155). Referred to three times in the monologue, always at a crucial shift in her consciousness, the statement provides a structure for her speech and her life, just as her own request to be buried in Jefferson provides a structure for her survivors' response to her death. Fittingly, as a philosophy, the statement represents an orientation toward death that is the extreme stasis of the completely grounded repetition. In fact, as in *Beyond the Pleasure Principle,* this grounding in death is a grounding in nothingness—not a grounding in the traditional sense, and yet capable of converting life into pure adjunct, no more than a downward slide into vacancy.

The vitality of Addie's life, however, has been her reinterpretation of that statement, her eventual possession of it as something of her own. In the first phase of her monologue, her memory of her father's statement produces in her a nihilistic desire never to have been born—"I would hate my father for having ever planted

me" (155)—and an awareness of the irrevocable privacy of being,
which results in her conviction that only through physical violence can she experience any communication with another person. Hardly communication, in fact, but only the harsh
registering of her identity in another's consciousness: "Now I am
something in your secret and selfish life, who have marked your
blood with my own for ever and ever" (155). But the climax of
this phase is Addie's first "answer" to the judgment that "living
was terrible" (157), which she finds implicit to her father's statement. This answer is her experience of the birth of her first
child, Cash, and a human communion like no other, violent or
sexual, that she has previously known. "My aloneness had been
violated and then made whole again by the violation: time,
Anse, love, what you will, outside the circle" (158). Thus a
transformation of aloneness and the meaning of violation: there is
an aloneness that is whole.

The second phase of Addie's life begins with the discovery that
she is pregnant with Darl, a fact to which she responds with
outrage. Perhaps this has to do with the reinvasion of "time,
Anse, love, what you will" into the circle of her wholeness. She
revises her father's statement again, this time into a cry of
vengeance against Anse, but more so against what she now
recognizes as the conditions of being: the virtual impossibility of
the wholeness she thought she had known, signalled by an even
more radical rupture between words and deeds than she had
once believed. With the birth of Darl she calls for the eventual
trip to Jefferson for burial—proposing this as the instrument of
her vengeance: an indelible exemplum, although not to be completely understood, of the fact that living really *is* nothing but
getting ready to stay dead a long time. "[B]ecause I knew that
father had been right . . . [and] I was wrong" (159), she admits,
and yet this is still a reinterpretation by Addie, another revision,
because father "couldn't have known he was right anymore than
I could have known I was wrong." Never having known the
wholeness with which Addie had first "answered" him, he could

not have known the outrage of Anse's violation of it, nor the murderous response of Addie to that violation.[25]

Addie's adultery with Whitfield is like an interlude, a momentary attempt, touched now with moral violence, to get outside her father and the determinacies of death; as if the answer, "it," might be "the duty to the alive, to the terrible blood . . . boiling through the land" (161), and the moral transgression a kind of garment which, in its shedding, might become a last means of reuniting word and deed, although it is a "forlorn echo of the dead word high in the air."

But with the knowledge that she is pregnant with Jewel, Addie moves to the last phase of her struggle with the past. Again she reinterprets her father's claim, who now not only couldn't have known he was right, as in the second phase, he "could not have known what he meant" (162). Getting ready to stay dead, Addie decides, is a matter of house cleaning, foreign to her father, presumably to any man, a cruel kind of accounting in which children become figures in the his and hers column of a ledger: "And now he has three children that are his and not mine. And then I could get ready to die" (162).

Addie's life is thus an originating bondage, locking her family into a structure as narrow as her father's, *and* a model of the revision of that structure. The father's statement abides, its language unchanged, the refrain of Addie's monologue and life. But meanings proliferate, each stage in Addie's life brings forth a new challenge, power is subverted—she reestablishes its significance.

Following her example, the Bundren family enacts Addie's statement as she in a sense has enacted her father's, both as a death-drive to be copied and, more so than Addie, as a springboard for repetition-forward. The immediate effect of the process of the dying of Addie Bundren is to hurl her family into a nearly total fragmentation. The isolation and alienation of each member, the hostility betweeen them, is comparable to that isolation of being Addie knew as a school teacher in the first phase of her response to her father's statement. This isolation never disappears, but once the journey to Jefferson begins, the family necessarily begins to act as a more coherent unit. Major instances of this coming together are the scene following the crossing of the river, as the family combines in concern for the injured Cash and in the effort to retrieve his tools. There is also Darl's monologue just before the crossing, in which he recalls the time when Jewel worked secretly at night in order to earn money to buy a horse and the family covered for his absences and weariness. There are also all the tangible contributions the family makes to the journey—some of them, of course, made grudgingly or even unwittingly: Jewel's horse, Cash's eight dollars saved for a graphophone, Dewey Dell's ten dollars to pay for a termination of her pregnancy. These contributions are the repeating backward of their fealty, their dedication to the journey Addie Bundren designed; but they are also the sign of their freedom and autonomy, the sign of those objects that are their transition *away* from Addie.

For even as the Bundrens carry out this incredible journey, doing serious physical and emotional damage to themselves, and no one knows exactly what violence to the corpse they bear, they are also releasing themselves from their originating structure into a new one, from the boundaries of death, and the instinct toward death that is at least one meaning of Addie's father's statement, into the openness of Eros. Freud's name for the life principle as opposed to the death, Eros is the movement out of atomization toward cohesiveness, the attempt to "hold . . . all living things together," to "establish ever greater unities and to preserve them thus—in short to bind together."[26] In a word, the Bundrens transform the journey from its origins in death into a narrative of comic integration, of survival and expansion: a marriage, a new mother, a new life—the coming baby Dewey Dell has failed to abort—and new acquisitions, however trivial, of bananas and a phonograph.

In one crucial matter the Bundrens repeat Addie exactly, and that is in the rejection of Darl—even as my discussion has, up to this point, rejected him and his subversive meanings. In specifying her final house cleaning, Addie says, "I gave Anse Dewey Dell to negative Jewel. Then I gave him Vardaman to replace the child I had robbed him of. And now he has three children that are his and not mine" (162). The child she "robbed" from Anse is clearly Cash. Darl is not referred to except in the collective "three children." One reads the sentence twice to learn what happened to him. Similarly, at the end of their journey, having buried Addie in an introductory adverbial clause, "But when we got it filled and covered" (220), the family brutally delivers Darl over to the men who will escort him to the asylum in Jackson, where he will spend the rest of his life.

The eloquence of Darl, the delicacy and depth of perception, the exquisitely modeled descriptions of scenes he is not even present to see—these qualities become in this novel the strange index of his remoteness from the rest of the family. Darl is rejected, it is important to notice, by both the source of the narrative (Addie) and the agents of its revisionary implementation. In the terms I have used in this analysis, Darl is the utterly ungrounded being—he has no past, no mother, no authority; and thus no received structure *within* which or *against* which he can act. Although on a number of occasions on the journey he lends his support and his quick-wittedness, he has no real place in it, because he neither wants to carry out Addie's desire literally, as Jewel does, nor to revise it. He wishes simply to stop it, negate the origin rather than repeat or recreate it. What we cannot help regard as the sign of his sanity—"'She wants him to hide her away from the sight of man'" (197)—is finally the sanity of the outsider, "same as you" (220) as Cash puts it, meaning us.[27] These are the onlookers, even the close friends of the family, who finally can only smell the rotting corpse, urge the Bundrens toward New Hope and a quick burial, and can never completely understand this journey because they, like Darl, are not inside of it. As Kierkegaard's narrator says of his efforts to understand Abraham, "only the one who draws the knife gets Isaac."

As Darl's monologues indicate several times, he is threatened with nonbeing itself: "I dont know what I am. I dont know if I am or not" (72); only through the most intricate ontological maneuvers can he prove his own existence. His understanding of repetition is unique in the novel: "How do our lives ravel out into the no-wind, no-sound, the weary gestures wearily recapitulant: echoes of old compulsions with no-hand on no-strings" (191). This is the repetition of Nietzsche's eternal recurrence, or Freud's repetition back into inanimacy: the echoes, the compulsion play with "no-hand on no-strings." The ground is gone.

As a result, there is no gap between presence and loss that Darl can fill with the transitionary objects of self-interest, no gap between word and deed that he can leap with his illusions: no gap because for Darl there has never been presence, never been deed, never been self. He is, as Calvin Bedient has described him, "absolutely naked" to the world.[28]

The danger of As I Lay Dying, which is of course part of its greatness, is that it never completely demolishes the possibility that Darl is *right* in his groundlessness. No modernist text, taking to itself the privilege of repetition forward, of subverting and revising a ground, can ever close the door again to the suspicion that the cost of our expanded freedom is that it is larger than we have supposed, that in challenging ground we have dispelled it for good. Darl *knows* what our identities are designed to protect, the void our fictions are designed to fill, just as he knows those truths of Jewel and Dewey Dell that they cannot bear to be known. This is the terrible knowledge for which they expel him from their lives, just as the narrative must expel him from its own. The sacrificial act of the narrative is to depict the ontological perception of Darl as madness.

One crucial level of this, as with all Faulkner's novels, is its formal enactment of the ungrounding that Darl endures: the narrative of voices, sharply edged by their intense privacy and isolation, ricocheting off each other as the Bundrens collide in their selfishness. But gradually these fragments add up to an accounting—structure and meaning. For some, this may be no more than the mechanics of house cleaning or the craftsmanship of the chicken coop. And yet there is a completion of a journey to death and life, from disarray to design. The narrative eventually confines the groundlessness which its own form of repetition must partially imply; it pretends to an order, the coherences of Eros rather than the blankness of death or that undecidability that is the critical mask for nothingness.

But we cannot claim too much. This novel is *about* not claiming too much. Robert Frost has a more suitably restrained version of what the achievement of design as a repetition forward looks like: "a clarification of life—not necessarily a great clarification, such as sects and cults are founded on, but . . . a momentary stay against confusion."[29]

NOTES

1. Mircea Eliade, *The Sacred and the Profane: The Nature of Religion*, trans. Willard R. Trask (New York: Harcourt, Brace & World, 1959), 30–31, 68–69. Also see 168, 202. On the acquisition of value in premodern societies, see also Eliade, *The Myth of the Eternal Return or, Cosmos and History*, trans. Willard R. Trask (Princeton: Princeton/Bollingen, 1971), 3–6. On Eliade, see Bruce F. Kawin, *Telling it Again and Again: Repetition in Literature and Film* (Ithaca: Cornell University Press, 1972), 90–94.

2. Eliade, *The Sacred and the Profane*, 12.

3. Ibid., 167.

4. Eliade, *The Myth of the Eternal Return*, 15. See also 5, 34, and *The Sacred and the Profane*, 100, 104.

5. Eliade, *The Myth of the Eternal Return*, 104.

6. See Eliade, *The Myth of the Eternal Return*, 90, and *The Sacred and the Profane*, 112. See also Karl Löwith, *Meaning in History* (Chicago: The University of Chicago Press, 1949).

7. De Man, *Blindness and Insight: Essays in the Rhetoric of Contemporary Criticism* (New York: Oxford University Press, 1971), 148.

8. Miller, *Fiction and Repetition: Seven English Novels* (Cambridge: Harvard University Press, 1982), 4–7.

9. Derrida, "Structure, Sign, and Play in the Discourse of the Human Sciences," in *The Structuralist Controversy: The Languages of Criticism and the Sciences of Man*, ed. Richard Macksey and Eugenio Donato (Baltimore: The Johns Hopkins University Press, 1972), 264.

10. Nietzsche, *The Will to Power: An Attempted Transvaluation of All Values*, trans. Anthony M. Ludovici, in *The Complete Works of Friedrich Nietzsche*, ed. Oscar Levy (New York: Gordon Press, 1974), 15: 1067, 1059.

11. For an important discussion of *Beyond the Pleasure Principle* in terms of origin and deferral, see Eric LaGuardia, "Priority and Deferral: The Text of Beyond the Pleasure Principle," *Psychoanalysis and Contemporary Thought*, 7 (1984), 269–88.

12. Kierkegaard, *Fear and Trembling/Repetition*, ed. and trans. Howard V. Hong and Edna H. Hong (Princeton: Princeton University Press, 1983), 131.

13. Louis Mackey, *Kierkegaard: A Kind of Poet* (Philadelphia: University of Pennsylvania Press, 1971), 17.

14. Heidegger, *Being and Time*, trans. John Macquarrie and Edward Robinson (New York: Harper & Row, 1962), 437. The passage is quoted and discussed in William V.

Spanos, "Heidegger, Kierkegaard, and the Hermeneutic Circle: Towards a Postmodern Theory of Interpretation as Dis-closure," *Boundary 2*, 4 (Winter 1976), 455–88.

15. Edward Said offers his own versions of "repetition forward" in his *Beginnings: Intention and Method* (New York: Basic Books, 1975) and "On Repetition," in *The World, the Text, and the Critic* (Cambridge: Harvard University Press, 1983). See for example his comments on Vico's distinction between sacred and gentile history, "where extraordinary possibilities of variety and diversity are open to it but where it will not be referred back docilely to an idea that stands above it and explains it" (*Beginnings*, 11–12, 349–50, and 377–78). See also Edward Casey, "Imagination and Repetition in Literature: A Reassessment," *Yale French Studies*, 52 (1975), 249–67.

The most commanding and comprehensive voice on the question of past and present contesting with each other for primacy is Harold Bloom's. If my own notions of repetition as a "middle ground," maintaining both source and creative autonomy, differ at all from Bloom's various ratios, it may be in the less adversarial quality I see in repetition— positioning myself somewhere between T. S. Eliot's idealization of the relationship between tradition and individual talent and Bloom's far more radical sense of tension.

16. Another example of this "repetition forward" can be found in Freud's accounts of psychoanalytic transference within the therapeutic encounter between patient and analyst. Basic both to the diagnosis and cure of neurosis is the patient's reenactment and revision of the narrative that has culminated in his present condition. Essentially he rewrites his story, without altering its facts, into "new editions of the old conflicts"; he engages again the formerly traumatic material, but this time chooses a course that can "lead . . . to a better outcome than that which ended in repression": *Introductory Lectures on Psychoanalysis*, trans. and ed. James Strachey (New York: W. W. Norton & Co., 1977), 454, 438. For a full discussion see my essay "Freud Reading" in *The Psychoanalytic Study of Literature*, ed. Joseph Reppen and Maurice Charney (Hillsdale, N.J.: Analytic Press, 1985), 3–36. For discussion of repetition as a theory of reading, see my "The Divided Protagonist: Reading as Repetition and Discovery," *Texas Studies in Language and Literature*, 30 (Summer 1988), 151–78.

17. *Faulkner in the University: Class Conferences at the University of Virginia, 1957–1958*, ed. Frederick L. Gwynn and Joseph L. Blotner (Charlottesville: University of Virginia Press, 1959), 1.

18. "An Introduction for *The Sound and the Fury*," ed. James B. Meriwether, *The Southern Review*, 8 (Autumn 1972), 705–8.

19. For full discussions of *The Sound and the Fury* as a text that defers its meaning see John T. Irwin, *Doubling and Incest/Repetition and Revenge: A Speculative Reading of Faulkner* (Baltimore: The Johns Hopkins University Press, 1975), John T. Matthews, *The Play of Faulkner's Language* (Ithaca: Cornell University Press, 1982), and my *The Fragile Thread: The Meaning of Form in Faulkner's Novels* (Amherst: University of Massachusetts Press, 1979).

20. *Light in August* (photographed copy of the first printing, 1932), (New York: Random House, Modern Library, n.d.), 363, 440.

21. *Absalom, Absalom!* (New York: Random House, Modern Library, 1951), 12.

22. *Go Down, Moses* (New York: Random House, 1942), 258–59, 178.

23. For a discussion of Faulkner in terms of repetition and revision, see Richard H. King, *A Southern Renaissance: The Cultural Awakening of the American South, 1930–1955* (New York: Oxford University Press, 1980), 77–145.

24. *As I Lay Dying*, The Corrected Text, ed. Noel Polk (New York: Random House, 1987), 48, 126, 217. Further references will be cited in the text. For discussion of Anse's generally unrecognized affection for Addie, see Robert Dale Parker, *Faulkner and the Novelistic Imagination* (Urbana: University of Illinois Press, 1985), 291–31.

25. See Parker, *Faulkner and the Novelistic Imagination*, 24–25.

26. Freud, *Beyond the Pleasure Principle*, trans. James Strachey (New York: W. W.

Norton & Co., n.d.), 27; *Outline of Psychoanalysis*, trans. James Strachey (New York: W. W. Norton & Co., 1949), 5.

27. On this point, see André Bleikasten, *Faulkner's "As I Lay Dying"* (Bloomington: Indiana University Press, 1973), 132.

28. Bedient, "Pride and Nakedness: *As I Lay Dying*" in *Faulkner: New Perspectives*, ed. Richard H. Brodhead (Englewood Cliffs, N.J.: Prentice-Hall, Inc., 1983), 145.

29. Frost, "The Figure a Poem Makes," *Complete Poems of Robert Frost* (New York: Holt, Rinehart & Winston, 1949), vi.

Compulsive and Revisionary Repetition: Faulkner's "Barn Burning" and the Craft of Writing Difference

Richard C. Moreland

While reading the typescript of *The Mansion*, Faulkner's Random House editor, Albert Erskine, kept finding "discrepancies and contradictions" between the earlier, already published novels of Faulkner's Snopes trilogy and this typescript of the last, in which Faulkner retold some of the same stories about some of the same events and characters, but retold them differently. As Erskine reported these discrepancies and contradictions to Faulkner, Faulkner became somewhat impatient with his editor's worrying so much about what Faulkner thought would pose problems only for readers he tended to call "academical gumshoes." He agreed to correct some such discrepancies, but eventually decided to let many more stand uncorrected, and decided to steal our gumshoe thunder by writing a prefatory note to the novel asserting his awareness of many of these discrepancies and explaining his reason for letting them show. Erskine had already offered what would have been a New Critical line of defense in suggesting that these three novels might not be a trilogy after all, [1] implying that Faulkner could fall back safely on the idea that each of his novels was an autonomous new creation by a peculiarly literary genius, who would therefore speak the language of poetry and religion, which was at that time identified as a language of paradox. [2] But this was not the explanation Faulkner gave. Instead, perhaps more candidly, he says in his prefatory note that over his life's work of writing he has continued to *learn* more than he knew before about the human heart and about his characters. If readers notice differences, then, in Faulkner's repetitions or rewritings of previous work, perhaps we should not gloat so thunderously that Homer nods, but *neither* should we pass over such discrepancies silently, apologetically, or sentimentally as part of this Mississippi native's woodsy wildness, something only a "better craftsman" like Pound or Hemingway would have bothered to prune and tame. These repetitions and especially the differences they emphasize might represent, instead, importantly critical, published revisions of Faulkner's ongoing thinking and writing, revisions not just of minor details but of whole plots and structures of thought. In the course of Faulkner's career, he constantly recycled and refit plots, episodes, characters, and phrases from poems to stories to filmscripts to novels to other stories and other novels: such repetitions and differences were in his case not only unusually prolific and undisguised, they amounted to an ongoing critical project in his career, as he repeated certain dominant structures of thought in the post–Civil War American South and the post–World War I United States and Europe, repeating these structures first to explore, elaborate, and understand their motivations and consequences, then critically to revise certain structural contradictions and impasses shared by both these postwar cultures, and elaborated in Faulkner's own and others' literary modernism.

Faulkner's revisions of his modernism involved an important shift in the function of repetition, both in his own work and also in his understanding of the historical and literary contexts in which he lived and wrote. In order to understand this shift, the notion of repetition with a significant, critical difference, which I will call *revisionary repetition*, should be distinguished from repetition of another kind which I will call, after Freud, *compulsive repetition*. Revisionary repetition repeats some structured event, in order somehow to alter that structure and its continuing power, especially by opening a critical space for what the subject might *learn* about that structure in the different context of a changing present or a more distant or different past.

As Sartre says, "a life develops in spirals; it passes again and again by the same points but at different levels of integration and complexity."³ This is the kind of repetition I have attributed to Faulkner's revisions of his modernism. But in compulsive repetition, it is precisely this unpredictable possibility of critically altering a familiar structure in the light of changing or different circumstances which repetition attempts to avoid. It attempts to expunge or ward off all such changes and variations as insignificant departures from an abstractly unchanged, unaffected original. Even the most unpleasant, restrictively habitual repetitions may seem in this way preferable to the unpredictability and impurity of change and difference. Inasmuch as every repetition, then, involves both an identity of the same content or structure and also a difference and change at least in time and context, compulsive repetition attempts to exclude that difference and change; revisionary repetition attempts to alter the structures of identity. It attempts to inscribe marks of change and difference within a linguistic, social, or psychological structure of such continuing power that it cannot be simply ignored, forgotten or denied, but must be acknowledged as a repetition, either compulsively or in a spirit of critical revision. Compulsive repetition repeats the familiar and the familial; revisionary repetition places these familiarities (with critical effect) in the midst of irrepressibly ambivalent, fearful but strong desires for other voices.

The issue of these two kinds of repetition arises in Faulkner's work in two ways, as method and then as topic—topic for a critique that led in turn to a shift in method. In his novels before *Absalom, Absalom!* Faulkner's method shared a tendency with that of other modernists toward repeated juxtapositions of various "unified sensibilities" from the past—Eliot's Elizabethans, Joyce's Greeks, Yeats's Byzantines and Celts, the Southern Agrarians' Agrarian South—over against the supposedly meaningless disarray and banality of everyday modern life, typically represented from an ironic distance as a "heap of broken images."⁴ As Faulkner extended his treatment of such broken

images in *Light in August* and especially *Absalom, Absalom!*
from the realm of the personal and familial toward the racial and
historical,[5] and from metaphysical themes of destruction and
loss toward social, historical themes of change and difference, he
explored and analyzed as a fictional topic certain compulsive
habits of memory, narration, and (in)action on the parts of Rosa
Coldfield, Mr. Compson, Thomas Sutpen, Shreve, and Quentin
that were in many ways similar to modernist methods of his
own—in their protomodernist vacillation between a more or less
explicit nostalgia for a diseased social structure and the ironic
contemplation of scenes of its inevitable and total collapse. After
interrupting his work on *Absalom* for a parodic treatment of
cosmopolitan literary modernism in *Pylon*, Faulkner continued
to examine in these characters of the postwar South the social
and historical motivations and consequences of their culturally
typical vacillation between forced nostalgia and bitter irony. In
Absalom Faulkner traces the motivations of such a vacillation not
to the deeper metaphysical nature of time and loss[6] but to the
social and historical climate of disillusionment and defeat after
the war, a climate of disillusionment already decades old (and
somewhat threadworn) as Rosa, Mr. Compson, Quentin, and
Shreve remember the course of postwar Southern history, and
well over a decade old again as Faulkner writes in the wider
climate of disillusionment in the United States and Europe after
World War I. Faulkner discovers and demonstrates how this
vacillation between nostalgia and irony in reaction to such disillusionment works retroactively to ward off and soften the impact
of a once unexpected blow, forestalling the implications of historical change and difference by insisting on the unchanging drama
of fated destruction and loss. While Faulkner thus comes to
understand the motivations of such a vacillation between
nostalgia and irony, he also comes to understand its consequences when it becomes a compulsive impasse attempting
indefinitely and sometimes violently to exclude change and difference. Faulkner's critical explorations of this repetitive impasse
as a historical topic in *Absalom* led him to seek a way out of these

historical compulsions in "Barn Burning" and *The Hamlet*, by revising a scene that in *Absalom* started a series of compulsive repetitions. In finding a way out of those repetitions for Ab Snopes, Faulkner also discovered his own way out of certain compulsive modernist methods, finding in this new process of revisionary repetition both a strikingly different fictional method and also openings for several new, formerly marginalized topics, notably in his treatments of the makeshift economy and precarious humor of the Old Southwest, in his attention to mourning as a way of working through the relentless repetitions of melancholia, and in his listening harder for blacks' and women's critically different voices. I will have space here only to point toward certain promising openings for such new topics, focussing instead on "Barn Burning" as a pivotal moment in Faulkner's career, poised between one method of repetition and the other, turning from the compulsive toward the revisionary for a change in method that made such changes in topics possible.[7]

An exemplary site for Faulkner's discovery of his way out of his native culture's and his artistic peers' compulsive repetitions is a series of repetitions and revisions of one particular structured social event in *Absalom, Absalom!* It is the scene where the ragged young Thomas Sutpen comes with a message from his tenant-farming father to the majestic front door of the planter for whom his father works. The liveried black slave who opens and bars the door tells Sutpen "even before he had had time to say what he came for, never to come to that front door again but to go around to the back."[8] Stunned and shattered here by his own social silencing and exclusion, Sutpen idealizes and internalizes the image of a planter perfectly purified, invulnerable, and invisible somewhere inside the house. Years later Sutpen represents this scene to General Compson as the determining "primal scene" at the very origin of his life's design to found his own family dynasty inside the same unviolated, unbroken Southern plantation tradition. He represents it as a primal scene, that is, in the sense of his being henceforth powerlessly compelled only to re-present and to repeat what he thinks he has learned here once and for all about the structure of his society and even of life in general. The rest of *Absalom* traces Sutpen's and his adopted culture's variously relentless, compulsive repetitions of this same structured social event, this apparently inescapable primal scene of purifying exclusion.

In "Barn Burning," which he published three years later, in 1939, Faulkner returns to this scene again, not compulsively, however, but in order to make significant revisions, and to open a critical space for reconceiving this oppressive primal scene. Again a poor-white boy inclined to idealize the planter's house sees his own way into the front door of that house barred by a liveried and insulting black servant; however, this time the boy, Sarty Snopes, is accompanied by his less impressionable father, Ab Snopes, who is not awe-struck by the insult but has clearly expected and provoked it, and who responds by pushing his way inside to deliver his message anyway by smearing horse-manure on the blond rug inside the door. After some ambivalence about his father's peculiar writing style, Sarty eventually repeats his society's tendency to refuse to read such gestures at writing difference, and repeats his society's violent condemnation and exclusion of Ab's social difference as only so much social filth. At least from Sarty's frightened and therefore humorless perspective, Ab's potentially critical difference seems here a failed and fatal alternative.

However, Faulkner himself would enlarge prolifically on this same critical and creative potential for revising the plantation society's primal scene, as he rewrites it once again as an opening episode of *The Hamlet*, published a year later in 1940.9 He now replaces Sarty's frightened, *humorless* perspective on Ab's "bad attitude" at the planter's door with V. K. Ratliff's *humorous* appreciation of Ab's singular history and his singularly unsettling provocations. Whereas in "Barn Burning" Sarty thinks Ab's attitude at the planter's door leads toward his inevitable, tragic death at the end of the story, in *The Hamlet*'s version Ratliff enjoys telling of Ab's repeated escape from that expected tragedy and of his surviving to outrage the planter's categories again and move on to Frenchman's Bend. In *The Hamlet*'s version of this repeatedly and undisguisedly revised scene at the planter's door, Faulkner places the scene at the opening of volume one of the Snopes trilogy, the longest, most sustained work of his career, making this episode a primal scene now of a different kind. It is now a primal scene not for compulsive repetition but for humorous appreciation and elaboration as an exemplary scene of critical escape from oppressive social categories and oppositions, a scene that points a way out for others without pretending to point the one new way.

I have mentioned humor, mourning, and different voices as three openings for critical escape from *Absalom*'s compulsive primal scene, openings which Faulkner discovered in his revisionary repetition of that scene in "Barn Burning" and which he explored further in his continuing revisions of that scene in *The Hamlet*. But in order to explain better Faulkner's discovery in his fiction of these openings for critical and revisionary escape, I should explain more fully the nature of those compulsive categories and oppositions in *Absalom* which Faulkner felt an increasing need to revise as he examined their social and historical implications. For in *Absalom*, while he does not yet open a way out of those compulsions, Faulkner does already discover and demonstrate the profoundly ambivalent motivations and the extremely violent consequences of those compulsive repetitions—ambivalent motivations and violent consequences in both the "innocent" and the "ironic" forms these compulsions tend to take in *Absalom, Absalom!*, as in much other modernist literature.

Thomas Sutpen's so-called "innocence" consists in his imitating and repeating, apparently without self-consciousness, apology, or extenuation, his society's essential gesture of self-purifying exclusion, that gesture he thinks he learned once and for all in his primal scene. In his internalization of his society's idealized image of the planter, Sutpen has purified his own later memory of the ambivalence of having been once, himself along with his closest family and friends, on the outside of that planter's door, wanting to get inside but all too closely tied emotionally and socially to those people and memories he would leave outside. It is this suddenly frightened and confusing ambivalence that motivates the violent imposition of the planter's idealized image in his consciousness. The emotional violence of this reductive, willful solution to his ambivalence has the social consequence that Sutpen repeatedly defends that same compulsively purified image of the planter and himself by violent social exclusions throughout his life—on the model of this first class exclusion, he later excludes his own first wife, Eulalia, then his own first son, Charles Bon, both because of their race, then he excludes his own second daughter (by Millicent Jones) because of her gender.

Faulkner makes both the emotional violence and the social violence of these repeated exclusions clear already in *his* representation of Sutpen's primal scene. It was "like an explosion," Sutpen said (238). His sudden internalization of the planter's monumental image with no remainder of "ashes" or "refuse" from his formerly groping ambivalence takes the form in the novel of a primal scene—not in the sense of an original, determining encounter with an unalterable knowledge, but in the sometime-Freudian sense of a "theoretical fiction" of such an origin—a fictional origin that is always already a simplifying, focusing repetition of more confusing earlier and later memories.[10] In Faulkner's novel Sutpen's primal scene imposes itself at the origin of his life's design as a violently reductive, purifying solution to his emotional confusion about two previous repetitions of this same socially structured event. In those two previous scenes, however, there had seemed to be more room for Sutpen's awareness of his own and others' ambivalence with regard to the violence of the event, whereas in the third that potentially critical awareness *of* ambivalence and violence is silently excluded from what has become a socially structured, ideologically naturalized event.

In the first of these three scenes, Sutpen is travelling with his father from the frontier society of the West Virginia mountains into the plantation society of Tidewater Virginia. While they are still on the margin of that plantation society Sutpen sees his first slave in the act of carrying and throwing Sutpen's drunken father out the door of a doggery; the slave's mouth is "loud with laughing and full of teeth like tombstones" (225): by comparison with Sutpen's later primal scene, here both the emotional ambivalence and the violence of this temporary, tenuous social exclusion are unmistakable. These become less clear, however, in the second scene, set farther into plantation country, as Sutpen watches his father being "not even allowed to come in by the front door" of taverns and then being ejected, but "with no laughter and jeers to the ejecting now, even if the laughter and jeers had been harsh and without much gentleness in them" (225–26). Sutpen still misses here the harsh laughter of the doggeries' frontier humor for what it *did* acknowledge of his and others' ambivalence toward, and mutual vulnerability to, such acts of physical and social violence. Sutpen can still notice here the absence of such laughter as a sign of this society's ideological naturalization of this still palpably unnatural event. In the scene I have called Sutpen's primal scene, however, this potentially critical but confusing perspective is eliminated from his henceforth compulsive repetitions of the scene, *as if* from the very start: Sutpen accepts and teaches himself once and for all (though the lesson must be learned and taught with repeated, increasing violence) this naturalization of a social act as a simple, even an unobjectionable fact, a fact that other re-presentations can only repeat, without significantly reinscribing or altering what they re-present.

These compulsive repetitions tend to take one other main form in their vacillations in *Absalom* and in Faulkner's earlier modernist work. Quentin Compson, in his self-conscious irony toward Sutpen's innocence, seems aware, as Sutpen was not, of what is repressed and excluded in these compulsive, repetitive acts of purificatory exclusion. However, Quentin's postwar Southern, postwar modernist irony offers only a mirror image of those same compulsions, an attempt to resolve at a higher

level—but in the same terms—those oppositions made uncom-
fortably clear by Sutpen's innocent imitations of this society's
defining structure. Irony here re-presents what has been repressed and excluded in innocence, but re-presents it only as the
still repressed and excluded, without giving any articulate voices
of their own to those repressed emotions or those excluded other
subjects. That is, irony here preemptively, cautiously represents
what innocence has repressed and excluded, but represents it
only in the safely generalized, still repressive terms of the same
opposition, in some version of what Conrad and Eliot called "the
horror," and what Joyce called the "nightmare" of history. It is
what Faulkner in *Absalom* represents as the repeatedly repressed and excluded voice of human suffering, desire, and grief
heard only in the safely inarticulate, undifferentiated sound of
the black idiot Jim Bond's howl.

The particular version of his society's compulsively repeated
primal scene on which Quentin himself gets stuck is the scene
where Thomas Sutpen's son, Henry, bursts into his sister's room
to announce he has just murdered her fiancé, Charles Bon, at
the front gate of the Sutpen plantation. Having been am-
bivalently attached to Bon as a friend, Henry has just repeated
his father's act of purifying exclusion at the plantation gate in a
gesture of protecting his sister's and his family's honor from the
"spot" of black blood he has discovered in Bon. Having thereby
secured his own place, as it were, in the *father's* place on the
inside of the plantation threshold, he enters now into his sister's
room as if "into his own," as if to claim now the father's oedipal
prize. But he discovers he is now again on the outside bursting
in, coming face to face in his sister's room with Judith half-naked
and sewing her wedding dress: he is coming face to face, that is,
with his own incestuous erotic desire and the violence it has
done to Judith by seeing her as an oedipal prize rather than as
another subject, capable of speaking from her *own* erotic desire,
if he could have listened. Quentin's ironic fixation on this scene
does represent some such discovery, on Henry's part, of the
violent repression of his ambivalance toward both Bon and Ju-

dith, as well as the violent exclusion of Judith's and Bon's own subjectivities, in Henry's compulsive repetition of his father's primal scene. Presumably Quentin also recognizes in this scene his own ambivalence toward his own sister Caddy and the violence his fixation on her virginity does to her as another subject, capable of her own erotic future. But if Quentin and Henry here do somehow confront ironically that other subjectivity which in their innocence they have previously repressed, it is not now to let that other subject speak in a different voice, but only to fixate on the scene of their own ironic discovery of the exclusion, represented here as a discovery not of particular other subjects but of their own mirror image in the form of the inescapable Other—the Other escapable only in Henry's death as in Quentin's impending suicide. As long as that other is only *the* Other, one can only be inside or outside the door, either father or son, either in possession or not in possession of the contested object of desire. Only when the contested object speaks as another recognizable subject, speaking thus outside the terms of this opposition—only then can the compulsive repetition of this opposition be broken. Here that other voice *might* have been that of the liveried slave whom Sutpen meets *on* the threshold of the plantation. Or it might have been the voice of the sister whom Henry finds in two places at once, both purified and protected *from* Bon *inside* the plantation ideal but also excluded and silenced as subject *with* Bon *outside* that same ideal, by Henry's attempt at purifying exclusion. Such voices are almost everywhere silent in *Absalom,* even though Faulkner's irony like Quentin's almost everywhere here *represents* their silence and the doors that repeatedly close them out.

In "Barn Burning" the critically different voice at the threshold of the plantation, though hard to read, is that of Ab Snopes. Standing alongside Ab on that precarious margin, Ab's son Sarty is tempted in his ambivalence and fright, as Thomas and Henry Sutpen were, to accept his society's compulsive resolutions of that fearful ambivalence. For the sake of such resolutions, Sarty is prepared to accept certain implicit oppositional terms for what he feels in his ambivalence, even though (or perhaps because) those oppositional terms violently bar the door on his father Ab and translate Sarty himself inside the house, in another compulsive insistence on self-purifying exclusion. Ab, however, here at the door and throughout the story, repeatedly provokes, frustrates, and escapes all such attempts by his society to account for him in terms of its usual mediations and resolutions: Ab provokes those resolutions to the point of exposing the violence of those oppositions they usually disguise, oppositions they usually disguise in order to preserve and repeat them still compulsively, though in apparently different forms. Ab also speaks and writes here and intermittently throughout the story in his own critically different voice and style, effectively setting these dominant oppositions *and* their resolutions off to one side of what they cannot account for—not by oversight but design—what those oppositions and resolutions are constructed in order to leave out of account. Thus Sarty cannot or will not listen to the singular impertinence of Ab's own history and potential humor, a voice the narrator here urges readers to read better than Sarty does. It is an impertinence that *Faulkner* would return to read much more elaborately and appreciatively in his next rewrite of this scene in *The Hamlet* another two years later.

In the "Barn Burning" version of the scene at the planter's door, set thirty years after the war, Sarty attempts two different currently available cultural means to resolve the ambivalence he feels. His first, more innocent attempt is in terms of a plantation myth that has become in many ways stronger after the war than before. It is the now nostalgically idealized myth of the plantation as trickle-down source of moral and even economic blessings to all its humble dependents. Sarty has felt with disturbing ambivalence the stark contrast between the apparently invulnerable "peace and dignity" of the planter's house, and his own father's world of frightening social and economic violence and indignity. Sarty seeks a sentimental resolution to that ambivalence in the hope for a moral change in his father's character under the influence of "the spell of the house": *"Maybe he will feel it too. Maybe it will even change him now from what maybe he couldn't help but be.*"[11] But instead of this baptism and redemption of Ab in the planter's image, Faulkner's revision here of the scene at the planter's door represents Ab's muddying of the water. Instead of dissolving Ab's difference into its mythically purifying solution, the spell of the house is broken by Ab's indelible signature on the blond rug placed just inside the door. Ab tests this false welcome by wiping the horse-manure on his boot on the expensive, imported rug, provoking another of his perennial exclusions in terms of those same compulsive social and economic oppositions that are only disguised and not revised by such mythic attempts to resolve the social division. Thus even Ab himself repeats the myth of the magical plantation house to Sarty, but in order to suggest a revision of what he knows is Sarty's awe-struck view of that mythic house: " 'Pretty and white, ain't it?' he said. 'That's sweat. Nigger sweat. Maybe it ain't white enough yet to suit him. Maybe he wants to mix some white sweat with it'" (12). As in his markings on the rug, Ab revises by smudging here Sarty's and their society's mythic image of the plantation as radiant and redeeming source of beauty, cleanliness, and moral improvement, to stress instead its relation to its dependents in the underlying, oppositional terms of purifying exclusion and exploitation. Its cleanliness functions not to redeem blacks and poor whites "from what maybe they couldn't help but be"; its cleanliness rather functions and exists at the direct expense of those blacks' and poor whites' excluded and degraded toil. Thus too when the planter brings the rug for Ab to wash the tracks out, Ab has his daughters wash the rug (and ruin it) with their own "harsh homemade lye" and a handy fragment of field stone: Ab here again rejects this ritual gesture at settling and resolving his differences with the planter, by instead exaggerating the compulsive violence of this compelled erasure of his signature, the planter's attempt to erase Ab's singular, ineradicable mark of his difference on the rug.

Let me point out, however, that Ab's apparent irony here, in his smudging of Sarty's innocence, and in associating himself with manure, with slavery, and with blackness, is in fact not irony but a potential humor, not a compulsive self-exclusion but a revisionary repetition of such exclusions. It represents a potential for speaking and writing humorously aside from those same compulsive oppositions. Quentin's irony in *Absalom* only represents and confronts, even if within himself, a blackness that he still finds, for all his irony, no less horrifying than Thomas or Henry Sutpen did. Quentin's irony is a cold comfort in private surrender and disillusionment—ultimately a suicidal disillusionment enforcing the same horror upon himself. Ab's potential humor similarly repeats those violent oppositions usually smoothed over but still compulsively repeated in his society's dominant gestures at resolution (including the gesture of irony). But Ab's potential humor is a much more active strategy than Quentin's irony, repeating and provoking those same inadequate oppositions, but only in order then to escape them, setting them critically to one side of what they cannot account for in his own singular history and peculiarly critical, potentially humorous stance. Even Sarty recognizes that Ab's character is captured and framed adequately by neither the spell of the plantation house nor their tenant house's squalor, where "his father appeared at the door, framed against that shabbiness, as he had been against that other bland perfection, impervious to either" (13). In other such overtly inadequate descriptions of Ab in terms of ready oppositions—as, for example, "at once formal and burlesque" in his dress or as "shabby and ceremonial" in his actions (20)—we can perhaps understand better now the function of Faulkner's often-noted stylistic tendency (I would say the subtly changing tendency) to oxymorons. These "uncorrected" stylistic discrepancies and contradictions are a sign not of Faulkner's bad habit of thinking in obscurantist paradoxes, as Walter Slatoff and others have charged, nor are they a sign of his achieving resolutions of such paradoxes in his art, as some have no doubt defended him on New Critical grounds.[12] They are rather instances in miniature of his increasingly revisionary repetitions of such inadequate ready oppositions, and of his rejection of those stylistic resolutions that would often only disguise those same inadequate oppositions.

Sarty's other attempt at a peaceable resolution of his emotional and social ambivalence is in terms of the law, another attempt at resolution that Ab sets aside as one more compulsive repetition only raised to a higher ground. When Sarty first sees the apparently magical plantation, he thinks, *"Hit's big as a courthouse"* (10), and this immediate association with the law suggests the force of this other main cultural alternative for resolution of social differences when the old plantation magic fails. Thirty years after the war, the planter's feudal privilege over his tenants still largely exists, but it is subject to question on supposedly higher moral and legal grounds, as even Sarty knows. Like irony in *Absalom,* here the law will recognize Ab's existence, but in implicitly repressive terms.

The background for the court-trial is that Ab's ruining the rug again in washing it has provoked the planter to an angry, indiscreet assertion of absolute legal sovereignty over his tenant, declaring he will write into Ab's contract unilaterally a charge of twenty bushels of corn. He says this figure is meant not to cover the damages to the rug, but to "teach" Ab to wipe his feet before he enters the planter's wife's house. The planter insists, that is, not on his own economic or legal rights, but on requiring from Ab a gesture of feudal obeisance to the lady of the manor (16). At these signs of an oppositional, arrogantly despotic relationship between planter and tenant, Sarty all too eagerly restores his allegiance to his father on now higher moral and legal grounds that offer him new hope for his father's moral and legal recognition and redemption, as well as his own emotional resolution: "'You done the best you could!' he cried. 'If he wanted hit done different why didn't he wait and tell you how?'" (16). This rather desperate moral claim for Ab's good intentions, however, completely misses the point—or avoids the point—of Ab's violent way of washing the rug. In pretending that Ab would have washed the rug in the way the planter wanted, if only the planter had made his instructions clear, Sarty is hoping again that his father did want to settle his differences with the planter, and wanted to settle them in the planter's way. Ab, however, harshly rejects any such moral whitewash of his contrary behavior, knowing that any such moral resolutions in this society will implicitly favor the planter, by leaving the deeper structural oppositions in place. He does not want to erase and be forgiven for his mark on the planter's rug; he wants a more adequate reading of that mark.

Ab's legal claim in his suit is only superficially the same as Sarty's moral claim. Ab, too, repeats the planter's instructions and claims he followed the letter if not the spirit of what the planter told him to do. However, the motivations and consequences of Sarty's and Ab's two repetitions of these instructions are altogether different (in ways that you may have guessed). Their two kinds of repetition reflect a radically different conception of law and language. Sarty hopes, compulsively, that in repeating and following only the letter of those instructions, their spirit should somehow follow. Their letter should have been an embodying *symbol* of the planter's intention, which Ab would have done his innocent best to read. The consequence of this conception of law and language when a difference exists in interpretation, as in Ab's suit, is that one meaning is judged more reasonable than another, one as the spirit or tenor and one as merely the letter or vehicle of the disputed language or symbol. Thus Ab loses his suit, for the social hierarchy in the trial matches this hierarchy of representation, with meaning conceived as an interior presence at the privileged center of all its different, but always secondary representations in language, representations that are either faithful to that true meaning or only literal-minded, poor imitations. On the other hand, Ab's own repetition of the planter's instructions in the trial is revisionary, repeating the letter of those instructions not as *symbol* but *sign*, not as an embodiment of only the planter's intention, but as a negotiable social contract or pact between them both, open to certain legitimate social differences of interpretation. Ab insists on his own contrary interpretation of the planter's instructions by refusing the vast, unspoken social

axiomatic of reasonableness and "mere" respect for the expectations of people like the planter and the planter's wife. When the
Justice rephrases and reinterprets the planter's instructions in
line with this socially reasonable interpretation, Ab's long silence
emphasizes the legal partisanship and privilege of the Justice's
decision against Ab, exposing it in its function not as an impartial
resolution but as another forcible exclusion of Ab's meaning in
favor of the planter's, making of Ab not another speaker of this
society's language, but one of its socially illiterate victims. Likewise Ab's suit focusses critical attention on the supposed fairness
of the Justice's "settlement" when that settlement has to be
imposed in a context of such extreme social and economic inequality that the planter's ninety-five dollar cash loss on the rug
has to be figured as equal with Ab's five-dollar loss in uncertain
future earnings.

This same extreme inequality is one reason barn burning was
such a favorite form of violent protest for Ab as for many others in
the postwar South, as Albert C. Smith has recently documented. [13] Those blacks and poor whites who owned virtually no
property had in that lack of property both a simmering motiva-
tion for arson and also a strong protection against a like revenge,
either by the property owner's violence or by legal punishment,
since their own property had always already been taken from
them. Ab can repeatedly set planters' barns on fire and move to
the side as the planter appears to battle his own shadow in a
rage. In battling the fire and then in trying to prosecute the
arsonist, the planter here rather more clearly than usual is
battling not against Ab himself but against a consequence of the
planter's own overextended monopoly on property and wealth.
The planter's repeated exclusion of the poor white from his
property reaches here its economic crisis, in an enraged attempt
to repeat the exclusion even when there is no one left there to
exclude.

Ab thus dangerously exacerbates his society's dominant oppositions to a point of crisis by provoking the planter to repeated
fits of rage. Sarty, in his mounting fright and confusion, is unable

to read Ab's critical, potentially humorous way out of those oppositions, and Sarty's own emotional ambivalence with regard to those oppositions reaches a crisis as well. Sarty finally cannot appreciate Ab's unaccountable difference from his society's dominant dialectics of master and slave, planter and tenant, white and black, clean and filthy, legal and criminal; unable to read Ab's difference as a potential criticism of the exclusive terms of those dialectics, Sarty reads that difference more simply as a condemnation of Ab and perhaps of Sarty himself. Sarty feels forced to choose, and in the terms most ready to hand, his choices are always already made, there merely for him to repeat. Earlier, Ab tried to describe their family "blood" to Sarty in terms of a shared kinship and loyalty. But when Sarty realizes that Ab is preparing to burn another barn, Sarty violently recoils from the blood—recoils as Thomas and Henry Sutpen did in similar moments of nauseated horror—from a "blood" that seems now hereditarily, almost inescapably tainted and cursed. Sarty therefore bursts out of his family's tenant house and bursts in through the front door of the planter's house. He thinks he can force an apparently final, apocalyptic resolution to all these frightening oppositions by enabling the planter to catch Ab in the act, Sarty effectively calling down on Ab both the planter's mythic power and the legitimating force of the law. When he later hears the planter's shots from the direction of the fire, Sarty turns away from the scene to light out for the territories, but the narrator comments that his terror seems resolved now, once and for all. His sudden grief when he thinks his father is dead threatens momentarily to upset this resolution again as Sarty calls out, "Pap! Pap!," but he is unprepared at this point for mourning, resorting for now to what Freud describes as the compulsive idealizations and repetitions of melancholia, idealizing the more personal, more ambivalent term "Pap! Pap!" into "Father! Father!" and introjecting his father's memory in his society's crudest terms of heroic idealization: "He was brave! . . . He was! He was in the war! He was in Colonel Sartoris' cav'ry!" As the narrator intercedes to object, this

idealization of Ab in his society's crudest terms completely ig-
nores and excludes Ab's own singular history as not a soldier of
either army but a professional horse trader throughout the war.
Sarty excludes that singular history to translate (and traduce)
Ab's memory instead to the inside of his society's most unam-
bivalently nostalgic, heroic myth, that myth according to which
Ab's violence is redeemed by his supposed service to the one
Cause, a cause that was defeated but supposedly without internal division, a cause whose despotism has supposedly been
focused only on another race and its violence focussed supposedly only on an "alien" army. Ab has provoked here that
myth's determined ignorance of his situation during the war as
also in his apparent murder now.

For one possible alternative to this apparently final, compulsive repetition of this society's self-purifying exclusion of its
own bad blood and the history of that bloodline, we might return
to the afternoon in town between the trial and the barn burning.
Ab is talking and listening at a horse-lot fence and in the black-
smith shop, where Sarty hears his father tell "a long and unhurried story out of the time . . . when he had been a professional
horse trader" (19–20). This is as much as we hear in "Barn
Burning" of such long and unhurried horse-trading stories, but
this is stuff of the same tradition of Old Southwestern and
frontier humor on which Faulkner would draw for a different
fictional method and different fictional topics from those of his
earlier, more modernist writing.[14] Instead of representing his
society's compulsively repeated exclusions of what it repeatedly
cannot exclude, and instead of repeating the intensities and the
inescapable ironies of this apparently unalterable, socially structured or metaphysical event, Faulkner would begin increasingly
himself to tell such long and unhurried stories. He would continue to repeat such powerful, restrictive oppositions and resolutions, but he would also rewrite them; he would critically and
humorously reshape and reconceive those dominant oppositions
in the presence of other unaccountably different voices. Thus his
novels would take the form of proliferating series of sketches, or

collections of short stories that repeatedly overflow their generic boundaries as stories of revealing single events.

Not only as method but also as topic, the tradition of horse-trading stories of Old Southwestern and frontier humor would become in Faulkner's work what Walter Benjamin discusses as an endangered and dangerous memory[15]—a precapitalist or marginally capitalist social and economic tradition on which Faulkner would draw in *The Hamlet* and steadily thereafter for his own critical alternative to both the property-based capitalism of the Old South and the money-based capitalism of the New. In stories of trading in *The Hamlet*, for example, when unexpected differences arise about a verbal or written agreement, there is no appeal to what the more powerful or respectable or wealthy party really meant, as in the case of the planter's instructions for cleaning the rug. The accepted challenge and the intersubjective appeal of trading for both parties is to read each other carefully and probingly for signs of differences, to try to account for or to accept the risk of those always unpredictable differences, and then to accept that a deal is a deal. To trade with Ab would mean to know you are risking trading at least partly on Ab's singular terms. In Ratliff's retelling of the "Barn Burning" story in *The Hamlet*, he stresses and appreciates both the potential humor and the potential for economic criticism and change in Ab's acute understanding of his own social and economic relationships with the planter. After ruining the planter's rug, bringing him to court, and burning his barn, Ab enters the planter's house on his way out of town the next morning to say, "It looks like me and you aint going to get along together, . . . so I reckon we better quit trying before we have a misunderstanding over something."[16] Of course they *have* had a misunderstanding, but the misunderstanding has been the planter's, who has consistently refused to read the signs of Ab's singular difference from the usual categories of planters and their humble tenants. The planter has been particularly unprepared for the unsettling possibility that Ab would repeatedly find more effective ways to take *advantage* of his lack of social dignity and property, particularly in daring to burn the barn. It is precisely this possibility that Ab's next landlord learns about in hearing Ratliff retell this story in *The Hamlet,* and this possibility becomes, for Ab's son Flem, a silent bargaining partner used to get himself some property.[17]

In conclusion, this humorous possibility of an unexpected economic leverage is by no means the only topical opening out of "Barn Burning" and into *The Hamlet* and Faulkner's later work. In *The Hamlet* Ratliff will expand on the "Barn Burning" story to remember Ab from a time before he was "soured," a time when his humor and love for his wife enabled him to escape not only the terms of the Old South's plantation myth and economy, but also the terms of the New South's money-based economy, those differently restrictive terms in which his son Flem would get so skillfully entangled. Ratliff's own ambivalent and affectionate memories of Ab's singular history and character will also provide an example of that same long and unhurried work of mourning that will become a more central topic in *Go Down, Moses.* In Faulkner's ongoing revisions of the primal scene I have discussed, as well as of other such socially structured events, he will listen more closely and specifically not only for the singular voices of poor-white males such as Ab and Flem, but also for other critically different voices that have been similarly concealed, such as those of blacks and women. These voices will suggest new topics; they will also throw into relief the fact that modernism's supposedly universal consciousness was a consciousness primarily middle-class, white, and male.

NOTES

1. Joseph Blotner, *Faulkner: A Biography,* 2 vols. (New York: Random, 1974), 1720–35.

2. Michael Millgate, for example, whose focus is the discrete, finished artifact and the original "conception" it completes in a "wholly organic structure," is surprised that Faulkner could ever have considered including a version of Wash Jones's story near the beginning of *The Hamlet,* taking Faulkner's hindsighted word for it that the story had no place in the book at all: "It seems remarkable that Faulkner should ever have thought that 'Wash,' much of which he had already incorporated into *Absalom, Absalom!,* might find a place in the "Snopes Saga'" (*The Achievement of William Faulkner* [New York: Random House, 1966], 184–86). I will suggest instead that much of Ab's story as Faulkner used it

near the beginning of *The Hamlet* had already been told as Sutpen's (and Wash's) story in *Absalom*, and that this is a typical and even crucial kind of connection between works that are rarely such distinct performances as Millgate often assumes, but repetitions and revisions of previous works, repetitions not at their unoriginal worst but sometimes at their critical best.

3. Jean-Paul Sartre, *Search for a Method*, trans. Hazel E. Barnes (New York: Random House, Vintage Books, 1968), 106.

4. My somewhat reductive characterization here of "modernism" addresses a set of oppositions actually quite important in modernist literature and society, but they are also a select group of oppositions that have been actively promoted and canonized by modernist writers themselves, notably Eliot, and by Southern Agrarians later turned founding fathers of the New Criticism, such as Tate and Warren. (See Michael O'Brien, *The Idea of the American South: 1920–1941* [Baltimore: Johns Hopkins University Press, 1979], 138–45.) Less critical of these oppositions than Faulkner was, although invaluably insightful in tracing these oppositions, the New Criticism has largely obscured the social and historical context of modernist strategies of irony, ambiguity, and unresolved tension in juxtaposition, for example, by making them into general criteria for aesthetic merit. The most influential and insightful Faulkner critic in this tradition is of course Cleanth Brooks, who tends to measure change and difference in Faulkner's work against a vast backdrop of "true community" (found in the agrarian societies and in the pastoral tradition of literature), a backdrop against which Flem Snopes, for example, takes his measure only as a "sinister deformation of universal human nature and a terrifying vision of appetitive man, modern style" (*William Faulkner: The Yoknapatawpha Country* [New Haven: Yale University Press, 1963], 368, and *William Faulkner: Toward Yoknapatawpha and Beyond* [New Haven: Yale University Press, 1978], xii).

5. Richard H. Brodhead (among many others) also sees the source of Faulkner's achievement in these two novels in his exploration of larger social and historical contexts. I disagree, however, that Faulkner reaches a "final knowledge" about certain "essential realities," especially "a past lost to memory but still so potent that it dooms the present to repeat it" ("Introduction: Faulkner and the Logic of Remaking," in *Faulkner: New Perspectives*, ed. Richard H. Brodhead, Twentieth Century Views [Englewood Cliffs: N.J.: Prentice-Hall, 1983], 9). This is precisely the kind of ironic repetition Faulkner subjects in *Light in August* and especially *Absalom* to social, historical, and critical scrutiny. The historical context provides not just variants of an essential myth (though characters try to think so), but challenges to that myth by other myths and by other excluded voices. The "logic of remaking" so well described by Brodhead in Faulkner's career up to *Absalom* also continues beyond *Absalom*, not merely into efforts at consolidation and completion (Brodhead; also Gary Lee Stonum, "Faulkner's Last Phase," *Faulkner's Career: An Internal Literary History* [Ithaca: Cornell University, 1979], rpt. in Brodhead, 195–207), but in a radical revision of his earlier work, looking progressively further back into increasingly difficult issues, first of class (in *The Hamlet*, 1940, looking back at *Absalom*, 1936), race (in *Go Down, Moses*, 1942, looking back at *Light in August*, 1932), and gender (in *Requiem for a Nun*, 1951, and *The Reivers*, 1960, looking back at *Sanctuary*, 1929). See Richard C. Moreland, *Faulkner's Modernism under Revision* (Madison: University of Wisconsin Press, forthcoming).

6. This is where my reading of *Absalom* differs most sharply from that of John T. Irwin, with its emphasis on an inexorable process of repetition and revenge in the artist's and the son's futile struggles with the immutable structures of time, originality, and secondariness as such. I would largely agree, though, with his reading of *The Sound and the Fury*, were he to consider the two novels more separately (*Doubling and Incest / Repetition and Revenge: A Speculative Reading of Faulkner* [Baltimore: Johns Hopkins University Press, 1975]).

7. See Moreland, *Faulkner's Modernism under Revision*, which returns in greater detail to the crises in one mode of repetition (especially in *Absalom*) that led Faulkner toward a mode of revisionary repetitions, especially in *The Hamlet, Go Down, Moses, Requiem for a Nun*, and *The Reivers*.

8. William Faulkner, *Absalom, Absalom!* (New York: Random House, Vintage Books, [1936]), 232. Page references are to this edition.

9. "Barn Burning" at first began Faulkner's manuscript of *The Hamlet*, then during the writing of the novel he detached this version (soon publishing it as a short story) and eventually replaced it in chapter 1 of the novel (15–21) with Ratliff's substantially rewritten version of the story as told to Jody Varner. See Michael Millgate, *The Achievement of William Faulkner* (New York: Random House, 1963), 185.

10. On this alternation in Freud's treatments of the primal scene, see Ned Lukacher, *Primal Scenes: Literature, Philosophy, Psychoanalysis* (Ithaca: Cornell University Press, 1986), 136–67. My use of the Freudian notion of primal scenes also resembles Jacques Lacan's "mirror stage" as an alienating, simplifying objectification of a previously more fluid and dismembered identity. Cf. the essay by Philip Weinstein in this volume.

11. William Faulkner, "Barn Burning," *Collected Stories of William Faulkner* (New York: Random House, 1950), 11. Page references are to this edition.

12. Walter Slatoff, *Quest for Failure: A Study of William Faulkner* (Ithaca: Cornell University Press, 1960).

13. "'Southern Violence' Reconsidered: Arson as Protest in Black-Belt Georgia, 1865–1910," *The Journal of Southern History*, 51 (1985), 527–64.

14. On the critical potential of humor in the history of American literature, and for useful distinctions between irony and humor, see especially Neil Schmitz, *Of Huck and Alice: Humorous Writing in American Literature* (Minneapolis: University of Minnesota Press, 1983).

15. Walter Benjamin, "Theses on the Philosophy of History," in *Illuminations*, trans. Harry Zohn (New York: Schocken, 1968), 253–64.

16. William Faulkner, *The Hamlet* (New York: Random House, 1940), 17.

17. Again, I am reading Ab's signature and his escape as one way out of one particular set of confining (mostly class-related) cultural alternatives, and not as the one new way out of all such cultural oppositions (assuming any such perfect escape from culture were either possible or desirable). His method of reinscription and escape serves here as a model for other more difficult escapes from other, more stubbornly naturalized oppositions, to be examined more critically later in Faulkner's career. Ab's violence toward blacks, toward women, and toward his son Sarty is obvious throughout the story. It is not in defense of this violence but in an effort to understand it—the "savage blows . . . but without heat" (6)—that I might add that Ab seems here to be passing on the social and economic violence he feels directed against himself, not in its usually more naturalized, axiomatic manifestations, but in a more explicitly despotic, violent form. That is, Ab savagely, bitterly exaggerates, while still repeating, the racism and patriarchal sexism of his society and class, a repetition that is in these cases unrevisionary and uncritical unless perhaps in the otherwise unaccountable, inarticulate *force* of his smoldering rage.

Faulkner's Narrative Frames

John T. Matthews

"For he knoweth our frame, he remembereth that we are dust."—Psalm 103: 14

Why doesn't Quentin Compson stay dead? If on June 2, 1910, Quentin concludes his last day on earth and commits suicide by the age of twenty—a fact confirmed by his family's later remarks in *The Sound and the Fury* and a fact foundational to the meaning of *Absalom, Absalom!*, then how do we explain Quentin's appearance as the narrator, now in his early twenties, of three short stories published in the 1930s? Usual explanations about authorial license remain perfectly acceptable; of course Faulkner is free to imagine alternative lives for his characters, or even to reject the need for absolute consistency from work to work. Yet encountering a once-dead character later in his life has startled many readers, and driven devout formalists nearly to deny that the various Quentin Compsons have anything at all to do with one another. [1]

Although these positions finally accommodate the fact of such a narrational anomaly, I doubt that either kind of response does much to explain Quentin's postmortem performances. On the one hand, describing alternative lives for a single character strikes at one of the fundamental premises of realistic fiction and, for all his technical experimentation, Faulkner never attains

I gratefully acknowledge a Fellowship for Independent Research from the National Endowment for the Humanities in 1984–85, which assisted my work on framed narratives.

quite so postmodernist a vantage. The stories in question, "That Evening Sun," "A Justice," and "Lion," nowhere make one confront the fictional "fact" of Quentin's 1910 demise; it is not as if we are being asked to entertain parallel fictive universes. On the other hand, denying that the Quentin Compson of the *The Sound and the Fury* has any relation to the narrator of the stories (or even to the character so named in *Absalom, Absalom!*) seems at the least counterintuitive to the conventions of reading, and it perversely disregards Faulkner's own remarks about the essential identities of the characters who appear in more than one of his works.[2]

Through an analysis of Quentin's position as a frame narrator, I think we can arrive at a more subtle account of the slippage or fissure that his reappearance indicates. The Quentin of *The Sound and the Fury* remains a largely silent witness to the dismantling of his life and world; the ghostly Quentin who survives through several textual avatars into *Absalom, Absalom!* becomes a narrator, one whose relation to narrative confines him both to the margins of life and the margins of story.

As a narrative component, framing is a staple of literary organization. Frames may contribute to the crafting of a work in a variety of ways—as discrete textual units such as purported editorial prefaces, as the introduction of narrators who relay another's story, as a host of secondary narrative trappings such as titles, epigraphs, notes, glosses, and so on. Though the effects of such framing gestures differ for each framed narrative, they all may be seen broadly as attempts to delimit the context of a work. Frames typically relate the circumstances of the narrative's production—how it originated, how it has been transmitted to the present circumstances of its recitation. Narrators frequently devote preliminaries to establishing their authority or dictating the conditions for a narrative's reception and interpretation. One recalls how the tale of the tale unfolds in the fictive overtures to *The Scarlet Letter*, "Rappaccini's Daughter," *The Narrative of A. Gordon Pym*, *The Turn of the Screw*, *Heart of Darkness*, or *The Great Gatsby*. The frame often serves as well to embrace disparate narrative units; one thinks of how the frame setting becomes a receptacle whose pretext unifies the tale cycles of the *Panchatantra, The Book of the Thousand Nights and a Night,* or the *Decameron.*

Faulkner deploys frame formats abundantly and adroitly. *Absalom, Absalom!* exemplifies the range of effects managed by frame devices: each version of Sutpen's story comes laminated to the highly motivated narrator who transmits it. Besides the framing narrator, the novel also presents instances of narrative embedding—the nesting of one telling inside the stories of other tellers.[3] I cite too the bracketing of some narrative portions by Mr. Compson's broken letter, or the careful prefatory narration that Mr. Compson crafts in preparation for the transmission to Quentin of Charles Bon's letter. Outlying matter includes the chronology, genealogy, and map in the first edition of the novel. A simpler frame device appears in *Requiem for a Nun,* the prose headnotes serving to set off the dramatic sequences. Like *Absalom's, Requiem's* reliance on the frame indicates a further characteristic of much of Faulkner's later fiction, the impulse to recast the material of earlier novels. The retrospective position— which perhaps reaches its most succinct formulation in the nearly zero degree frame attached to *The Reivers* ("Grandfather said:")—that retrospective gaze leads much more routinely to the frame format. The device emphasizes the recessed position of its subject.

More often in the later fiction, but not exclusively (as we shall see in the case of the three stories affiliated to *The Sound and the Fury*), Faulkner's efforts to recast earlier material constituted efforts to recontain it. The great early novels like *The Sound and the Fury,* the final version of *Sanctuary,* and *As I Lay Dying* might be seen as radically *unframed.* These novels stand free of outer scaffolding that would encase their fragmentariness or compose a framework for their innovative forms. *Sanctuary* serves as an illuminating example in this regard, for Faulkner's first impulse clearly involved registering the resonance between Temple's story and its narrative reflector, Horace Benbow. In the original version, Horace verges on becoming a Conradian narrator, but he remains mute before the horror he has discovered. Revising, Faulkner all but pries Temple's story free from Horace's involvement, turning it into a piece of highly stylized, free-standing statuary. The corruption bemoaned by the novel, like the innocence lamented in *The Sound and the Fury,* by default seems a universal state of affairs. The absence of frames often indicates a crisis transcending the determinants of history, region, and class. *The Sound and the Fury,* for example, segregates its definition of loss from its social context; for the purposes of the novel, loss is strictly personal and seems to impinge on characters purely in psychological and emotional registers. Reframing material typically introduces the force of these contextual elements; the frame opens the plot's relation to social, economic, and political conditions—in precisely the way *Absalom, Absalom!* places the demise of the Compson family in a historical framework.[4]

This function of frames in Faulkner—that they typically introduce the social and historical contexts kept at bay by the narrative's longing for purity—brings us to the double bind of framing, a double bind that will form the basis of my analysis of the three Quentin Compson stories that succeed *The Sound and the Fury.* If the impulse in the early unframed works involves banishing historical frameworks, then another impulse in framed narratives involves the recontainment of that unruly material by the frames themselves. That is, the frame promises to be the site of fuller comprehension and the point of contact between the plights of the individual characters and the historical realities that condition the narrative. But the frame also becomes a site of stress at which the frame narrator works to cover over the very insight the story has put him in a position to grasp. The frame labors to re-cognize and to resist comprehension at the same time, in the same gesture. In Faulkner's texts, the frame often forecloses precisely what it promises to open.

Why should this be so? The cluster of documents constituting the Compson material in Faulkner's oeuvre follows a model for literary production that involves processes of both expression and suppression on the part of the text. Poststructuralist analyses of discourse have established this view of textuality over the last two decades, but I hope to show quite specifically how these three Quentin Compson stories found themselves on this double movement. In part this dynamic organizes the tensions within each story. "That Evening Sun," "A Justice," and "Lion" all display standard features of framed narratives. Each is narrated by an older Quentin looking back on a significant moment in his childhood; each points to the significance of the remembered incident in Quentin's later understanding of his culture; and each observes a formal break or shift between the present narrator's backdropping and the episode's occurrence. And in each, the frame narrator identifies a moment of *in*comprehension as the product of the story.

I want to contend as well that these stories also stand as frames themselves to the centerpiece of the Compson material, *The Sound and the Fury*. Though I cannot develop this part of my argument, I will posit that *The Sound and the Fury* achieves its remarkable concentration on the eccentricities of its characters' minds, its extraordinary devotion to the memory of one missing sister, its utter preoccupation with the misfortune of a single family, by shutting out the social and historical contexts for these phenomena.[5] As Benjy's section first teaches us, deeply personal visions rule the novel and generate its crises. In the manner of high modernist literature, the novel's aesthetic eschews social background and presents its characters in isolation from the human community.[6] This aesthetic finds its match in the subject matter of the novel—the private, personal loss that is reinforced by Faulkner's own remarks about shutting the door on all publishers and all readers in order to make a vase for his own ecstatic delight.

Yet the novel's will to self-sufficiency founders on the admission that something remains missing. Each section, as Faulkner was so fond of repeating, called for its own replacement as he composed.[7] No telling seemed complete; the mechanism of supplementarity drove the writing. Even after Faulkner let "Faulkner" have his chance, the novel was not finished, only abandoned. In the wake of the enormous work of sustained concentration on his "heart's darling,"[8] Faulkner supplements the novel with a series of fictional and nonfictional pieces. The three additional Quentin stories bob to the surface along with other submerged matter, some of it in the form of Faulkner's draft introduction to the proposed 1933 edition of *The Sound and the Fury, Absalom, Absalom!* itself, of course, and the 1946 Appendix for the Viking Portable edition. Each of these documents works to acknowledge social and historical questions that have been sacrificed to the purity of the virginal text about Caddy. Each seeks to settle the Compson material as well, to recontain it in the process of reframing it.

"That Evening Sun" and "A Justice" comprise a brace of stories exploring the issues of economic and racial injustice that surface only between the lines in *The Sound and the Fury* "proper." The stories share a concern with the breakup of an established social order, the shift from codes of moral and economic behavior whose pedigree allegedly descends from antebellum aristocracy. The destruction of communal cohesiveness and tradition ruins the world as Quentin knows it, and these stories, unlike *The Sound and the Fury*, attempt to register its implications for populations marginal to the Compsons. Both stories give voice to the black man's outrage at dispossession, "That Evening Sun" in Jesus' furious resentment, and "A Justice" in the wronged husband's hysterical mutilation of Craw-ford's cock. Such a take on historical injustice occurs to Quentin only after he is in effect dead. As we shall see, the consequence of such knowledge is the loss of all he knows, all he loves. *The Sound and the Fury* represses the recognition of the historical dimensions of Quentin's malaise—postpones it until he can accomplish his suicide.

The frame portions of "That Evening Sun"—the opening two paragraphs and one passage toward the end—place the time of narration "fifteen years"[9] after the episode, which takes place

when Quentin is nine (294). At age twenty-four, Quentin believes that he looks across a gulf, from a modern world filled with
automobiles and an impersonal mass economy to a simpler, more
natural time. The tone of the overture laments the displacement
of shade trees "to make room for iron poles bearing clusters of
bloated and ghostly and bloodless grapes" (289), the branches of
telephone and electric service. Automobiles slice through town
"with a long diminishing noise of rubber and asphalt like tearing
silk" (289). Quentin's bitter imprisonment in the "now"—a word
he repeats contemptuously in his first sentences—cuts him off
from a world remembered as "quiet" and "steady." Quentin's
image of tearing silk transmits his sense that the town's social
fabric has been rent by change, just as the automobiles' "irritable
electric horns" mark his own vexation.

Quentin's nostalgia, however, tenses against a more damaging
kind of recognition in the frame. The old order may be desig-
nated natural and serene, but it also predicates inequity and
oppression. The "old custom" of Monday morning laundry popu-
lates Quentin's memory with streets "full of Negro women with,
balanced on their steady, turbaned heads, bundles of clothes
tied up in sheets, almost as large as cotton bales, carried so
without touch of hand between the kitchen door of the white
house and the blackened washpot beside a cabin door in Negro
Hollow" (289). On the one hand, Quentin's description emphasizes the naturalness of this scene, the Negro women's graceful
execution of their work. Like the other laundresses, Nancy
balances a bundle on her head, "then upon the bundle in turn
she would set the black straw sailor hat which she wore winter
and summer" (289–290); her burden, her labor, becomes her
accepted uniform. Quentin admires how she is able to keep the
bundle balanced as she walks down the ditch separating her
house from the Compsons', even managing to "go down on her
hands and knees and crawl through the gap, her head rigid,
uptilted" (290).

But Quentin's evocation subverts its own innocence. The comparison of the bundles to "cotton bales" puts black domestic

labor in its proper historical context, just as the reference to "the white house and the blackened washpot" points to a legacy in which whites own and occupy the house while blacks serve as their tools of maintenance. That Nancy must "go down" to cross the line between white and black, employer and servant, marks a debasement hardly assuaged by Quentin's appreciation. The very syntax of Quentin's narration registers this tension. The sentence I quoted above halts awkwardly on a preposition, as if incorporating the questionable balance it describes: "Negro women with, balanced on their steady, turbaned heads, bundles of clothes tied up in sheets, almost as large as cotton bales, carried so without touch of hand" (289). The sentence's wobble may make us pause to wonder if the steady balance it celebrates does not arise from an imbalance of race and class.

As the image of the white property being carried "without touch of [black] hand" might suggest, one of the story's abiding anxieties centers on the need to maintain categories of segregation and discrimination.[10] As children, the Compson siblings struggle to keep their world separate from Nancy's. Jason continually seeks reassurance that he is white:

"Jesus is a nigger," Jason said.
   . . .
"Dilsey's a nigger too," Jason said.
   . . .
"I aint a nigger," Jason said. (297)

Mr. Compson wryly endorses the family's conviction that Negro and white behavior remain fundamentally different; he reassures his wife that she has nothing to fear from *his* absence since, unlike Jesus, he is "not lying outside with a razor" (299). And Mrs. Compson redraws a familiar Southern line: "'I cant have Negroes sleeping in the bedrooms'" (299)

These boundaries would be less actively policed were it not for a mood of reversal or overthrow in the relations between the races and classes in "That Evening Sun." Nancy's husband complains directly about that inequity: "When white man want to

come in my house, I aint got no house. I cant stop him, but he
cant kick me outen it. He cant do that" (292). Nancy's infidelity
to Jesus prompts this resentment and the accompanying boast
that he "can cut down the vine" responsible for her pregnancy.
The story's descriptive language underscores the fear that blacks
will reverse the violence they have suffered. Quentin notes the
"razor scar on [Jesus'] black face like a piece of dirty string"
(292), but later reports Nancy remembers "[t]hat razor on that
string down his back" (295). The trace of Jesus' victimization by
violence becomes, through the action of the figurative language,
the literal weapon whereby Jesus may avenge himself. Jesus'
threats, moreover, must be deflected onto Nancy because Mr.
Stovall's liaison with her involves more than simple *droit de
seigneur;* Nancy has put herself on the market, and her exploitation by the Baptist bank cashier underscores the complexity of
economic relations between the races in the so-called new
South. Mr. Compson deliberately misconstrues her motive as
mere sexual mischief ("'And if you'd just let white men alone'"
[295]), but Nancy's question carries a demand with more dis-
quieting social consequence: "'When you going to pay me,
white man?'" (291).

If economic relations snarl with violence between and within
the races, surely part of the force of this fact for Quentin inheres
in his suspicion that his own family are about to embark on a
period of distasteful financial and social dealings with those
formerly beneath them. This repugnance shoots through Quentin's attitudes toward money matters of all sorts in *The Sound
and the Fury*—from Herbert Head's crude blandishments to the
justice of the peace's levy against Quentin to indemnify an
immigrant worker. Jason's rage in the novel over Miss Quentin's
behaving like a "nigger," and his own resentment at having to
"slave" his life away, point to a reversal in racial categories. The
new South forces a recognition that blackness and whiteness
reflect economic and social status rather than biological in-
nateness. The novel dreads the detection of resemblance between "Compson" and "Gibson," say, and the story struggles to

distinguish merging doubles: "'It's the other Jesus she means '"
(297); "it looked like father had two heads" (309); "Nancy held
the cup in both hands, looking at us, making the sound, like
there were two of them" (298).

There are two Nancys of course. The other one is the dead
animal in *The Sound and the Fury* used as an illustration of how
dying is like undressing. That Jesus threatens to kill Nancy and
leaves a hogbone on her table as the sign of her fate ("with blood
meat still on it") (307), leads Malcolm Cowley to assume that it is
Nancy's corpse discussed in *The Sound and the Fury*. Stephen
Whicher has corrected this rather ghoulish mistake, but perhaps
overcorrects in the process: "Obviously she is some animal, and
the name is only coincidence."[11] I think the confusion is more
significant, and contributes to the pattern of doubles, a pattern
that betrays white dread about the confusion of opposites. The
human Nancy carries a mulatto child, and that she is a "transformation" of the novel's dead mule may supply a subterranean
recognition of the link between two beasts of burden. Nancy's
fate in "That Evening Sun" may strike Quentin with special force
because she so resembles Caddy, for that matter. Both make
their first textual appearance stooping through gaps or breaks;
both trade on their bodies to protest their confinement and earn
their own ways; and both are "blackened" by their sexual and
fiscal "corruption."

The denial of similitude colors the rhetoric of "That Evening
Sun." Throughout the story Quentin proposes analogies or
makes assertions that he immediately cancels out or refutes. It is
as if Quentin so fears the possibility of social and racial combination that he sabotages the very combinational power of language
itself. At a number of rhetorical pressure points Quentin's language betrays the fundamental indecision of his class and race at
the prospect of social upheaval. Notice, to begin with, his description of Nancy's wash bundle carried "steady as a rock or a
balloon" (290). Which is it? The incompatible alternatives measure the distance between indictment, which would view the
black woman's plight as insupportable, and nostalgia, which

would view it as no burden at all.[12] Or consider Quentin's repeated description of Nancy's cry: "It was like singing and it wasn't like singing, like the sounds that Negroes make" (296; also 300 and 309). The attempt at analogy dismantles itself, providing Quentin a language that shortcircuits when he tries to decide how to interpret the sounds Negroes make. Likewise, Quentin says that Nancy "was looking at us, only it was like she had emptied her eyes, like she had quit using them" (302); seeing but not seeing characterizes Quentin's evasiveness throughout. Elsewhere, her eyes look "like when your eyes look up at a stick balanced on your nose" even though "[s]he had to look down to see Caddy" (303). Looking up, seeing down: contradiction is the rhetorical order of the story.[13]

Perhaps the most telling moment of undecidability occurs when Caddy asks the terrified Nancy if she has fallen asleep yet. Quentin's description of this scene marks how profoundly he wills not to have to reckon with her fear, with her victimization and dependence on the Compsons, with the Compson's dependence on their black supporters, indeed, with the whole structure of a society threatened with torture and death: "Nancy whispered something. It was oh or no, I dont know which. Like nobody had made it, like it came from nowhere and went nowhere, until it was like Nancy was not there at all" (296). The possibility of a black voice without source or destination that would just disappear, of a vowel that might be assent ("oh") or denial ("no") undecidably.

Quentin's management of his narrative conforms to the dynamic of expression and suppression I suggested at the outset. The closure of the formal frame reinforces this blockage of comprehension. The voice of the adult narrator does not reemerge fully at the end of the story. The closing lines record a childhood squabble between Jason and Caddy. But just before the last section Quentin interrupts his narrative to explain briefly Nancy's reference to having her coffin money already saved up with a Mr. Lovelady. We learn that Lovelady is a "short, dirty man who collected the Negro insurance" (308), and that one day his wife, who lived with him and their daughter at the hotel, "committed suicide." The word *suicide* punctures the adopted point of view of the child narrator and suddenly opens up a passage of communication with *The Sound and the Fury*. Quentin as narrator notes the fate of one contaminated by financial dealings with Negroes, one who parasites the former parasites. Mrs. Lovelady's suicide responds to the ignominy of her life; that Quentin reports no motive for her makes the suicide all the more a commentary on his own. The feminine response, in Quentin's eyes, to such social displacement and humiliation would be suicide—"just passed out like a girl"[14] Quentin thinks to himself of his failure to stand up to Dalton Ames. (We might recall that Nancy too tries to commit suicide, in her jail cell, and that the jailer finds her contradictorily hanging from the window bar but unable to make her hands release their hold on the ledge. The image captures Quentin's intuition that his suicide may be a destructive act designed to preserve what he cannot reconcile himself to lose.)

At the last, the story closes ranks to protect Quentin from a comprehension of racial and economic suffering. The uncanny trick of the story involves the undecidability of Quentin's summarizing question. Inferring that Nancy will indeed be murdered by Jesus, the child Quentin asks, "Who will do our washing now, Father?" (309). Taken as an index of the child's innocent selfishness, the question might suggest that the adult possesses a deeper appreciation of Nancy's terror and misery, which constitute the avowed concerns of the story. Yet the frame refuses to establish that perspective, and instead we may be left wondering if Quentin's question is not the real one after all. If the South's old order of economic and racial hierarchy has been overthrown, who will do the washing?[15]

Both "A Justice" and "Lion" continue Quentin's meditation on the loss of a world. The first story begins with the words "[u]ntil Grandfather died" (343) and the second ends with Major de Spain's withdrawal from the annual hunt after Old Ben's death. Yet the pressure of Faulkner's work invariably reveals that the loss of the old order cannot be dated from a single event, from the death of any grandfather, whether Colonel Sartoris, General Compson, Sam Fathers, or even Old Ben. Rather, innocence appears fallen originally. This always already corruption is not only a linguistic phenomenon, but a socioeconomic and historical one as well. Quentin's considerations of his heritage will show that ownership and exchange—of the land and of other humans—constitute the primal crime, and that the world preceding such a state of affairs cannot be imagined.

According to Quentin, the issue of "A Justice" involves the origin of Sam Fathers' given name, "Had-Two-Fathers." The narrative frame places this particular question in a larger context, for Quentin notices that though white poeple call Sam simply a Negro, and Negroes call him a blue-gum, Sam is not a Negro: "That's what I'm going to tell about" (343), says the narrator. The adult Quentin seems to use the frame to introduce his sympathetic effort to establish the closer facts of Sam's heritage and history. Looking back on the story Sam has told him at twelve, the narrator seems to structure his story as an initiation into knowledge about his culture. Not then, but now, Quentin implies, I see the unjustness of racial categories like white and Negro; I see that "Had-Two-Fathers" did not sound like a name at all to me once, was "not anything" (345) to me until I could place Sam's story in the larger framework of my region's history.

Taken on its own terms, "A Justice" shows how the Indian chief Doom resolves a dispute between one of his black slaves and the Indian Craw-ford over the black man's wife. Though married to the slave, the woman and Craw-ford seem to conduct a dalliance that produces a "fine yellow" child. The husband takes the child's color as proof of Craw-ford's continued transgression against his rights, about which he has protested to Doom before. Doom agrees, and arranges for Craw-ford to help build a fence around the black family's house that will prevent future meddling. In honor of the child's contested parentage, Doom names him "Had-Two Fathers."

Sam Fathers clearly takes Craw-ford to be his father; throughout the story and to Quentin he refers to him as "my pappy." As the story would have it, then, Doom does enact a kind of justice. He defends even a slave's right to his wife and property; or, as he puts it: "Any man is entitled to have his melon patch protected from these wild bucks of the woods" (357). The metaphor recalls Jesus' remark about Nancy's melon, and might sharpen the contrast between the black man's inability to get justice from the white man and his success in doing so from the red. [16]

Moreover, Doom's willingness to recognize two fathers for one child strikes at the very heart of patriarchal practice. [17] Doom's decree announces that biological and social paternity may be sundered, that fatherhood may be a social fiction as much as a natural fact. Such an insight would have profound consequences for Quentin, of course, since his destiny is to confront that crisis in the Sutpen family as well. As a child, Quentin protests that "Had-Two-Fathers" is "not a name. That's not anything" (345) because the very principle of language rests on an ideological relativism he cannot see. The coordinates of class, race, and gender constitute the patriarchal discourse of Quentin's world; he takes his language to be the only one imaginable.

At first blush, Quentin's narration puts him in a position to identify a historical reality represented by the true story of Sam's name and paternity, and by the achievement of justice for the black man. As we have seen in the case of "That Evening Sun," however, Quentin's willingness to comprehend stimulates a process of self-protective incomprehension. Within Sam's story this incomprehension takes the form of a fundamental un-decidability. Some early interpretations of "A Justice" argued that Doom's resolution of the dispute actually serves his own self-interest. [18] We learn from *Go Down, Moses* that Sam knows his father to be Doom himself, not pappy Craw-ford. If it is Doom who actually deceives the husband, making Craw-ford his fall guy, then the story reverses its meaning. Justice becomes nothing but a charade, a cover-up and frame-up designed to perpetuate the privilege of those holding power. Such a view certainly accords with Doom's career of deceit and intimidation, and it helps to explain some oddities in the story, such as Doom's postponement of awarding the slave to Craw-ford, to whom she has been promised in exchange, apparently, for Craw-ford's acquiescence to Doom's original political coup.

Even so, the evidence for this reading does not cancel out the other. Now if we were capable of choosing between these views—either that the black man does or does not receive justice—then the story would contribute to Quentin's critique of racial inequity and the legacy of ownership in the old South. But the insistent irresolution distracts the story from its point. Quentin uses it as the feature by which he can avoid comprehension since it renders the difference between justice and injustice undecidable.

The formal frame sections of "A Justice" reinforce this stance. Even as the retrospective narrator, Quentin does not seem to see what his language implies about the perpetuation of social inequity. His description of the ancient Sam emphasizes that the Compson farm is "kept whole and sound" by the "clever carpenter" (343). Sam's labor in the service of a culture that continues to keep him bound by false social constructions ought to remind us of his pappy, who helps build the very structure of his own dispossession. But Quentin refuses to drive the story to the point of his own discomfiture. Instead, he reserves the knowledge carried by the story to an unspecified zone associated vaguely with death.

After Grandfather calls him to the surrey to leave the farm, he asks Quentin what he and Sam were talking about. Here are the closing words of the story:

> We went on, in that strange, faintly sinister suspension of twilight in which I believed that I could still see Sam Fathers back there, sitting on his wooden block, definite, immobile, and complete, like something looked upon after a long time in a preservative bath in a museum. That was it. I was just twelve then, and I would have to wait until I had passed on and through and beyond the suspension of

twilight. Then I knew that I would know. But then Sam Fathers
would be dead.

"Nothing, sir," I said. "We were just talking." (360)

Even without the pun on the original title of *The Sound and the
Fury* manuscript, Quentin's passage beyond the suspension of
twilight issues in death. The subject of knowledge is dead,
known because it is dead. The adult narrator picks up his earlier
impression of Sam as a museum piece, preserved, perhaps, but
only as a curiosity, an antiquity. The museum, of course, was the
residence of the muses; the remoteness of his subject serves as
the inspiration for Quentin's art. Quentin's narratives are
postmortem because they identify knowledge with loss, and loss
with death. Only the ruse of turning the story into "nothing"
enables Quentin to keep on talking.

I shall conclude by suggesting only briefly how the third of the
Quentin stories, "Lion," displays many of the same marks of
repression. Like "The Bear," the story it grows into for *Go
Down, Moses*, "Lion" is meant by Quentin to celebrate a world of
experience lost to the destruction of the wilderness. The hunting
party appears to represent the closest approximation to that
"communal anonymity of brotherhood"[19] who might occupy the
land without saying "this is mine." Quentin's immersion in the
woods stimulates the sensation of "something breathing out of
this place which human beings had merely passed through without altering it, where no axe or plow had left a scar, which looked
exactly as it had when the first Indian crept into it and looked
around, arrow poised and ready."[20] When Lion dies in the fatal
embrace of Old Ben, it seems to Major de Spain as if an order
has passed: Quentin laments that de Spain "never went back
again" (197), and he appreciates that gesture since his own return
shows him that the wilderness is "the same, yet different" (198).

Quentin insists that a kind of panequality prevails in the
woods. Despite Boon's comic ineptness and declined status,
despite Ad's being a Negro, despite Lion's being a dog, the
wilderness seems to make the distinctions of race, class, and
even species drop away: "we were not men either while we were

in camp: we were hunters, and Lion the best hunter of us all"
(186). Yet Quentin's narration crawls with casual references to a
state of affairs among the hunters that scarcely annuls the evils of
ownership and domination. In the opening paragraph Quentin
lauds the talk and the whiskey that hunters share:

> I know certainly that the best, the finest talk about dogs which I have
> heard took place over a bottle or two bottles maybe, in the libraries
> of town houses and the offices of plantation houses, or better still, in
> the camps themselves; before the burning logs on hearths when
> there were houses, or before the high blazing of nigger-fed
> wood . . . when there were not. (184)

The best talk remains shut up in the command posts of the
culture, isolated from many populations of the dispossessed—
including women and all men who happen not to own libraries,
plantation offices, or hunting woods. Those "nigger-fed" camp-
fires might actually illuminate more a young man's initiation into
the seats of his society's private power than into any genuine
experience of freedom or equality.

Quentin celebrates the apparent freedom from ownership
Lion enjoys: "Because you didn't think of Lion as belonging to
anyone, any more than you thought about a man belonging to
anybody, not even to Major de Spain" (186) Of course, were
Quentin to continue the career as woodsman that Isaac McCaslin
eventually takes over from him, Quentin could not help but
think about men belonging to other men. But Quentin uses his
romanticization of the wilderness to avoid the persistent legacy
of slaveholding in his world. Notice, for example, the way he
turns the anecdote illustrating Boon's marksmanship away from
its tragic implications. Quentin reports that Boon "never had
killed anything bigger than a squirrel that anybody knew of,
except that nigger that time. That was several years ago. They
said he was a bad nigger, but I don't know." What he knows
about the incident is that "Boon shot four times and broke a
plate-glass window and shot in the leg a nigger woman who

happened to be passing before he managed to hit the nigger in the face at six feet with the last shot. He never could shoot" (189). Quentin realizes that he cannot turn the episode into inconsequential slapstick, yet he goes as far as one might imagine. The repression of the black victim's story strains Quentin's narrative and contributes to its tendency to blank out whatever might distract from the nostalgic celebration of the hunt.

As in "That Evening Sun," Quentin's language strikes at the root of its own power. The narrative repeatedly denies its capacity to describe what it sees: Boon, for example, bundles himself up against the cold, "his feet wrapped in towsacks and a quilt . . . wrapped around him and over his head so that he didn't look like anything at all" (186). Or it remarks the failure of referentiality implied by Big Ben's name: "so he should have been called Two-Toe. . . . Maybe it was because Old Ben was an extra bear . . . and everyone knew that he deserved a better name" (187). What has "Ben" to do with being an "extra" (special) bear? Or the language attempts to make distinctions that come close to parodying nuance and turning it into nonsense: "I was not shivering, I was just shaking slow and steady and hard" (185)

Quentin's strategic verbal impotence accords with his refusal to see some of the ramifications of his story. Quentin describes both Boon's and Lion's eyes as having nothing in them at all. Boon's are like "shoebuttons, without depth, without meanness or generosity or viciousness or gentleness or anything at all" (185); Lion's "were as impenetrable as Boon's": "he would blink and then you would realize that he was not looking at you at all, not seeing you at all. You didn't know what he was seeing, what he was thinking" (190). Only once, when he verges on death, do Lion's eyes fill with content for Quentin: "as if he was looking at the woods for a moment before closing his eyes again, remembering the woods again or seeing that they were still there" (197). Like Quentin himself, Lion sees the woods only when they are about to vanish and he is about to die. As in the earlier stories, comprehension is a kind of death, the narration a kind of border mortality.

Quentin nearly makes the connection between the rhetorical figure of blindness and the interests of privilege. When he describes Lion's gaze as looking at you but not seeing, he goes on: "It was like when you are sitting with your feet propped against a column on the gallery and after a while you are not even aware that you are not seeing the very column your feet are propped against" (190). The social structures that prop up Quentin remain virtually invisible to him. One of the enduring strengths of Faulkner's craft arises from his willingness to enact the contradictory impulses toward comprehension and evasion. The device of the frame provides one site upon which that struggle can be played out. By framing telling moments in his personal past, Quentin appears to place them in contexts that might allow them significance in the representation of his heritage. But because these frames work to resist their own insights and identify knowledge as the realm of death, these narratives confirm the career of the Quentin Compson who, in *Absalom, Alsalom!*, must listen to himself being a ghost.

NOTES

1. François Pitavy, for example, argues that "Faulkner's different works are autonomous, despite the obvious 'factual' links between them . . . each text begins a new *experience* in the author's reflection upon creation." See "Through the Poet's Eye: A View of Quentin Compson," in *William Faulkner's "The Sound and the Fury": A Critical Casebook,* ed. André Bleikasten (New York: Garland, 1982), 98, n. 8. Pitavy makes this point to counter views that all of the material dealing with Quentin Compson can be read as a single extended text.

2. About the servant Nancy in "That Evening Sun" and *Requiem for a Nun,* for example, Faulkner says, "She is the same person actually. These people I figure belong to me and I have the right to move them about in time when I need them." See *Faulkner in the University,* ed. Frederick L. Gwynn and Joseph L. Blotner (New York: Random House, 1959), 79.

3. See Gérard Genette, *Narrative Discourse,* trans. Jane E. Lewin (Ithaca, New York: Cornell University Press, 1980), 227–34 and passim, for discussions of the distinction between narrative levels generally and frame possibilities in particular.

4. Kenneth S. Lynn points to the relation between formal strategy and class interests in remarks on the frame device in the Southwestern humor tradition: "By containing their stories within a frame, the humorists also assured their conservative readers of something they had to believe in before they could find such humor amusing, namely, that the Gentleman was as completely in control of the situation he described as he was of himself" (*Mark Twain and Southwestern Humor* [Boston: Little, Brown, 1959], 64).

5. I consider the unframed status of *The Sound and the Fury* in a separate paper, "The Rhetoric of Containment in Faulkner," forthcoming in the volume of proceedings from the International Faulkner Symposium 1987.

6. The classic view of modernism from this standpoint remains Georg Lukács's *The Meaning of Contemporary Realism*, trans. John and Necke Mander (London: Merlin Press, 1963). Lukács argues that modernist fiction leads to an "atttenuation of actuality" (25) by rejecting narrative objectivity and surrendering to subjectivity. Lukács has in mind, for example, Kafka's "descriptive detail," which though of "extraordinary immediacy," is dedicated strictly to the "substituting of his *angst*-ridden vision of the world for objective reality" (25–26). This attenuation of actuality is produced by Joyce's stream-of-consciousness experimentation, too, an effect "carried *ad absurdum* where the stream of consciousness is that of an abnormal subject or of an idiot—consider the first part of Faulkner's *Sound and Fury* [sic]" (26). For Lukács, the attenuation of actuality accompanies the privatization of experience in the modernist work: "Man, for [modernist] writers, is by nature solitary, asocial, unable to enter into relationships with other human beings" (20). Such a state implies a fundamental isolation of the individual from others and from history.

7. See, for example, *Faulkner in the University*, 32.

8. *Faulkner in the University*, 6.

9. William Faulkner, *Collected Stories* (New York: Random House, 1950), 293. I shall quote from this edition for both "That Evening Sun" and "A Justice."

10. In *Figures of Division: William Faulkner's Major Novels* (New York and London: Methuen, 1986), James A. Snead studies the patterns of segregation and amalgamation in the fiction as they reflect Faulkner's struggles with the problem of racial relations and his effort to find a rhetoric to express a transcendence of that division.

11. "The Compson Nancies: A Note on *The Sound and the Fury* and 'That Evening Sun,'" *American Literature* 26 (May 1954), 254.

12. Mae Cameron Brown studies Quentin's style as a reflection of his unique sympathy for Nancy's plight in the story ("Voice in 'That Evening Sun': A Study of Quentin Compson," *Mississippi Quarterly* 29 (1976), 347–60). The older narrator lets his feeling for Nancy's victimization "by the cruelty of the actions and attitudes of the adult whites" show through his childlike narration. Brown notices the contradictory aspect of the rock/balloon comparison, but attributes it only to Faulkner's general preference for paradox (351).

13. Others include Nancy's swallowing and not swallowing (298) and Aunt Rachel's position on her relation to Jesus: "Sometimes she said she was and sometimes she said she wasn't any kin to Jesus" (294). Laurence Perrine annotates a long list of questions that remain unanswered in the story's plot ("'That Evening Sun': A Skein of Uncertainties," *Studies in Short Fiction* 22 [Summer 1985], 295–307).

14. William Faulkner, *The Sound and the Fury: The Corrected Text* (New York: Vintage, 1987), 186.

15. James B. Carothers, in *William Faulkner's Short Stories* (Ann Arbor: UMI Research Press, 1985), remarks that the closing question's "ironic inadequacy is not lost on the mature Quentin who tells the story" (13). I agree, though I suggest that he may choose to ignore its ironic adequacy.

16. According to Lewis M. Dabney, Indian slaveowners were more humane masters than their white counterparts (*The Indians of Yoknapatawpha* [Baton Rouge; Louisiana State University Press, 1974], 84).

17. Dabney makes the claim that Doom becomes "a benevolent paternalist" (ibid., 76), and M. E. Bradford argues that through Doom's action "the basic principle of patriarchy is broken" ("That Other Patriarchy: Observations on Faulkner's 'A Justice'," *Modern Age* 18 [1974], 269).

18. See, for instance, Elmo Howell, "Sam Fathers: A Note on Faulkner's 'A Justice'," *Tennessee Studies in Literature*, 12 (1967), 149–53.

19. William Faulkner, *Go Down, Moses* (New York: Modern Library, 1955), 257.

20. William Faulkner, *Uncollected Stories*, ed. Joseph Blotner (New York: Random House, 1979), 192. I shall quote from this edition.

A Trap Most Magnificently Sprung:
The Last Chapter of *Light in August*

CHRISTOPHER A. LALONDE

> Did you hear the one about the travelling salesman? It goes like this: "Byron Bunch knows this: 'most of what folks tells on other folks aint true to begin with.'"

I begin with a joke in order to make an initial connection between my beginning of this paper and William Faulkner's close of *Light in August*. I am concerned with closure. Given the structural complexity of *Light in August*, a novel where the two major characters never meet, it is apparent that the issue of closure is centrally important. More specifically, the reader must deal with the open-endedness of Lena Grove's strand of the novel. A few words on strand are necessary: I am not referring to a length of string or thread; rather, the word as I am using it here is meant to convey something of the sense of that part of the shore that lies between tide marks—that place or location that is constantly being both hidden and revealed. The sea, then, bounds and unbounds the strand. The reader has the luxury, if I may subtly pervert that word, of having Joe Christmas's death serve as the capstone of Christmas's strand of the novel. Lena Grove's strand does not end so cleanly; David Minter argues that Lena gives Faulkner an "unforgettable beginning" and an "ending to match his [Faulkner's] beginning," but that ending leaves Lena still on the road, still proclaiming that "a body does get around," still marvelling that "we aint been coming from Alabama but two months, and now it's already Tennessee."[1]

Lena Grove's strand of *Light in August* ends with a statement of movement through physical space. Like Joe Christmas, Lena

Grove climbs through a window in order to achieve passage into the world of sex, but, unlike Christmas's movement, Lena's journey is firmly grounded in temporality and physicality. The reader is never allowed to be unaware of how far Lena has come and how long the journey has taken her. Lena sees things on a spatial plane; her movement is linear and nonpsychological. Her sexual rite of passage begins and ends when she moves across the threshold for the first time; and her swollen belly, and later her child, is the exclamation point at the end of her cry of woman-hood.

At the beginning of *Light in August* Lena Grove is a naive backcountry woman, and there is little evidence that she has changed over the novel's course. She does, of course, have a physical rite of passage, from pregnant woman to mother, but she does not grow psychologically or emotionally throughout the course of the novel. As such, Lena is not an exceptionally attractive character. She has a certain charm, to be sure, and her passivity and self-posturing allow her to receive aid from men, but her character seems to lack depth and development, especially when one considers her in relation to Joe Christmas. Looking at the last chapter of *Light in August*, then, beyond giving one clues in a search for the novel's closure, enables the reader to understand, at least in part, some of the reasons behind this deficiency of characterization.

That last chapter almost reads as an addendum to *Light in August*, in something of the same way as the final chapter of *Sanctuary* can be viewed as an addendum to Popeye's story as it is revealed in the body of that text. Chapter 21 of *Light in August* could, I believe, stand alone as a short story divorced from the novel proper. However, the chapter is crucially important to the novel. Any examination of this curious chapter, in an attempt to understand both it and its importance, must in turn deal with Faulkner's manipulation of narrative voice, as he turns the novel over to a new narrator who closes *Light in August* with a set piece that illuminates both Lena Grove and Byron Bunch *and* the problems Faulkner had in closing Lena Grove's strand of the novel. Faulkner chooses to have a nameless furniture repairer and dealer close the book on Lena Grove by having that man tell his wife the story of his encounter with Lena and Byron Bunch. Throughout the first twenty chapters of *Light in August* the narrator had exhibited ample control of both the narrative and the story. Consider two examples: "From that face squinted and still behind the curling smoke from the cigarette which was not touched once with hand until it burned down and was spat out and ground beneath a heel, Joe was to acquire one of his own mannerisms. But not yet" (196); and the shorter and perhaps simpler, "This is not what Byron knows now" (38). In both instances what is suggested is that the narrator knows the story, knows what is yet to come, and that on occasions such as the two I have pointed out the narrator takes pains to show us what he knows—what, that is, is already there but which he chooses not yet to reveal. Why then this sudden shift from an omniscient third person narrator to a furniture salesman? Answering that question can inform the reader of the difficulty Faulkner had in concluding Lena's rite of passage.

The last chapter of *Light in August* begins with a prefatory paragraph that sets the stage for the travelling salesman's tale:

There lives in the eastern part of the state a furniture repairer and dealer who recently made a trip into Tennessee to get some old pieces of furniture which he had bought by correspondence. He made the journey in his truck, carrying with him, since the truck (it had a housed-in body with a door at the rear) was new and he did not intend to drive it faster than fifteen miles an hour, camping equipment to save on hotels. On his return home he told his wife of an experience which he had had on the road, which interested him at the time and which he considered amusing enough to repeat. Perhaps the reason why he found it interesting in the retelling is that he and his wife are not old either, besides his having been away from home (due to the very moderate speed he felt it wise to restrict himself to) for more than a week. The story has to do with two people, passengers whom he picked up; he names the town, in Mississippi, before he entered Tennessee. (545)

Several things are revealed in the first paragraph of chapter 21. First, the absolute break between itself and what precedes it: there is no mention of anything in this paragraph which would suggest that there is a link between it and the previous chapters of the novel. That there is of course a connection, a connection to be revealed slowly across the next page or so but not made explicit until the last third of the chapter, is not so important as is the fact that Faulkner uses the first paragraph to divorce the last chapter from the first twenty. This disruption both creates a special space for the last chapter and, in a cunning rhetorical move, forces the reader to the realization that he or she must make, forge, and/or understand the connection between the salesman's story, Faulkner's marginalization of that story, and the novel as a whole. Second, the oral nature of the prefatory paragraph, its "once upon a time" quality, both foreshadows the orality of the travelling salesman's story and begins to fix him within an established oral tradition. Third, the dramatic nature of the paragraph, with the stage direction quality of the last line—"The story has to do with two people, passengers whom he picked up; he names the town, in Mississippi, before he entered Tennessee"—serves to frame the salesman's tale and hint at the salesman's role in part of the story. That is, the salesman casts himself in the role of audience as he watches the short play starring Lena Grove and Byron Bunch. Moreover, the dramatic nature of the last line also serves to turn over the story to the salesman. The earlier omniscient narrator divorces himself from the ensuing tale, and, save for a few minor intrusions, that narrator remains removed from the story. Fourth, the reason given by the narrator for the salesman's decision to recount the story makes no sense. Consequently, Faulkner's erasure of his omniscient narrator literally forces the reader to take an active role in interpreting the travelling salesman's story—as well as his reasons for telling it.

The salesman tells his narrative to his wife, in their bed, after intercourse. The location and timing, as I mentioned earlier, are telling. The tale told in the dark, reminiscent of the pillow talk between Joe Christmas and Bobbie after they had made love, stands in juxtaposition and direct contradistinction to Lena and Byron's situation; Lena and Byron do not talk in bed, in the dark, after making love. The travelling salesman's narrative carries or contains a voice of experience that is completely incongruous with Lena and Byron's situation, at least insofar as the location is completely alien to their experience together. What Faulkner gives us is a tale told out of marriage and born out of sexual intercourse that is conceived from, concerned with, divorce and separation. It is important here to remember that, as John T. Matthews points out, there is throughout Faulkner's fiction a correspondence "between verbal discourse and sexual intercourse." In the case of the last chapter of *Light in August*, the travelling salesman's narrative can be seen as generated from the earlier act of sexual intercourse. Matthews goes on to state that the relationship between discourse and intercourse "suggests that teller and listener, or writer and reader, surrender themselves to engagement, exposure, embrace, intimacy, and creation"; Faulkner prefigures the necessity of audience involvement and a dynamic between author and reader, narrator and audience, when he writes that Mrs. Hines only learns the story of her life, her daughter and grandson, when she tells it to Hightower and they see it together: "Very likely that was the first time she had ever told it. And very likely she learned it herself then for the first time, actually saw it whole and real at the same time with Hightower" (493). Matthews also states that, "narratives repeatedly issue from marriages in Faulkner,"[2] but the travelling salesman's narrative, while generated from sexual intercourse, does not issue from a marriage between Lena Grove and Byron Bunch. The travelling salesman can term Byron one of Lena's husbands, but his tale issues from separation. The location, the context, of the salesman's narrative, therefore, is laced with irony. If, as Booth suggests, irony is any disparity between utterance and meaning, then Faulkner uses irony to force the reader to call into question the whole of the travelling salesman's narrative.

The nameless furniture man who serves as the narrator of the last chapter is a character straight from humorous oral tradition in America. He is the travelling salesman, that stock figure who is both a part of and the brunt of a part of American humor. The man is a fine storyteller, he knows how to pace a tale and manipulate an audience, he is adept at wordplay, and he laces his story with a healthy dose of sexual innuendo. For instance, in response to his wife's query regarding Byron's intentions toward Lena, the salesman responds, "You wait till I come to that part. Maybe I'll show you, too." Shortly thereafter, he answers his wife's question of what Byron Bunch had "desperated himself" up to do by saying that he had "just showed [her] once," and then adds, "You ain't ready to be showed again, are you" (550)? The salesman is also a perceptive reader of other people, as evidenced by his remark that Byron Bunch looked "like a fellow that aint used to lying" and his further comment that Byron knew that his lies would not be believed. Most importantly, at the climactic moment of *his* role in the action of the tale he is telling, the travelling salesman falls back on oral tradition in order to make an analogy to the situation in which he finds himself. As such, the salesman comes out of and is situated in late nineteenth-century American humor.

We must, however, be careful of how we take Faulkner's nameless narrator. By the 1930s his star is on the descent; he has begun to be replaced by a new type of humor.3 Writers of that older tradition were finding that audiences wanted humor of a more subtle sort. Leading the rise of this new, subtler nonrural humor was *The New Yorker* magazine. Walter Blair writes that, even from its beginning in 1925, *The New Yorker* had no interest in rural and small-town readers, precisely the audience for which characters such as the narrator at the end of *Light in August* would have been created:

The New Yorker [said the Prospectus] will be the magazine which is not edited for the old lady in Dubuque. It will not be concerned with what she is thinking about. . . . The New Yorker is a magazine avowedly published for a metropolitan audience and thereby will escape an influence that hampers most national publications. It expects a considerable national circulation, but this will come from persons who have a metropolitan interest.4

Blair points out that the humor in The New Yorker, humor from writers such as Clarence Shepard Day and James Grover Thurber, was in direct opposition to the sort of humorous tradition out of which Faulkner's travelling salesman comes. Given Faulkner's interest in and concern with magazines such as The New Yorker (he was after all constantly attempting to place stories in major Eastern publications), it seems reasonable to assume that he understood the fragility of the travelling salesman's narrative position. While it is an extreme position to argue that one should deny the legitimacy of the travelling salesman's voice simply because he is something of an anachronism, I do think that one has to be careful of taking what this jokester says straight. This cautionary attitude increases when one realizes the importance of the specific folk ballad he refers to during his climactic moment in his tale.

Byron Bunch leaves Lena and the furniture salesman after Lena rejects his sexual advances. Lena, according to the salesman, physically removes Byron from her bed while admonishing him for his actions. Lena puts Byron in his place, and that place is clearly not in her bed. Consequently, Byron is not back the next morning when the travelling salesman is ready to start out. The salesman and Lena break camp and start travelling on toward Tennessee. The salesman hangs "out the seat to look back, hoping that he [Byron] would show up before we got around the curve" (557). Byron does not show up before they round the curve, and the travelling salesman tells his wife that he felt like "a fellow being caught in the depot with a strange baby on his hands" (557). The salesman is drawing an allusion to a cycle of thematically connected railroad ballads that were first

heard in America in the 1860s. The travelling salesman alludes
to the folk ballad "Fooled in a Railroad Car" and the related "The
Charming Young Widow I Met in the Train." In both ballads the
theme is one of deception and robbery by an artful maid.5 The
young woman in "Fooled in a Railroad Car" charms an un-
suspecting young man, and then leaves him at the depot with
her "baby." The young man discovers that he has been robbed
and that the baby is only a dummy. The innocent and naive
young man falls prey to the young woman. The travelling salesman seems here to suggest that he assumes the role of the
innocent young man to Byron's assumption of the trickster role.
But Byron Bunch is no trickster; he does not use language nearly
well enough. Furthermore, the travelling salesman *knows* that
Byron is not a trickster; the salesman is well aware of Byron's
inability to lie successfully. The salesman, then, perverts the
allusion by both misusing it and by interpreting incorrectly.

How could the travelling salesman make such a mistake?
Perhaps the root of the error reveals no error whatsoever. Rather,
the travelling salesman could well make the allusion to suggest a
connection between the woman trickster and Lena Grove.6 The
travelling salesman clearly places Lena in kinship with that sort
of woman who beguiles and deceives. He tells his wife that he
thinks Lena

> was just travelling. I don't think she had any idea of finding whoever
> it was she was following. I don't think she ever aimed to, only she
> hadn't told him [Byron] yet. . . . I think she had just made up her
> mind to travel a little further and see as much as she could, since I
> reckon she knew that when she settled down this time, it would
> likely be for the rest of her life. That's what I think. (558)

The salesman is ashamed to look at Byron after Lena rejects him.
He is afraid "to let him know that any human man had seen and
heard what happened. I be dog if I didn't want to find the hole
and crawl into it with him. I did for a fact" (555). The salesman's
narrative, both the story and the tone, makes it clear that he
feels that what happened to Byron does not happen to real men;

a real man, like the salesman I suppose, would have made love to Lena long before the night in question. In revealing this prejudice, then, the narrative also reveals that the travelling salesman sees women as sexual objects.

Lena is, then, according to the travelling salesman, a trickster, but not simply a trickster in the ordinary sense of a character who uses language to deceive. Rather, it is also, indeed primarily, from womanhood and motherhood that Lena gets her power. It is precisely Lena's physicality, first as a pregnant woman and then as a mother with a newborn child, which enables her to receive things from men. So it is that early in the novel Harry Armstid can voice the realization that "she'll [Lena] walk the public country herself without shame because she knows that folks, menfolks, will take care of her" (15). *Light in August* certainly bears out Armstid's prediction. But no matter where Lena gets her power, and no matter how rightly or wrongly that power is conceived and utilized, the fact is that the travelling salesman sees women as sexual objects, and he sees Lena as the sort of woman who deceives and manipulates.

The salesman is both a dated character and sexist. We would do well here to remember that for the travelling salesman both sex and language are power. He holds sway over his wife by his use of both intercourse and discourse. His sexual banter cannot disguise the fact that he perceives his ability to give his wife sex as a source of power; similarly, he perceives his ability to give his wife the story as a source of power. Lena is, then, threatening to the salesman because of her denial of the power men receive from both intercourse and discourse. Early in the novel Lena tells "them [the men at Varner's store] of her own accord about that durn fellow like she never had nothing particular to either hide or tell" (21). In the last chapter the salesman tells his wife that "I just lay there" and listened to "them talking, or him talking" (552–53). Lena listens to Byron, but she does not care what he says. His words, his discourse, are powerless to move her. Byron gets no power from intercourse either. Lena refuses sex and is only concerned with her story. It is no wonder then that the salesman considers Lena a trickster, but the fact that Lena has nothing to hide suggests that she is not one. Teresa de Lauretis reminds us that, "As social beings, women [and men] are constructed through effects of language and representation,"[7] and the travelling salesman wrongs the allusion in his overdetermined attempt at figuration. Lena and the baby are left "on" the travelling salesman's hands: left, that is, to be dealt with, to be taken care of, but the salesman, because he cannot see Lena as anything save an object to control or master, can only fault her.[8] We therefore simply cannot and must not trust the voice of the travelling salesman, but Faulkner's use of the travelling salesman as narrator enables him to make a statement about Lena, and to some extent about women in general.

In *The Sound and the Fury* Faulkner does not allow Caddy to speak in a section of her own. Faulkner felt that Caddy was his "heart's darling," and he came to her almost immediately after deciding that he would write first and foremost for himself:

> One day I seemed to shut a door between me and all publishers' addresses and book lists. I said to myself, Now I can write. Now I can make myself a vase like that which the old Roman kept at his bedside and wore the rim slowly away with kissing it. So I, who had never had a sister and was fated to lose my daughter in infancy, set out to make myself a beautiful and tragic little girl.[9]

Despite Caddy's obvious importance and significance to Faulkner, however, he chooses to allow the reader to see her only through her brothers—through their representations of her. It is significant and suggestive that the third-person omniscient narrator of the fourth section never discusses Caddy, never mentions her. Caddy remains locked inside the discourse of her brothers; Caddy remains trapped inside male discourse. Each brother attempts to define her (or her surrogate Miss Quentin) in order to sublimate his desire for her. Caddy herself is meaningless, but it is precisely her meaninglessness that enables her to be meaningful. Each brother's discourse tries to rule Caddy by defining her, by trapping her within its individ-

ual phallocentric language. Lena Grove also remains trapped
inside male discourse: she ends up within the confines of the
bantering, sexually ripe talk of the travelling salesman. It is
precisely that talk, furthermore, that is most telling, most indica-
tive of the travelling salesman's need to rule Lena Grove.

In Caddy Compson and Lena Grove one can see the problems
Faulkner had in dealing with women and their emergence from
rites of passage. David Minter suggests that Faulkner tended to
think of himself "as a man who wrote to or for some woman."[10]
Faulkner, however, has trouble dealing with the central women
in *The Sound and the Fury* and *Light in August*. Throughout his
life it seems as though Faulkner looked at the movement of
women to adulthood in the same way that he looked at his
daughter's movement to adolescence and womanhood: with fear
and some lack of understanding. He would say, about his daughter's maturation, that "this is the end of it. She'll grow into a
woman."[11] In *Mosquitoes* Dawson Fairchild remarks that
women get into life and become a part of it by conceiving and
bearing children. Men, Fairchild states, can only look on as
women make this rite of passage into life. The ending of *Light in
August*, indeed the whole of Lena's portion of the novel, suggests that the Dawson Fairchild voice continues to live in
Faulkner's fiction and in Faulkner. Byron Bunch can only look
on, in fact he can only arrive too late, when Lena gives birth.
Moreover, chapter 21 suggests that one can come to terms with
Lena's passage in the way the travelling salesman does, but to do
so is to lock that woman into a male grid of perception so tainted
that it allows for only a skewed perception. I have tried to point
out how the use of that voice—its incorporation (or lack thereof)
with *Light in August*, and what the voice says and how it says
it—suggests that Faulkner was knowingly depotentiating and
delegitimizing it. The other alternative to the male voice at the
end of the novel, then, is the realization that Faulkner, like
Fairchild, is dealing with something he cannot close properly,
cannot close well. Faulkner's use of the travelling salesman as the
closing voice, bearing in mind where that voice comes from,

serves to close the novel the best way that Faulkner, in 1932, is able. Unreliability is better than uncertainty and ambivalence, and it is up to the reader to see Faulkner's dilemma and advance any alternatives to the travelling salesmen's statement.

This is not to say, however, that Faulkner might not have felt a certain allegiance with the sentiment expressed by the travelling salesman. The early part of his relationship with Estelle Oldham ended in betrayal. The glamorous, popular Estelle had promised herself to Faulkner. The knowledge of the secret promise enabled Faulkner to adopt the role of watcher and the posture of waiting while other suitors pursued Estelle. Estelle reneged on her pledge, however, and married Cornell Franklin. Faulkner allows another voice to make a statement in *Light in August*, and it is the employment of that other voice that allows Faulkner the luxury of avoiding direct confrontation with women and their movement in and into the human race. Torn between the voice that sees woman as deceivers, beguilers, and agents of betrayal, and the voice that wrote everything to or for some woman and who considered Caddy his heart's darling, Faulkner leaves Lena the only way he can. She has come "a fur piece," and yet in some sense she has gone nowhere at all.

Using the travelling salesman's narrative, with its carefully embedded allusion to a revealing cycle of nineteenth-century ballads, is, it seems to me, a stunningly crafty and craftful move on Faulkner's part. The salesman's voice allows Faulkner the luxury of sidestepping what he found most difficult to write about, and alluding to the nineteenth-century ballads reveals the prejudice of the salesman's position with regard to women. The carefully calculated freeplay of that last chapter forces the reader, as Matthews suggests, to engage the text and participate in both its act of creation and a creation itself. Let me return to my initial act of creation, my joke:

Did you hear the one about the travelling salesman? It goes like this: "Byron Bunch knows this: 'most of what folks tells on other folks aint true to begin with.'"

My joke both hides and reveals. My joke is not funny; consequently it perverts the genre in which it attempts to belong. I have wronged language, wronged my subject, and wronged my audience. The travelling salesman also wrongs language (with his misappropriated allusion to the railroad ballads), wrongs his subject (Lena), and consequently wrongs his audience (both his wife and us readers). Faulkner lets us know, if we are sufficiently aware, of the travelling salesman's acts of perversion. Faulkner lets us know that "most of what folks tells on other folks aint true to begin with" (59). There is *nothing* funny about the travelling salesman's joke, about his comic narrative. Faulkner empties the strand for us, pulls back the boundedness of the salesman's narrative, so that we might better see not Lena so much as the problem of figuring her. Lena Grove's strand of the novel, then, is closed without closure. Lena travels onward, chapter 21 suggests, but Faulkner lets us know that she travels in the trapped, closed space of male perception, valuation, and figuration.

NOTES

1. William Faulkner, *Light in August* (New York: Vintage, 1987), 559. All subsequent references are to this edition.

2. John T. Matthews, *The Play of Faulkner's Language* (Ithaca, New York: Cornell University Press, 1982), 17.

3. Walter Blair, *Native American Humor* (San Francisco: Chandler Publishing Co., 1960), 168.

4. Ibid.

5. Norm Cohen, *Long Steel Rail: The Railroad in American Folksong* (Urbana: University of Illinois Press), 50.

6. The argument suggests that Faulkner has his character both appropriate and pervert the folk ballad in order that we can see both the travelling salesman and Lena. Daniel Hoffman points out that this same strategy of appropriation and perversion is evident in Faulkner's "Was." See "Faulkner's 'Was' and 'Uncle Adam's Cow,'" in Doreen Fowler and Ann J. Abadie, eds., *Faulkner and Humor* (Jackson: University Press of Mississippi, 1986) 57–78.

7. Teresa de Lauretis, *Alice Doesn't: Feminism, Semiotics, Cinema* (Bloomington: Indiana University Press, 1984), 14.

8. On fault in *Absalom, Absalom!*, see Matthews, *The Play of Faulkner's Language*, 15–17.

9. William Faulkner, "An Introduction to *The Sound and the Fury*," ed. James B. Meriwether, *The Southern Review*, n.s. 8, 4 (Autumn 1972), 710.

10. David Minter, *William Faulkner: His Life and Work* (Baltimore: The Johns Hopkins University Press, 1980), 35.

11. Ibid., 93.

Faulkner's Patriotic Failure: Southern Lyricism versus American Hypervision

WILLIAM E. H. MEYER, JR.

All spiritual discoveries are transforming.
Jonathan Edwards, Religious Affections

INTRODUCTION: Faulkner's Rhetoric-of-Reality-as-Failure

And then the black blood failed him again, as it must have in crises all his life.

Light in August

One gets more than a little weary, in reading *Faulkner in the University*, of the writer's insistence that his productions are always failures—"it ain't good enough"[1]—until one realizes that the author is operating with a system of ultimate values wherein "failure" is the highest metaphysical or aesthetic "truth." Whether we read how Hightower "failed his wife" or "failed himself," or whether we read how *The Sound and the Fury* was "the most gallant, the most magnificent failure," or whether we observe Faulkner's critique of Thomas Wolfe's "splendid magnficent bust" for "trying to put the whole history of the human heart on the head of a pin"[2]—in each and every instance Faulkner is reliving or *vindicating* the experience of his own environment, with its shrinking wilderness, postbellum consciousness, and its ultimate guilt for having to choose between the aural/lyrical "thunder of hooves" or "ricklickshun en de blood of de Lamb!" and the hypervisual "genius in America, with tyrannous eye."[3] Indeed, until his death, Faulkner filled his speeches and essays with the insistence that "the American

Dream" had failed to deliver the promised "privacy" or freedom from "fear" or the necessary "individuality" that he craved.[4] But, again, this is by no means the negation of art or the spirit of the South—it is failure as the *sine qua non* of reality. It is, finally, Faulkner's inability to succeed as the *American* writer because of his *Southern* high-priestess, failure; or, as he declared of his fourfold failure in *The Sound and the Fury*— "it's the one that I love the most."[5] Or of the "deep South" and its "curse" of "slavery"/failure—"It's my country, my native land, and I love it."[6]

As I hope to make plainer, this rhetoric or metaphysic of failure will have immense consequences for not only interpreting but also evaluating Faulkner—and indeed the whole "South"— vis-a-vis the American/Emersonian *optimism* that the hyper-visual ideal or the triumphant "*White*-Whale" ideal and not the failed Southern/lyrical/"black" ideal must be definitive for the evolution of *American* culture:

> The eye is final; what it tells us is the last stroke of nature. Beyond color we cannot go.[7]

O Say, Can *YOU* See the real conflict between the "blue" and the "grey"?

> Over the river a golden ray of sun came through the hosts of leaden rain clouds.[8]

Nor should we neglect to add that the very concept of "patriotic failure" has a double implication or potential: the "good" failure *because* of patriotism, *i.e.*, the "patriot's failure"; and the "bad" *failure to be* patriotic at all. Of course, too, "patriotism" itself may be a very ambiguous notion for a Southerner. Finally, I hope that this paper stimulates each reader to a better understanding of what Melville touted in "call him an American and have done"—of who, indeed, will "endure" in the difficult twenty-first and twenty-second centuries ahead.

The Magnificent Failure of Southern Sound

I think of myself as a failed poet, not as a novelist at all.

Faulkner in the University

It was inevitable that Faulkner should have moved from *The Sound and the Fury* to *Light in August*—not in now "turning to the light" or finally "seeing the light," but in having postulated his first love, his ultimate love, he should thereupon take up the crisis in American fictional identity which he intuited that the "tyrannous eye" created. That is, having postulated and grounded himself in "sound," this "Southern boy" should have felt compelled to confront the *originating* cause of the Civil War—the hypervisual "light" that demands that no "inscrutable" condition or color-coded injustice should prevail or go unseen. As we shall observe, Faulkner will, in *Light in August*, attempt to "domesticate" or "lyricize" this proto-American light, only to discover that, like Joe Christmas, "the black blood failed him again" and thrust him outside the pale of what we may call "the American Religion of Vision."9 All in all, both novels illustrate the irony of the great Southern/lyrical writer thereby damning himself as a great American/hypervisualist.

Here, however, we first of all need to emphasize that *The Sound and the Fury* is the "magnificent failure" of the Southern lyricist/novelist attempting to transcend Shakespeare via an American tragedy wherein sound, even meaningless sound, is made the ultimate value—far beyond even that of honor, glory, region, and womanhood. *The Sound and the Fury*, then, is Faulkner's attempt to transcend his own identity as a "failed poet" by turning the craft of fiction into the original craft of sound/song:

> I would say that music is the easiest means in which to express, since it came first in man's experience and history. But since words are my talent, I must try to express clumsily in words what the pure music would have done better . . . that is, *the thunder and the music of prose* take place in silence.10 (italics mine)

This meaningless "thunder and music of prose" in that novel which Faulkner "loved the best" has forever kept him from that outstanding front rank of *American* writers who understand their milieu as a Puritanical/Emersonian "clean, well-lighted place," wherein "you do not want music; certainly you do not want music."[11]

Moreover, *The Sound and the Fury* is a kind of "four quartets" or ensemble of choruses/solos with a concluding coda. Here, the sights and visions of the characters—even Faulkner's own famous initial vision of Caddy's muddy drawers in a pear tree—have all been apotheosized in sounds/words or what we may call the Old-World hyperverbal ideal. That Faulkner realizes that this "tradition" cannot coexist with the "individual talent" of hypervisual America forms the true pathos and theme or failure-metaphysic of his works: again we stress the proud failure—

> I must try to express clumsily in words what the pure music would have done better.

Let us note, for example, the short lyrical "cadences" of Benjy in part 1—metrical grunts which, for all their simpler coordinators, no one would mistake for Hemingwayesque simple diction/observation:

> Caddy's head was on Father's shoulder. Her hair was like fire, and little points of fire were in her eyes, and I went and Father lifted me into the chair too, and Caddy held me. She smelled like trees.
> *She smelled like trees. In the corner it was dark, but I could see the window. I squatted there, holding the slipper. I couldn't see it, but my hand saw it, and I could hear it getting night, and my hands saw the slipper but I couldn't see myself, but my hands could see the slipper, and I squatted there, hearing it getting dark.*[12]

Here, unlike Thomas Wolfe's fiction of the "tyrannous eye" wherein "that *vision* of the city blazed outward not only from the images and objects which would evoke it literally . . . it came in all the *sounds and noises* of a carnival, in the *smell* of confetti and gasoline"[13] (italics mine)—wherein "vision" comes to usurp and absorb all the other senses, of ears and nose—Faulkner's passion is to create the idiocy of simple music from the secondary or extraneous elements of the other "senses." In essence, Faulkner wants to *lyricize* the "little points of fire" and *"she smelled like trees"* into "a tale told by an idiot" that will transcend the American hypervisual norm and in fact reclaim or revindicate the "honor" and "glory" and "worship of woman" and "song" that is basic to the chivalric/Southern/Old-World past. Benjy, however, as he finally, in periodic position, *"squatted there, hearing it getting dark,"* represents "the magnificent failure of Southern sound" to reach the *positive*—not "failed"—certitude of America's "Battle Hymn" wherein "Mine Eyes Have Seen the Glory of the Coming of the Lord." Indeed, as Quentin emphasizes, Benjy's great power is his voice, not his uncoordinated bulk: *"pulling at her dress and bellowing his voice hammered back and forth between the walls in waves . . . his voice hammering back and forth as though its own momentum would not let it stop."* Benjy's solo is essentially a failed dialogue between Faulkner and America on his love for *The Sound and the Fury;* it stands as an idiotic momentum-monument to "bellowing" Southern isolationism.

As Faulkner goes on to tell us, the eldest brother, Quentin Compson, also necessarily "failed" to tell the story of the lost Southern sister. And I think it is no accident that here the novel's lyricism and obsession with sound reaches its greatest crescendo. Quentin has taken Benjy's raw power and nascent harmony and has attempted to annihilate all reality via rhetoric. Indeed, from the opening sentences, wherein Quentin awakens, "hearing the watch" and musing on failure—"victory is an illusion of philosophers and fools"—to the suicidal close, wherein "the last note sounded," we find the most excruciating outburst of damned Southern "thunder and music of prose" as ever has been penned. No wonder Faulkner exclaimed that "I don't have the feeling toward any of them that I do toward that one"[14]— toward *The Sound and the Fury*. It was the one wherein he pushed Southern lyricism to its ultimate expression—to its ultimate *Shakespearean* crisis—from whence he would turn to a novel titled from his own more "Americanized" experience—of "light in August."

In fact, if we compare Benjy's outbursts and murmurings with Quentin's, we find that the *maddest* character's outpourings are heard in Quentin's section, not Benjy's. Here there is no Keatsean "sense" to the nightingale's tune—only Quentin's attention to how some "bird whistled again, invisible, a sound meaningless and profound, inflexionless, ceasing as though cut off with the blow of a knife." Here, "meaningless sound" becomes the be-all, end-all of culture and art—the *"Oh Oh Oh Oh"* and *"did you hear what I said"* and the *"oh oh oh oh"* of frustration and magnificent failure. Again, this is no Wolfean transmogrification of reality into "a stream of swarming images, stamping a thousand brilliant pictures on his brain with the speed of light";[15] it is the overcoming of all pleasure and pain in the idiot's cradle of furious Southern song:

> I would lie in bed thinking when will it stop when will it stop. . . .
> Sometimes I could put myself to sleep saying that over and over until
> after the honeysuckle got all mixed up in it the whole thing came to
> symbolize night and unrest I seemed to be lying neither asleep nor
> awake . . . the rest of the time just voices that laugh when you see
> nothing to laugh at, tears when no reason for tears.

Here, the "saying over and over" comes to function as its own highest good—a metaphysic of failure which both author and character perceive but have no will to change, no matter what the cost:

> I have sold Benjy's pasture and I can be dead in Harvard Caddy said
> in the caverns and the grottoes of the sea tumbling peacefully to the
> wavering tides because *Harvard is such a fine sound forty acres is no
> high price for a fine sound.* (italics mine)

Although Faulkner realizes the irony of his "fine dead sound" and the tragedy of the loss of the Emersonian "pasture" for a "fine dead sound," he can no more than his young lyricist, Quentin, halt the impending suicide of trading America or "the land that was ours before we were the land's" for the magnificent failure of *The Sound and the Fury*. The tradition out of which Faulkner wrote was too strong to escape, yet ultimately too weak to reach beyond the ears of modern Americans to their eyes:

> Grandfather wore his uniform and we could hear the murmur of their voices from beyond the cedars they were always talking and Grandfather was always right.

It is quite fitting, then, that Quentin's final lyric free-association should attempt to outrace even the reverberations of the campus bell, should attempt to "say it all" in the space of time created as "the first note sounded, measured and tranquil, serenely peremptory, emptying the unhurried silence for the next one"—should find itself veering towards irrevocable insanity as the "failed poet" knows that he "could hear whispers secret surges smell the beating of hot blood." This tormenting "incest" is the failure of the European immigrant to "couple" the South with America the Beautiful rather than with the ingrown Old-World aristocracy or "kin." Truly and pathetically, Quentin/ Faulkner wants to rid himself of the guilt, wants to penetrate hypervisual America and its *rite de passage "beyond the clean flame"*—wants to "isolate her out of the loud world"—but traditional expectations and conditioning make this impossible: Harvard is such a "fine dead sound" and one must not "disappoint a lady," especially if that lady is the Southern muse of Lyricism itself. If Quentin had understood *why* the Liberty Bell had cracked upon its first ringing and had become another icon or "Eye-con" in the American Religion of Vision, he might have been able to cope with the trauma of a cultural ethos drowning as "the last note sounded."

Moreover, it is no accident, I think, that section 3—Jason's "song"—should be or at least *appear* to be the least "lyrical" of the major divisions of *The Sound and the Fury*. For here, unlike Benjy or Quentin, Jason professes an enormous hatred for the fallen Southern sister/lyrical muse—"once a bitch always a bitch"—and refuses to "sing," at least ostensibly, on her or her offspring's behalf. Jason's only hope is that he can tame or subdue this passionate ideal/child by the strict demand for hypervisual righteous *appearance* or by the projection of *image:* "Everybody in this town knows what you are. . . . I've got a position in this town, and I'm not going to have any member of my family going on like a nigger wench." Jason is enraged that the preservation of this old, crumbling family and lyric ideal has unfairly fallen upon his shoulders—that what should have been his Emersonian inheritance and provision for the future was squandered on a "bellowing" idiot and a suicidal romanticist/rhetorician. Jason, in short, represents the Southern writer *in extremis,* attempting to "educate" or control his unpredictable and dangerous hyperverbal heritage: "If I *hear* one more time that you haven't been to school, you'll wish you were in hell" (italics mine). The wild Southern muse must be domesticated or "changed," or it must be expelled, destroyed. Again, it is no wonder that Jason's cold and vindictive method of discipline and keeping-up-appearances should be for the passionate Southern novelist another excruciating "magnificent failure."

In truth, however, Jason can no more escape the "thunder and music of prose" that is his birthright and blessing/curse than can any of the other characters; and section 3 is, in essence, a kind of natural symphony of voices or everyday cacophony, ranging from the almost mellifluous to the thought-drone. Here, to take one example, Uncle Job reveals how a love for the "darkie-dialect," with its rhythm, personification, and rhyme, can pop up in the most mundane of circumstances—while assembling cultivators at the store where Jason works. For purposes of demonstration, I have set up Uncle Job's dialogue in the form of "failed poetry":

> "Boll-weevil got tough *time.*
> Work ev'y day in de week out in de hot sun, rain er *shine.*
> Ain't got no front porch to *set on*
> en watch de watermilyns *growin*
> and Sat'dy dont mean nothing a-tall *to him*." (italics mine)

This natural black lyricism, with its "unconscious" preference for the sonority of repeated vowels, consonants, and trochees, surrounds Jason despite his austere attempts to exist by a revengeful calculation alone. In fact, in a long, impassioned outburst akin to an "atonal" virtuosity, Jason manifests his own fundamental relation to the Compson hyperverbal muse and its volleys of insane monodies:

> I could see the bottom of his nightshirt and his bare legs and hear the decanter clinking until finally T. P. had to pour it for him and she says You have no respect for your Father's memory and I says I dont know why not it sure is preserved well enough to last only if I'm crazy too God knows what I'll do about it just to look at water makes me sick and I'd just as soon swallow gasoline as a glass of whiskey . . . I've got respect for a good honest whore because with Mother's health and the position I try to uphold to have her with no more respect for what I try to do for her than to make her name and my name and Mother's name a byword in the town.

While this extended "thought-chant" certainly lacks the melodious character of Quentin's lines, it does betray Jason's "failure" to entirely escape the "fallen" muse for some "good honest whore." Indeed, Faulkner is really talking here about the broad problem of culture and aesthetics—the impossibility of denying one's own "wise blood" for any kind of logic or sentience which eschews "the thunder and the music" of Southern prose:

> If it's in her blood, you cant do anything with her. The only thing you can do is to get rid of her.

But in this desire or monomania to "educate" or "discipline" or "purge" what is inexorably fixed in the "blood," one indeed runs the danger of losing all—of having the sister/muse declare, " 'I wish we were all dead,' " and of having any ill-gotten "material fortune" or fame snatched from out one's psychic "hoard."

All in all, Jason has come dangerously close to losing it all, both in his attempts to repudiate the "fallen" sister or hyperverbal South and in his simultaneous inability to truly understand and appreciate the wider concerns of hypervisual America. Undoubtedly, then, Jason's "failure" is the most alarming of all the "lyrical" failures of *The Sound and the Fury*—a failure which matches that of Joe Christmas in *Light in August* because Jason, too, "didn't know what he was." Indeed, perhaps the ironic solution/fate for everyone in the South lay in the amusing "failure" of even emasculation/castration/defeat to alter the power of the lyrical/hyperverbal ideal—it merely strung one's vocal cords up a notch:

> I read somewhere they'd fix men that way to give them women's voices. But maybe he didn't know what they'd done to him.

And perhaps that "Southern boy" or "failed poet," William Faulkner himself, really "didn't know what they'd done to him" either.

The last section, or what the novelist called the "failure" when "Faulkner tried to tell it," seeks to create an even greater distance and objectivity concerning the plight of the hyperverbal South than was possible in the narratives of the three brothers. But here, in what is essentially the "negroes'" story, we have more striking evidence of the firm grip of lyricism on the struggling Southern consciousness. Luster might attempt to shoo away the "five jaybirds" or hyperverbal furies flocking among the mullberries—"'Whoo . . . git on back to hell, whar you belong at'"—but the "maddening" and "terrific slowness" of the deeply ensconced lyrical muse would never be so summarily dismissed from *The Sound and the Fury*.

Indeed, just as James Baldwin declares that "it is only in his music . . . that the Negro in America has been able to tell his story"[16] or just as W. E. B. Du Bois reports that he only emphatically discovered his "roots" in the "Sorrow Songs,"[17] so the African/aural character of the Southern blacks in *The Sound and the Fury* is what finally accounts for Faulkner's famous and ironic encomium—"They endured":

> As she ground the sifter steadily above the bread board, *she sang*, to herself at first, something without particular tune or words, repetitive, mournful and plaintive, austere. (italics mine)

This Southern "plaintive number" or austere, even meaningless "sorrow song" presently begins to "thaw" and will later reach its fervid culmination in the "sonorous echoes" of the black Easter sermon.

Truly, in this famous black worship service, Faulkner has

provided us with a paradigm for the quintessential "fall" and "redemption" of the rhetorical South. First of all we note how the blacks themselves have to transcend the hypervisual bias or their own state of "consternation" as they "watched the insignificant looking man" who was to be the featured speaker—a visual disappointment which leads Frony to whisper, " 'En dey brung dat all de way from Saint Looey.' " Indeed, the preacher himself has to pass through the crucible of "sounding like a white man" until he can recall the "negroid" intonations and pronunciations. And finally here, then, in the lyrical/aural " 'I got de ricklickshun en de blood of de Lamb' " we find that the blacks, Faulkner, and the whole South meet head on that unsurpassable wall, "the voice which consumed them." An Emerson may confess, as the "transparent eyeball," that "I am nothing; I *see* all,"[18] but a Faulkner must shout as "the voice consumed him"—

> He was nothing and they were nothing and there was not even a voice but instead their hearts were speaking to one another in *chanting measures* beyond the need for words. (italics mine)

Here is the paradigm for that silent "thunder and music of prose" that Faulkner craves above all else. It is an aesthetic/faith that can only elicit more vocality/aurality—

> "Yes, Jesus!"

A Hawkeye on Mount Vision may wax emotional as he "saw all that God had done, or man could do, far as the eye could reach"[19]; but what unshackles Dilsey is "the *voice* that took them to itself" (italics mine):

> Two tears slid down her fallen cheeks, in and out of the myriad coruscations of immolation and abnegation and time.

This "little Jesus" about to be "killed"—not the "winking" infant of "untempered light" that Hester Prynne brought forth into the sunlight upon the Boston scaffold—is the lost Southern child, the *hyperverbal* God-as-Word, the liberator of the "murmuring" congregation:

> "Mmmmmmmmmmmmmmmmmm!" The woman's voice said, "Yes, Jesus! Jesus!"

This salvation, by "voice" and "sonority," is akin to that Old-World *geist* that drove Yeats to exclaim, "I *hear* it in the deep heart's core," and that compelled Wordsworth to flee the "world" for the right to "*hear* old Triton blow his wreathed horn"[20] (italics mine). The black preacher, in fact, offers the final vindication for the entire traditional "South," which demands that it "shall rise again," as he "*hears* de golden horns shoutin down de glory, en de *arisen dead* whut got de blood en de ricklickshun of the Lamb!" (italics mine).

Finally, however, this hyperverbal/lyrical ideal has come under attack by neon signs that demand, "Keep your 👁 on Mottson, the gap filled by a human eye with an electric pupil," or by billboards that, in Fitzgerald's *The Great Gatsby*, sport "the gigantic pale blue eyes of Doctor T. J. Eckleburg," brooding over our hypervisual "valley of ashes" with retinas "one yard high."[21] And, here, is it any wonder that in this "tale told by an idiot," Benjy should, in the final paragraphs, find himself "in an utter hiatus" and should give stentorian vent to his amazement and sense of betrayal/rage:

> Then he bellowed. Bellow on bellow, his voice mounted, with scarce interval for breath. There was more than astonishment in it, it was horror; shock; agony eyeless, tongueless; *just sound* . . . Ben's voice mounted toward its *unbelievable crescendo*. (italics mine)

Indeed, this is Ben's—and Faulkner's—own "Southern sermon"; and it is one that we shall have to confront again in the "siren mounting toward its *unbelievable crescendo*" announcing the castration/death of the "hero" of *Light in August*.

THE DOMESTICATED FAILURE OF SOUTHERN LIGHT

> Do we fear lest we should *outsee* nature
> and God, and drink truth dry? (italics mine)
> > Emerson, "The American Scholar"

One can by no means describe or evaluate Faulkner's "craft of fiction"—his rhetoric, his narrative poetics, his employment of temporal patterns and points of view—until one has come to terms with the foundational problem of lyricism and vision as that manifests itself in both of his *magna opera,* in *The Sound and the Fury* and *Light in August.* While there is a continuity between the two novels in Faulkner's ongoing preoccupation with the tragedy of the South, there is also a new note struck or attempted to be struck in *Light in August*—the attempt to turn the art of the novel toward the transcendent hypervisual norm. And, of course, with this attempt comes the challenge for the writer to refine his techniques of observation and description beyond that of the dialogues/monologues of a fallen Southern clan in *The Sound and the Fury.* This casting of one's eye over a wider panorama of characters, places, and events is what gives *Light in August* its own distinct "feel" vis-a-vis *The Sound and the Fury.*

However, one is never allowed to forget that this ephemeral "light in August" is more closely tied to provincial, Southern interests than to the Melvillean "fiery hunt" for the White Whale as the "great principle of light."[22] Indeed, Faulkner goes out of his way to stress that the "luminosity" with which he is concerned is *not* that of Emerson's "original relation to the universe" but is, in good Southern/traditional fashion, akin to "the old classic times" of Grecian fauns and satyrs.[23] Moreover, although Faulkner has ostensibly left the Shakespearean title and influence for a local phenomenon, he nevertheless still writes with the Old-World hyperverbal assumption that "all the world's a stage":

> Now the final copper light of afternoon fades; now the street beyond the low maples and the low signboard is prepared and empty, framed by the study window *like a stage.* [24] (italics mine)

This domesticated and dramatized attitude toward the American sight-geist ideal again makes it most difficult for Faulkner to really *see* beyond his first love—"the thunder and the music of prose." That he attempted to do so, or that he at least tried to match the hyperverbal with the hypervisual ideal—that he wished to wrestle with "white" blood and "black" blood and the primal Mother Nature as she wants "to see as much as she can" before settling down—reveals a courage that will redound to his artistic and social honor. However, that Faulkner understands this peculiar Mississippi phenomenon of luminosity as essentially tied to "old classic times" will forever separate him from a Thoreau who radically demands "old deeds for old people, and new deeds for new."[25] William Faulkner will never be accounted among those quintessentially *American* heroes whom D. H. Lawrence noted for their "*new* consciousness" and "alien character"—qualities that would "hurt horribly" yet cause Europeans to "open new eyes" to the art and culture of the New World.[26] That is, Faulkner lacked the courage or perhaps simply the ability and environment to *fully* confront the power of the "tyrannous eye" to absolutely enlighten and reveal the defeated Southern landscape. Faulkner's lyricism acts as a kind of shield or blinders against the Medusa-like "transparent eyeball" of the American Religion of Vision. This is really the "failure" that Faulkner repeatedly senses as the reality behind each of his forays into "the craft of fiction."

Turning briefly, now, to what is the apparent heart of Faulkner's experiment in *Light in August*—an expanded descriptive technique—we find that the story or set of stories is encompassed by a primal seer, Lena Grove, who begins by "*watching* the wagon mount the hill" and *looking* for the father of her child, and who concludes by "traveling a little further and *seeing* as much as she could" (italics mine). Indeed, in this ocular trial, both Lena and Faulkner are "*further from home than I have ever been*" as they search through Alabama, Mississippi, and Tennessee. Yet the *South* is never actually transcended or escaped in this exploration of identity and culture, in this "hot still pinewiney silence of the August afternoon." Moreover, in his portrayal of Lena or what *should* be Miss America's "groves" as an Old-World/Keatsean muse "moving forever and without progress across an urn," Faulkner again reveals his fundamental allegiance to an Old-World hyperverbal/lyrical ideal and not the "grove" of the Emersonian/American "woods" wherein any "old classical" lack of progress is superceded by originality or "living ever in a *new* day"[27] (italics mine).

Here, the descriptive power of the "transparent eyeball" is lost in the monotonous cadence of the wagon—"the eye loses the road as sight and sense drowsily merge and blend"—and audition becomes the primary reality:

I will be riding within the hearing of Lucas Burch before his seeing.

This is, finally, a realm of narrative description—of Southern half-vision—that the hypervisual Great Awakening cannot, perhaps will never or must never, touch:

They draw slowly together as the wagon crawls terrifically toward her in its slow palpable aura of somnolence and red dust in which the steady feet of the mules move dreamlike and punctuate by the sparse jingle of harness and the limber bobbing of jackrabbit ears, the mules still neither asleep nor awake.

We should note here, too, that while not only do so many of the chapters open with what promises to be keen observation— of how "the group of men at work . . . saw the stranger standing here, watching them," or how "from the study window he can see the steet," or how "they sit facing one another across the desk"—but also how again these observations grow dim or too soft in the Southern lyrical light, as at the beginning of chapter 11, with its erroneous, "romanticized" vision:

By the light of the candle she did not look much more than thirty, in the soft light downfalling upon the softungirdled presence of a woman prepared for sleep.

In fact, perhaps the "observations" of Hightower, preferring to utilize his window for evening sound, not daylight vision, best reveal the domestication or lyricizing of the lost hypervisual opportunity:

Then, as though it had waited for his signal, the music begins. The organ strains come rich and resonant through the summer night, blended, sonorous, with that quality of abjectness and sublimation, as if the freed voices themselves were assuming the shapes and attitudes of crucifixions, ecstatic, solemn, and profound in gathering volume.

This is "heaven" for Hightower/Faulkner—"*listening,* he seems *to hear* within it the apotheosis of his own history, his own land, his own environed blood" (italics mine). Indeed, there is absolutely no way to reconcile Hightower's feeling that "Sunday evening prayer meeting," with its profound, provincial sonority, was the hour wherein "man approached nearest to God," and Thoreau's enthusiasm for "Morning air!" or Emerson's diurnal ecstasies wherein "I am nothing; I see all" and so become "part or parcel of God."[28] A Hightower/Faulkner may "*hear* . . . the apotheosis of his own history, his own land," but an Emerson declares that "that which others hear, I *see*" and a Dickinson touts the eye-epistemology of our "very Lunacy of Light":

> Omnipotence—had not a Tongue—
> His lisp—is Lightning— . . .
> "How shall you know"?
> Consult your Eye![29]

There can simply be no comparison between the ephemeral and fading and lyrical "light in August" and the constant, dominant, hypervisual power of *The Sun Also Rises*.

Finally, as we have indicated above in passing, William Faulkner and Joe Christmas share an identical crisis of identity— the tragedy of being a divided man, a black man in a white world, or of being a Southerner in America, or of being a hyperverbalist in our artist's milieu, our "clean, well-lighted place."[30] Christmas/Faulkner, as he moves into "the cold hard air of white people" and observes "on a lighted veranda . . . the white faces intent and sharp in the low light, the bare arms of the women glaring smooth and white above the trivial cards," confesses to himself and his "craft of fiction" that this *should* be the ideal—"That's all I wanted . . . that dont seem like a lot to ask." But "the black blood failed him again"—the "wise blood" that amalgamated Negro and Southern white in the blessing/curse of lyricism: "*blended,* sonorous, with the quality of abjectness and sublimation, as if the *freed voices* themselves were assuming the shapes and attitudes of crucifixions." Even Christmas's death itself, for rebelling against both the hypervisual color "code" and the hyperverbal ideal in attempting to escape that "woman" or muse who could surrender only in "words" and who would try to force him to "pray," must be given that "apotheosis" which Hightower *heard*—a meaningless/all-meaningful sound which seeks to transcend even itself:

> Again, the scream of the siren mounted toward its unbelievable crescendo, passing out of the realm of hearing.

Who could believe that this "unbelievable" scream of self-awareness issues forth from that same artist who dared to complain of the hyperverbal *threat* to America—

> Now we hear only the mouthwords; the loud and empty words which we have emasculated of all meaning whatever—freedom, democracy, patriotism.

Faulkner's own Southern passion for "the wild bugles and the clashing sabres and the dying thunder of hooves" or what he called "the thunder and the music of prose" has made it impossible for him to transcend his "magnificent failure" in the craft of fiction for that reality which even an "ex-patriot" like T. S. Eliot saw—

> Looking into the heart of light, the silence.[31]

A SELF-EVIDENT *AMERICAN* CONCLUSION

See if you can grasp the reason why Faulkner spoke of his "demon" as "the mosquito that won't let you sleep . . . it keeps on whispering to you,"[32] while Hemingway "lit a match" and destroyed the humming mosquito in the light "and went to sleep."[33] Or see if you can understand why Faulkner's assertion that, among his contemporaries, "Wolfe failed the least because he had tried the hardest, had taken the largest gambles, taken the longest shots,"[34] will have to be reevaluated in light of Faulkner's own magnificent Southern failure and Wolfe's own furious obsession to achieve what in *The Web and the Rock* he called his "superhuman intensity of vision."[35]

O Say, Can *YOU* See a whole new set of problems facing the critic of Southern writing in hypervisualistic America—or simply why, instead of the bear or the roaring lion, the "eagle-eyed" Eagle of 6X-vision is our national symbol?

NOTES

1. William Faulkner, *Faulkner in the University*, ed. Frederick L. Gwynn and Joseph L. Blotner (Charlottesville: University of Virginia Press, 1959), 90.

2. Ibid., 144.

3. Ralph Waldo Emerson, "The Poet," *Selections from Ralph Waldo Emerson*, ed. Stephen E. Whicher (Boston: Houghton Mifflin, 1960), 238.

4. Faulkner, *Essays, Speeches, and Public Lectures*, ed. James B. Meriwether (New York: Random House, 1965), 62, 68.

5. Faulkner, *Faulkner in the University*, 77.

6. Ibid., 83.

7. Emerson, *Journals and Miscellaneous Notebooks, 1854–61*, ed. Susan Sutton Smith (Cambridge, Mass.: Belknap, 1978), 14: 166.

8. Stephen Crane, *The Red Badge of Courage*, ed. William Gibson (Dallas: Holt, Rinehart and Winston, 1968), 538.

9. William E. Meyer, Jr., "The American Religion of Vision," *Christian Century*, 16 November 1983, 1045–47.

10. Faulkner, "William Faulkner: An Interview," in *William Faulkner: Three Decades of Criticism*, ed. Frederick J. Hoffman and Olga W. Vickery (East Lansing: Michigan State University Press, 1960), 76.

11. Ernest Hemingway, "A Clean, Well-Lighted Place," *Short Stories* (New York: Scribner's Sons, 1966), 383.

12. Faulkner, *The Sound and the Fury* (New York: Vintage Books, 1956), 88–89.

13. Thomas Wolfe, *The Web and the Rock* (New York: Sun Dial Press, 1940), 92–94.

14. Faulkner, *Faulkner in the University*, 61.

15. Wolfe, *The Web and the Rock*, 455.

16. James Baldwin, "Many Thousands Gone," in *Black Literature in America*, ed. Houston A. Baker, Jr. (New York: McGraw-Hill, 1971), 310.

17. W. E. B. Du Bois, "Of the Sorrow Songs," in *American Literature: The Makers and the Making*, ed. Brooks, Lewis, Warren, 2 vols. (New York: St. Martin's, 1973), 2: 1762.

18. Emerson, "Nature," *Selections*, 24.

19. James Fenimore Cooper, *The Pioneers* (New York: Dodd, Mead and Co., 1958), 300.

20. William Butler Yeats, "The Lake Isle of Innisfree," in *Selected Poems and Two Plays*, ed. M. L. Rosenthal (New York: Collier Books, 1968), 14; William Wordsworth, "The World Is Too Much with Us," *Anthology of Romanticism*, ed. Earnest Bernbaum (New York: Ronald Press, 1949), 404.

21. F. Scott Fitzgerald, *The Great Gatsby* (New York: Scribner's, 1953), 23.

22. Herman Melville, *Moby-Dick*, ed. Charles Feidelson, Jr. (Indianapolis: Bobbs-Merrill, 1964), 264.

23. Faulkner, *Faulkner in the University*, 199.

24. Faulkner, *Light in August* (New York: Vintage Books, 1972), 441.

25. H. D. Thoreau, *Walden*, in *American Literature*, 1: 775.

26. D. H. Lawrence, *Studies in Classic American Literature* (New York: Thomas Seltzer, 1923), 1–2; *The Symbolic Meaning*, ed. Armin Arnold (New York: Viking, 1968), 17.

27. Emerson, "Self-Reliance," *Selections*, 77.

28. Emerson, "Nature," *Selections*, 24.

29. Emily Dickinson, poem #420, *The Complete Poems*, ed. Thomas H. Johnson (Boston: Little, Brown and Co., 1966), 201.

30. Meyer, "The Artist's America: Hemingway's 'A Clean, Well-Lighted Place,'" *Arizona Quarterly* (Summer 1983), 156–63.

31. T. S. Eliot, *The Waste Land*, in *American Literature*, 2: 1778.

32. Faulkner, *Faulkner in the University*, 205.

33. Hemingway, "Big Two-Hearted River: Part 1," *Short Stories*, 218.

34. Faulkner, *Faulkner in the University*, 143.

35. Wolfe, *The Web and the Rock*, 273.

"Drowsing Maidenhead Symbol's Self": Faulkner and the Fictions of Love

Judith L. Sensibar

Obsessed, mad Labove. His name prefigures his ludicrous "final disaster" at the hands and by the words of the sixteen-year-old girl he fictionalizes as "the drowsing maidenhead *symbol's* self."[1] Faulkner clearly and humorously marks the immense disparity between Labove's fiction and Eula's reality. When Labove tries to rape her, Eula effortlessly slams him to the floor. Standing "over [*above*] him, breathing deep but not panting and not even dishevelled," she drawls, "Stop pawing me. . . . You old headless horseman Ichabod Crane" (122). Labove's dismal failure in love is comic, but the fictions that feed his desire are similar to and thus anticipate the desires that drive Jack Houston and Mink Snopes to their deaths. Labove's vision insists that Eula is "at once supremely unchaste and inviolable" (115). Labove speaks of his love in a series of ludicrous antitheses enveloped in a haze of romantic and melodramatic language he has gleaned from books. Eula is like "one of the unchaste and perhaps even anonymously pregnant immortals eating bread of Paradise on a sunrise slope of Olympus" (123). The telltale sign of Labove's own imaginative origins is there. His legs are "haired over like those of faun" (118). And like Joe Christmas, his earlier tragic counterpart, Labove "knew that sooner or later something was going to hap-

My research for this article was supported by an Arizona State University Women's Studies Faculty Summer Stipend (summer 1987) and an American Council of Learned Societies Fellowship (partially funded by NEH) 1988–89.

pen" (119). Yet, knowing that he will be destroyed, he helplessly wallows in his vision of desire. What is this vision? Again Labove evokes a panoply of Faulkner's *pierrotiste* protagonists including Quentin Compson, Addie Bundren, and Joe Christmas—desire is not gender specific—when he says:

> That's it. Fight it. Fight it. That's what it is: a man and a woman fighting each other. The hating. To kill, only to do it in such a way that the other will have to know forever afterward he or she is dead. Not even to lie quiet dead because forever afterward there will have to be two in that grave and those two can never again lie quiet anywhere together and neither can ever lie anywhere alone and be quiet until he or she is dead. (121)

Permutations of Labove's fiction or vision of love pervade Faulkner's fiction and, as I have shown elsewhere, his poetry.[2] Antitheses, tension, and conscious theatrics are love's essence whether its form is tragic, comic, or tragicomic. Think, for example, of how Joe Christmas and Joanna Burden act out their meticulously staged desire. Their affair proceeds in three "phases" or acts whose climax is Joanna's violent murder. Joe claims that Joanna has produced and directed the show. She throws "fits of jealous rage . . . and there was neither reason for the scene nor any possible protagonist: he knew that she knew that. It was as if she had invented the whole thing deliberately, for the purpose of playing it out like a play."[3]

She insists on an elaborate means of secret communication, a pitiful parody of pastoral in which the "place for concealing notes, letters" is a "hollow fence post below the rotting stable" (245). But Faulkner makes it clear that Joe can ham as well as his female twin and that he is equally steeped in the trappings of romance and melodrama. Although the door to her ancestral home is unlocked, Joe first enters Joanna's house by crawling through a window. His immediate and subsequent descriptions of Joanna reveal clearly that his relation to her is consummately theatrical. He constantly frames her in windows or doorways, and always in light—candlelight, lamplight, firelight. He sees her as an actress making a stage entrance: "the door opened and a woman entered. . . . She carried a candle, holding it high, so that its light fell upon her face" (217–18), or as an art object: "her calm profile in the peaceful firelight was grave and tranquil as a portrait in a frame" (254). He speaks of the scenes of their coupling as acts: "the scenes, the faultlessly played scenes of secret and monstrous delight and of jealousy" (249). And he maintains the high level of tension throughout by insisting that "something is going to happen." Joe heightens and prolongs their drama by refusing to go away because—like Labove, or Jack Houston, or Mink Snopes in *The Hamlet*—he insists that he is bound to Joanna "with a lock and chain" (257).[4] Like Labove's, Joe's image for desire is war. In the final phase "neither surrendered; worse: they would not let one another alone; he would not even go away" (264). Costume and masking are as important as action and lines. Joe's descriptions of Joanna's amazing physical transformations are matched by his own split-second costume changes as he slides continuously between his black and white identities.

These are marvelous renderings of love or desire: marvelous because, despite their similarities, and no matter how many times we read and reread them, we are still caught in the drama and seduced by Faulkner's language. Such renderings of love and desire are a central trope in all his art. These fictions, which are grounded in antithesis and theatricality, pervade his mythical yet very real world. He writes obsessively and with great sensitivity about the ways men and women fail and, more rarely, succeed in love. He is preoccupied with the ecstasy and pain of desire. Unlike the novels of his modernist counterparts like Fitzgerald or Hemingway, Faulkner's greatest novels—*The Sound and the Fury, As I Lay Dying, Light in August, Absalom, Absalom!*—are about families, generations of Mississippi families, and—perhaps most of all—they are about marriage. In current critical terms we would say that the politics of desire are central to Faulkner's imaginative vision.

And yet, to date, Faulkner's biographers have not traced out those politics in his life or in his family history. We have no sense of the relation of Faulkner the Southerner, the son, lover, husband, or parent to the tortured marriages and love affairs in his fiction. In current biographical assessments, Faulkner and his actual world remain essentially one-dimensional; the Faulkner women appear as caricatures or shadow figures. There is an underlying assumption working in Faulkner studies which results in a portrayal that conforms to the popular and essentially romantic stereotype of the Great (Male) American Writer. Insistence on this myth is one reason why, until recently, Faulkner's very *un*romantic but fascinating ten-year self-apprenticeship to poetry was ignored; the myth requires no hint of effeteness and an instantaneous transformation to genius. In Faulkner biography the driven, lonely, misunderstood artist is judged, ultimately, a magnificent Failure—a man consumed by two fatal obsessions—his dependence on alcohol and his lifetime attraction for and marriage to a helpless hysteric. There is some truth in all myths, but this picture is not accurate or complete. The myth also insists that the most significant positive influences on Faulkner's creative development were men. Since clearly Faulkner's father, Murry, was not one of these, attention centers on a host of other dead and living father surrogates.[5] In contrast, the imaginative and creative women with whom the artist was first surrounded and later chose to surround himself are simultaneously distorted and marginalized. We know practically nothing about these other family influences who were *alive* when Faulkner was and who were at least as important—the four generations of Mississippi women whose voices, indistinct in Faulkner biography, are heard across the entire spectrum of his imaginative domain. Looked at together with those men to whom they are joined, they can teach us much that is fresh and new about the origins of the art and craft of Faulkner's fiction.

This is what I wish to discuss here—some aspects of work-in-progress, a family narrative about William Faulkner and the four women with whom he lived most of his life: his "two mothers," Maud Butler (1871–1960) and Caroline Clark Barr (c. 1840–1940); his wife, Estelle Oldham (1897–1972); and his daughter,

Jill Faulkner Summers (1933–).[6] My earlier book established the organic stylistic and thematic connections between Faulkner the young poet and Faulkner the mature artist. It also noted the importance of Faulkner's erotic attachments to the women who are now my focus in shaping his literary strategies and affiliations. But my earlier emphasis was a comprehensive treatment of Faulkner's poetry. Thus I only touched on the delicate transactions between his art and life suggested by the intriguing biographical information I had collected in initial interviews with Faulkner's daughter and other women he had loved.

Since then, more interviews and new primary-source materials have further confirmed the rich reality of Faulkner's relations with the four crucial women I focus on. These different perspectives provide an unfamiliar view of the artist's inner life and his creative process, a view which suggests strongly that while his relations with both sexes naturally formed and informed his vision of sexuality, his fictions of love and desire, his relations with the women in and outside of his family, rather than his connections with a tenuous and questionable masculine ideal, shaped both his understanding of what it meant to love and his optimistic and positive vision of what an artist and a man could be.

The biographical, critical, and historical groundwork for my book has been laid by Faulkner scholars and others and encompasses a multiplicity of disciplines.[7] But, as the recently published *Faulkner and Women* essays and Minrose Gwin's analysis and summary of the literature make clear, the debate on the nature of Faulkner's fictional men's and women's sexuality has only just begun.[8] The larger question of the origins of Faulkner's perceptions of the relation of creativity to sexuality has similarly received little attention. Despite the growing literature on Faulkner's women characters, no one has yet attempted to relate fiction to fact—to the politics of sexuality in his actual world. Nor is there a description and analysis of these politics as they were experienced and taught by the four generations of black and white women among whom Faulkner lived. My narrative seeks a more balanced approach for by so limiting our view, we have missed a large subject in the expansive field of the human scene that Faulkner inhabited and transmuted into art. By writing these women back into Faulkner's life, I want now to fill out the canvas. In doing so, I take my lead from Faulkner's art. There family and erotic relationships are central and *women and men* are portrayed as subjects, not objects. My focus is Faulkner and these women in relation to each other and to the culture in which they all lived.

Who was Caroline Clark Barr, the "salty-tongued" and bossy ex-slave who ran Maud's and then Estelle's households? Her stories spellbound three generations of Faulkners. She often told Jill, when she misbehaved, that if she weren't careful, she would end up like her grandfather Murry. Faulkner's stepson Malcolm claimed that Caroline Barr ruled the roost. Jill says that "the women Pappy most loved and admired were Granny, Mammy Callie, and Aunt Bama."9 What was Caroline's relation with Maud and, later, Estelle? What did Faulkner learn from this illiterate black woman about narrative structures and strategies? How do his dark and light "mothers" fuel his imaginative images of psychic fragmentation and of sexuality? What does the trope of seeing but not touching have to do with the politics of race and gender in his fiction?

We can caricature Maud Butler as a little old lady in Buster Browns (she did wear them, as her feet were too small for women's shoes) but that fails to illuminate. She was certainly controlling and probably "tough as whip leather."10 But these and other descriptions don't touch on the extent and nature of her imagination, her creative sensibilities, her iconoclasm, or her quiet but sometimes withering humor. Nor do they explain her sons' and women friends' devotion or the wistfulness with which these friends say, "I still miss Miss Maud's wit."11 She is pictured as a loner. This complex and intelligent woman was certainly difficult, but she was not isolated and she maintained a life apart from her family. My interviews reveal an intricate and tightly knit group of women friends

of all ages with whom she played bridge, went driving (she loved
to drive—not be driven), and attended the Memphis dog races.
She was reserved but she was also full of life. In her own
paintings she practiced a fervid realism. How did her imaginative perceptions of reality transmute to Faulkner's art? What
strengths did these two "mothers" give Faulkner? Why, faced
with their intense disapproval, did he drink? And why, in his
fiction, is alcohol (another pervasive trope) always an anodyne for
unbearable loss?

In contrast to Maud's and Caroline's materially austere lives,
Estelle Oldham's world was rich in all variety of outward show.
The Oldhams were social snobs. But with Republicans on both
sides, and only Lida Oldham's mother's *maternal* pedigree un-
sullied, their veneer of class and caste, their pretentious claims
to "family," were thin. It is a constant refrain among the women
of Oxford and of Kosciusko that Lida Oldham "pushed Estelle."
Jill Summers says:

> I think that all of Nanny's children were a disappointment to her—
> her only son for dying in the flu epidemic, and the pretty daughter
> [Victoria] who married well and then promptly died. And Ma-ma—
> whom they thought they'd married off—and then she made a botch
> of it. And then Aunt Dot just generally making a botch of life. That
> didn't please Nanny at all. Those children just didn't do what they
> should have done. Nanny was very easy-going as far as I was con-
> cerned. But I think she was extremely hard on her own children.
> There was not much love lost between Nanny, Aunt Dot, and Ma-
> ma.

Lida Oldham worked by indirection:

> Nanny had the delightful habit that seems to run in the family—of
> talking about people when they were in the room. For example,
> Aunt Dot would be in the room and Nanny would start discussing
> her in definitely uncomplimentary terms like, "Isn't Dorothy's hair-
> do terrible?" or something unkind like that. She did that all the time
> to both Ma-ma and Aunt Dot. But she never said anything mean or
> ugly to them directly. It was just as though they were not there.[12]

Her mother could not complain about Estelle's looks because her daughter was always immaculately groomed. So instead she'd criticize her for her housekeeping or for not being a dutiful daughter. Lemuel Oldham was equally controlling. He determined

> that Ma-ma would marry well—to a family that could trace every ancestor back a long time. In Mississippi particularly, family is important. And when Ma-ma was twelve or thirteen, Grandaddy and Nanny started scouting the eligible families and decided which direction they intended Ma-ma to go. Marrying Cornell Franklin was strictly an arrangement between Grandaddy and Mr. Franklin. [13]

Faulkner chose to be an outsider. And he had strong support from his mother. In what ways were Estelle's parents outsiders too? Were the Oldhams as wealthy as they claimed? Did parental and other constraints keep Estelle from leaving what appears to have been in many ways a lonely and unsatisfying second marriage to Faulkner? With no independent income and no family support, could she, like her friend Ella Somerville, have gone into business for herself? (Estelle was an exquisite seamstress, and loved this work. She often designed her own and her daughter's clothes, and she sewed without patterns. At least twice she organized a showing of her gowns, using as models students at Ole Miss and her friends from Oxford and Memphis.)

Like Maud Butler, Estelle Oldham began painting after her husband's death. But Faulkner's wife's surreal and impressionistic transformations of reality in her art were the antithesis of Maud's realistic primitives. Estelle also wrote fiction and humorous verse. She was no Zelda Fitzgerald, but her unpublished short stories, written in the '20s, are competently crafted and particularly insightful on subjects as wide-ranging as social tensions in the pre- and post–Civil War South and the casual and deadly racism of American Colonials in Shanghai during the '20s. Aside from their iconoclasm, these two women seemed to have little in common. Yet, apparently, Faulkner needed both. He was neither naive nor young when he and

Estelle Oldham married. Why, despite much talk of divorce, did it last? We have read about his infidelities, Estelle's hysteria, her drug dependency. Viewing her as Disease and Faulkner as Myth, we have effectively silenced both. Estelle is much more than a spoiled Southern Belle. Her total life tells a great deal about her husband's life and art. In his fiction, Faulkner writes about families. Yet we know little about his relations with his parents, his wife, and his daughter.

When he was writing, Faulkner closed out the world. But he did not *live* an isolated life. Although Rowan Oak, the Faulkners' house in Oxford, is large enough that Faulkner could have chosen a quiet upstairs bedroom for his study, he chose instead a light and airy groundfloor room adjacent to the front door and opposite the living room, with doorways to both the front hall and what was originally the gallery. Faulkner's daughter explains:

> My friends and I almost always came through as a matter of course and the colored people who worked for us never hesitated to beat on the door to ask him for something. When he was at the typewriter, he was just playing. The only time they didn't disturb him was when he was asleep on the couch. There was no such thing as the library ever being off-limits. I spent much of my childhood reading on the couch while he was working. I could even talk at him, make comments and such; but I wasn't supposed to ask direct questions, and I wasn't to *expect* an answer. When Pappy was really concentrating, he didn't hear anything anyway. Nothing could bother him.[14]

My narrative focuses on four main historical and biographical issues that directly inform structure, characterization, and intention in Faulkner's poetry and fiction. The first is the writer's earliest experiences with women in what Anne Firor Scott, and others, have shown was a patriarchal but matrifocal world. Faulkner reveals an important part of its essence in a screen memory of his "two mothers," Caroline Barr and Maud Butler. He remembers a small, three-year-old, homesick boy walking through the night between two women who simultaneously attract and repel him. One is dark, warm, and sensual: "she must have carried me." The other is blond, cold, and "aloof," but "she was holding the lamp."¹⁵

This remarkable conflation of racism and sexuality is a core fantasy that fuels Faulkner's imaginative visions of desire from *The Marionettes* to *Absalom, Absalom!* and beyond. Often in Faulkner's fiction, a tortured and torturing *pierrotique* male lover merges these two images in one woman (as Joe Christmas does with Joanna Burden in *Light in August*). In *Absalom, Absalom!* Faulkner invents black and white brothers and sisters (races are literally split and merged) to continue his imaginative exploration into the meanings of and relations between racism, gender, love, and sexuality. Since this splitting or doubling is a constant source of creative tension in his poetry and fiction, it is worth looking at its extraliterary origins. From whom did Faulkner learn to split and why? What are the implications in a culture where white men and women say again and again that their black nurse "was my real mother"? Are his changing relations with the women in his family and with other women in his life reflected in the increasing complexity, dexterity, and brilliance with which he gives imaginative form to these questions? I have begun to trace out a pattern of splitting that Faulkner imposed on all the women he loved. Most vividly, his daughter was alternately "Jill" and "Bill."

My second and third biographical issues are Faulkner's imaginative representations of the relation between creativity and sexuality and the relationship of a four-generational family history of alcoholism to Faulkner's fictional tropes of self-destruction, distrust of words, and psychic numbness and to his recurring figure of the silenced poet. We have understood the sense of impotence—the inability to sing that Faulkner's earliest personae experience—as his creative response to the loss of Estelle. That loss was doubtless a precipitating event. But we must look futher back to understand both the formal and psychological implications of his ultimately triumphant fictional blurring and merging of gender distinctions, and the consummate ease with which he handles his polymorphic characters.

Were his "two mothers" an important source of his fears of
artistic impotence? After all, these two mothers were potential
artists.[16] In a family headed and supported by Faulkner's inarticulate and hard-drinking father, these two women, Maud
Butler and Caroline Barr, controlled the word and, between
them, taught the young artist the word's practical and imaginative powers. They also had little use for the grown men in
their lives, sons excepted. What did they say about their husbands and about women and other men? What expectations did
they place on Faulkner? What was the significance of art as a
vocation if only women and men like Stark Young and Ben
Wasson (both of whom had left Mississippi) attempted to be
artists? In this context it is important to remember that Faulkner
was the South's first great novelist. He really had no significant
male models. And the great storytellers and the visual artists in
his family were all women.

Of equal importance in exploring the relations between creativity, sexuality, and alcoholism is Faulkner's figuring of Estelle
Oldham in his recurring trope of the Fatal Dancer. Discussion of
the Dancer includes Pierrot, her paralyzed partner. The most
interesting of Faulkner's poems and poem sequences center on
these two central images of late romanticism, symbolism, and
early modernism. Did their original attraction to Faulkner stem
merely from their literary ancestry? Or did these highly charged
symbols of desire draw their power as much from Faulkner's own
reality? My research suggests that Faulkner chose them, or they
chose him, because they mirrored central aspects of his relations
with women, but especially with Estelle. She once said that
while she never recognized any of Faulkner's characters as herself, she had noted that her husband's more savage inventions
often displayed some of her own worst qualities. This frank and
insightful remark is characteristic of the woman who is beginning
to emerge from my research. That Estelle was the seductive and
exhibitionistic Dancer and Faulkner the voyeuristic and often
sadistic watcher is well documented. Estelle was quintessentially theatrical and her theatricality played directly into

Faulkner's. But, in Faulkner's poetry and fiction, why is the dance so threatening?[17] Why must Pierrot always silence and literally still the Dancer in order to hear his own "silent music"? Why did Faulkner create rivalries between the women he loved, especially (as the letters show) between his mother and wife and between his wife and his sister—rivalries that mirror his own fictional battles between mothers, daughters, and sisters?[18]

Whether Faulkner drew a line between his art and his life leads to my fourth biographical issue: What was the relation of masking and theater in his love relationships and in his art? This issue and the part it played in Faulkner's marriage is my focus here. In Faulkner's poetry and fiction, masking as well as racial and gender transformations constantly attend the consciousness of characters who ask, in one way or another, "Who am I?" in *The Marionettes*, Faulkner's 1920 dream-play, Pierrot woos Marietta in the guise of his shade and, as I have shown in *Origins*, Faulkner's drawings of his heroine bear an uncanny resemblance to photographs of Estelle Oldham, photographs taken shortly before and in the early years of her marriage to her first husband Cornell Franklin. Thus masking and theater figure prominently in one of Faulkner's earliest imaginative productions, which was in part a reworking of his long relationship with Estelle Oldham, a relationship begun in 1903 when her family moved from Kosciusko, Mississippi, to Oxford. It is well known that Faulkner delighted in role playing in his life as well as in his art. What is not common knowledge is that his wife joined him, that the two had acted together since childhood and shared equally in an attendant love for costume and that their private theater remained central to their marriage. It is this aspect of their relationship that I want to discuss, because it illustrates vividly one of the many ways in which Faulkner's marriage, contrary to popular conceptions, fueled his creativity. Let me first sketch briefly the outlines of that popular conception.

In Faulkner biography, Estelle Oldham is, to use one of Faulkner's favorite poetic adjectives, an "opaque" but negative and somewhat pitiful figure. By all accounts, including

Faulkner's own, she is the millstone around the great author's neck. Coming to him as used goods, she merely repeated the role she had played with her first husband before he divorced her in 1929.[19] Faulkner's letter to his editor Hal Smith asking to borrow $500 to finance his marriage establishes the basis for this interpretation. In it, he claims dramatically that he is marrying because

> [I] [b]oth want to and have to. . . . For my honor and sanity—I believe life—of a woman. This is not bunk; neither am I being sucked in. We grew up together and I don't think she could fool me in this way; that is, make believe that her mental condition, her nerves, are this far gone. And no question of pregna[n]cy: that would hardly move me: no one can face his own bastard with more equanimity than I, having had some practice. Neither is it a matter of a promise on my part; we have known one another long enough to pay no attention to our promises. It's a situation which I engendered and permitted to ripen which has become unbearable, and I am tired of running from the devilment I bring about. This sounds a little insane, but I'm not in any shape to write letters now. I'll explain it better when I see you.[20]

I will not stop to analyze the stagey quality of Faulkner's cleverly balanced rhetoric, his piling up of negatives, his hyperbolic exaggeration as, like Rosa Coldfield, he denies only to suggest and claims to accept blame only to shift charges of manipulation to his lover. I quote from this letter because it conveys in Faulkner's own words the accepted version of why he and Estelle Oldham married and why, despite his many affairs, they remained married. A new biography's description of Oldham's state of mind shortly before her marriage to Faulkner is typical:

> [Faulkner's] stalling and uncertainty [about whether to marry her] threw Estelle into a panic. Unless he married her, how could she go on living—she, a 32-year-old divorcee with two children? A failure in the eyes of her family and friends, worse than that to the town at large? Without him she felt she had nothing, was nothing. For the sake of her sanity, of her life, he must marry her. She had no one else to turn to. Her nerves were gone, her mind, too. He was her last hope.[21]

Here, as in previous biographies, she appears as a caricature of
the helpless and hysterical Southern belle (a role which, when it
suited her purposes, she could play to the hilt). Note that
Faulkner is also stereotyped, as a dutiful son and honorable
Southern gentleman: "Estelle's frantic helplessness appealed to
his sense of honor. . . . Here was a chance to prove to his father
and Major Oldham . . . that he was a *man,* not a wastrel" (84).
Such biographical fictions distort our perceptions of Faulkner
the human being and Faulkner the artist. For example, Faulkner
has a history of seldom concerning himself with others' opinions.
That he would allow one of the most important decisions of his
life to be dictated by the opinions of two men he neither loved
nor respected seems farfetched at best. But, perhaps most dis-
turbingly, this portrait insists, in the face of the *facts* of a virtual
lifetime of mutual attachment which began when William and
Estelle were eight or nine years old, was continued throughout
Estelle's eleven-year marriage to her first husband, and concluded with the Faulkners' own thirty-three-year marriage
that—again according to this newest biography—"there was a
wall of irreconcilable difference between Faulkner and Estelle
which made real intimacy impossible."[22] The deletion of all
erotic and affectionate material from surviving letters Faulkner
wrote his wife from Hollywood and New York in the '30s and
early '40s in the published *Selected Letters* reinforces such interpretations, especially in the light of Meta Carpenter's memoir of
her affair with Faulkner during just those years. To suggest that
Faulkner spent his life with a woman with whom he had no real
relationship demeans both partners.

But in virtually every Faulkner biography Estelle Oldham's
hysteria, her alcoholism, her narcissism, her profligacy, her
exhibitionism, and her stupidity are her most commonly noted
qualities. While there is truth in some of these charges, the
picture is not accurate or complete.

Let's take another look at the letter to Hal Smith. Our interpretation changes if, rather than allowing ourselves to be seduced by its histrionics, we remember its intent—to get a loan,

an advance on *The Sound and the Fury*. Our interpretation also changes if we look for the letter's fictional parallels, and read it as part rhetorical ploy and part practice arena for Faulkner's fictions of love and desire. For besides being rhetorically convincing, this letter is a shorthand version of some of the most redundant and powerful images of desire in his novels. Like Joe Christmas and Jack Houston, Faulkner too is tired of "running" from his own devilment. Like Houston and his wife, Estelle Oldham and he have known each other forever.

In *The Hamlet* Faulkner elaborates on this fiction. There Jack Houston says of his desire, "it seemed to him that it had been in his life always, even between those five years between his birth and hers; . . . that he himself had not begun to exist until she was born, the two of them chained irrevocably from that hour and onward forever" (206). Like Joe Christmas's, Houston's organizing fantasy, or fiction of love, fuses preoedipal with mature erotic desire: the woman he marries has been in his life before he was born. Houston wants it all. But because this fusion is incestuous, and therefore forbidden, his conscious response must be to fight it. He sees himself chained "not by love but by implacable constancy and invincible repudiation—on the one hand, that steadfast and undismayable will to alter and improve and remake; on the other, that furious resistance" (206).

Theater springing from the tension of yoking antitheses was as important to the structure of Faulkner's love affairs as it was to the formal concerns of his poetry and fiction. One thinks of Faulkner insisting to the middle-aged Meta Carpenter that she wear hair ribbons like a teenager and of her comment that he was more passionate in letters than he ever was in the flesh. Or of the transparent fiction he and Meta Carpenter imposed on his wife when Meta came to dinner at the Faulkners' as Ben Wasson's date. There are dozens of examples. A recent brief reminiscence, "Faulkner: A Flirtation," in the *New York Times Sunday Magazine*, provides a nice vignette of Faulkner flirting with a young admirer. In this instance, he assumes the guise of Januarius Jones, one of his earliest self-parodies.[23] The *Times* essay aptly illustrates Faulkner's habit of almost immediately imposing his own fictional frame upon any potentially romantic relationship. During the ten years he wrote poetry almost exclusively, his most favored persona was Pierrot, the quintessential masker. Cyrano de Bergerac, who wooed his true love in the guise of another man's voice, was another of Faulkner's favorite characters: throughout his life he cribbed from Cyrano to woo a series of women, including Helen Baird in the '20s and Joan Williams in the '50s.[24] In short, when we read Faulkner's 1929 letter to his editor in the dual contexts of his erotic and aesthetic life, its meaning changes. The letter's drama and the practical and artistic function of that drama are revealed.

Faulkner's daughter, Jill Summers, describes growing up in a household in which masks were the order of the day:

> Living with Ma-ma and Pappy was like living on a stage-set. Everybody was playing a role. You never knew who was being what today. They played roles to each other and, largely, I was left out of it. There was always lots of storming up and down the stairs and threats, on my mother's part, to slash her wrists. She really liked playing tragic parts. They both enjoyed it, and even I got to know it was not for real. But it was pretty exciting. The only time I touched base, you know, hit the ground in the real world, was when I went to school. When I walked back through the gates at Rowan Oak, it was like Alice going down the rabbit hole. I never knew exactly what would be at the end of the hole when I reached my front porch. . . . Pappy always—it would be hard for me to say that I could look at him at one point and say, "this is who he really is," because, almost always he was playing a part. When I was young, it gave me a feeling of unreality. I never knew whether I was real to them.[25]

As it had been in Estelle's and William's childhood games, costume was part of this theater. When she grew older, Jill could often predict the tone and theme of the evening's performance when she saw what her mother was wearing as she came down to dinner:

> When Ma-ma was getting ready to really have a major scene, she wore major clothes for it. I could pretty much predict what an evening was going to be like by what Ma-ma wore to dinner. If we

were going to have a real confrontation—you know, "My life is wasted, I've been abused"—then it would usually be something really elegant. If it were going to be a fairly smooth, uneventful evening, it would just be an ordinary, decent type of dress. And then, if it were going to be a "Aren't we all happy together in this nice little threesome here in the country" sort of thing it would— there was just a difference in her dress that would fit that too. Life was never dull at Rowan Oak. Pappy did the same thing. He liked to play the country squire but he also liked to play the good ol' boy with all the men from the fishing camp or the hunting camp and he changed his clothes and his accent accordingly. To a certain extent Ma-ma was the same way.

So often what was said was said for effect, and so often the position that was taken was taken for effect. It didn't really reflect anyone's true feelings on the matter. What I'm really trying to say is that people had roles. Everyone had—they were standing back and watching themselves play this particular part.[26]

Theater was not reserved for special occasions. It often entered into the daily routine. A friend of Jill's loved life at Rowan Oak because it was so much more interesting than any place else in town. "It was the atmosphere—I always felt like they sort of— it was like a play, maybe." Even a family meal at Rowan Oak was a performance:

Well, to me Mrs. Faulkner—she was not the greatest housekeeper, but she had a lot of flair. I mean you could have the simplest food but it would be served up buffet on silver platters. It was just great. Nobody's mother actually cooked. But she could cook when she wanted to. She was very inventive, very artistic with whatever she did—cooking, gardening, sewing—she made beautiful clothes. It was a household that was so entirely different from anything I knew. I enjoyed going down there so much. It was just highly entertaining.

Jill's friend makes the following comparison:

At our house, we ate in the dining room only for Sunday dinner and when company came. Well, the Faulkners always ate in the dining room—except for in the winter when everything was frozen as we didn't have any central heating. But, no matter how simple the meal was, it was very elaborately served. Mr. Faulkner was at one end and the plates were stacked and he served the dinner—he served the meal and everything, always. And even if it were bacon, lettuce, and tomato sandwiches, it would all be on silver trays with the lettuce beautifully arranged. I thought it was the greatest. I think they all enjoyed it.[27]

Faulkner's daughter's comments about her parents reveal more similarities in her parents' likes and dislikes than differences:

Both my parents always went out of their way to make my friends feel welcomed, and they always enjoyed them. Pappy was much happier with my friends than he was with adults anyway. And he would go well out of his way—tell stories and that sort of thing. They both tried to be careful that none of my friends saw them drinking. There were exceptions like the time that I told you about—when Pappy ruined my birthday.

Estelle also told Jill and her friends stories she invented based on characters in Hawaiian folklore. Jill says:

These were two actual people but Ma-ma would weave all sorts of fantastic tales around them which we would mix in with our own remake of whatever movie was playing at the matinee that week. Our main props, besides our ponies, were the trees and grapevines in the garden at Rowan Oak. We'd do a lot of climbing and swinging.[28]

Besides making up tales for her daughter, Estelle wrote some fiction of her own. In fact, in the late '20s Faulkner sent Scribner's a coauthored story which they rejected.[29] Estelle's known surviving manuscripts are competent magazine-quality work. One is particularly interesting because it's consciously autobiographical and tells much about Estelle's feelings when, as an almost eight-year-old girl, she was just about to move from Kosciusko to Oxford. Here she already privileges the imagination and sees herself as, therefore, different. After offering her good-night prayers, she is admonished for asking God to "deliver me from playmates. Grown-ups—white and colored—were far superior company."[30] One reason she prefers grown-ups is that they tell stories. These details about Estelle Oldham tend to call into question biographers' insistence on her as a totally depen-

dent lightweight whose greatest concern was her reputation in
the community.

Unlike other children's, Jill's parents seemed generally available. Her Mother is supposed to have craved a more active social
life. Perhaps she did. Yet her daughter says:

> She wasn't interested in the activities of the other ladies' clubs and
> bridge. She loved to fiddle around the garden. She wasn't doing the
> gardening herself, but she was out there supervising and cutting
> flowers. I don't think there was ever a problem as far as Ma-ma was
> concerned—not at the beginning of her life or at the end either. It
> was not a question of "what I am going to do with myself for the next
> hour because there's nothing I don't have to do." Time was some-
> thing to be enjoyed.[31]

As for Estelle's availability, again her daughter's comments suggest a kind of self-sufficiency and independence that is at odds
with current biographical assessments:

> She was ready to listen, always wanted to help. But if I didn't come
> with a specific problem, she was perfectly willing to let me fend for
> myself. She wasn't intrusive, but also she was very wrapped up in
> her own self and in her own thoughts. I was more important to her
> than anything else other than Pappy. At the same time, she herself
> was very important to herself. I realized early—and it probably
> saved me too—that I was not of primary importance to either one of
> them. You know, some people tend to forget that there is a "me."
> They are *always* concerned with other people. But she wasn't. It's
> probably one of the reasons she and Pappy stayed together.[32]

After Faulkner's death in 1962, his wife began painting, something she hadn't done since she lived in Shanghai. Her abstract
impressionist style was precisely the opposite of her mother-in-
law's primitive realism. Maud's interest in accuracy led to detail
such as including a photograph of Eleanor Roosevelt in a painting of the inside of a black sharecropper's cabin. Estelle Oldham
had several exhibits of her paintings in Charlottesville. In one
interview she remarked, "I have never been bored in my life—
lonely, maybe, but never bored."[33]

While Rowan Oak may have been fun to visit, it was more complicated to live there. When it became too much, Jill could go the the cabin where first Caroline Barr (Mammy Callie) and, later, other black women who cared for her lived: "It was sometimes a happier place to be. There was no feeling of tension there. It was the difference between sitting under a nice cool shade tree and sitting on top of a volcano."[34] But I suspect that the tension that their daughter experienced as dangerous and unpleasant was a sustaining and enlivening force in the Faulkner's marriage, a point Summers makes herself:

> Ma-ma and Pappy were two very different and difficult people trying to coexist. They walked on tight wires around each other, and I walked an equally tight wire around the two of them. But I think they both enjoyed it. I think *I* was the only one who felt uncomfortable.
>
> There was always the feeling that something was getting ready to happen. I'm trying to think if there was ever any time when life was simply there. There wasn't. There were always undercurrents and just a feeling of tension. There's no other way to describe it.[35]

Her description of their marriage sounds eerily similar to Faulkner's fictional portrayals of desire. Elaborating, she contrasts her mother's two husbands.

> Judge Franklin was a delightful man, but pretty pedestrian. He had money, he liked the things that money provided—polo ponies and steeplechase horses. But, despite all the places he'd been and things he'd done, he was really pretty dull and predictable. I think *that*, as much as anything, caused the problems between them, because Ma-ma didn't care for the pedestrian aspects of any life. I think that, because she enjoyed living to some degree in a fantasy world. Because she didn't like the pedestrian aspects of any life or thing, she completely enjoyed the sort of life she had with Pappy even though it was difficult. I'm not sure Pappy would have stayed married to anyone else. He married an idea; he didn't marry a person.
>
> Ma-ma was very good and so was Pappy—if something was distasteful or wasn't quite as it should be, they could simply not see it. I think moving into Rowan Oak to begin with was something of a lark. It was a romantic adventure sort of thing. And both of them liked that. For example, if there were no electricity, they'd say "Oh, isn't

candlelight nice?" instead of "Oh, what am I going to do without any electricity?" There is no running water; a bottle of wine on ice is better than water coming out of a tap. That's what I'm trying to say about their fantasy world. And remember, everyone had help.[36]

To say that Faulkner's marriage translated directly into his fiction (that it was an instance—to use Faulkner's words—of sublimating the actual to the apocryphal) is simplistic. But their daughter's observations on why her parents stayed married, despite much talk of divorce and desertion, give one a sense that it was a stimulating relationship for both partners. In many respects, Faulkner very consciously used the tension and theater in his marriage—a theater in which Estelle was an adept player—for imaginative experimenting. His marriage and love affairs functioned somewhat like his role playing.

Elaborating further on the tension she experienced, Jill Summers says:

Ma-ma herself was not a tense, uptight person. I think a lot of people got the impression that she was a little high-strung and tense. I don't really think she was. I think that the tension that I'm talking about was between her and Pappy, and in a situation where the two of them were involved. But I don't think that she, herself, was tense. It may, in part, have been a way of their maintaining in their marriage the illusion of unattainability that seemed to have been so important to Pappy.[37]

And, I might add, to Estelle.

If we misread the intentions of the fictions of love Faulkner and his wife created in their lives, we risk misreading the fictions of love and desire in Faulkner's art.

Maud, Caroline, Estelle, and Jill and their world were the circumstances in which Faulkner chose to write. They both hindered and nourished his art. Clarifying the significance, complexity, and richness of these relations, and suggesting their relevance to central concerns in Faulkner's fiction, releases fresh perceptions of the artist and his art. Faulkner is, perhaps, our best twentieth-century novelist. In many ways his life *is* a Type for the artist in America. Perhaps this is why the myth to which I referred earlier is so compelling. However, by relinquishing this one-dimensional myth and attending instead to those dimensions previously obscured by its romance, we can take a major step forward in our understanding of Faulkner's tremendous achievement and of the peculiar place of the artist of language in our culture. Here too, I take my cue from the Master of Yoknapatawpha.

NOTES

1. William Faulkner, *The Hamlet* (1931; New York: Random House, Vintage Books, 1964), 123 and 114 (my italics); subsequent citations to this edition are given in the text.
2. Judith L. Sensibar, *The Origins of Faulkner's Art* (Austin: University of Texas Press, 1984).
3. William Faulkner, *Light in August* (1932; New York: Random House, Vintage Books, 1972), 244–45; subsequent citations to this edition are given in the text.
4. Faulkner's earliest known version of this image occurs in his love poem "After Fifty Years." See *Origins*, 73–76.
5. Many books, articles, and book chapters (including a chapter of my own) have been written about the importance of the Colonel W. C. Falkner legend to his great-grandson's imaginative vision. Despite the Colonel's death eight years before Faulkner's birth, despite the fact that Faulkner's mother's opinion of the great man was deeply ambivalent, his is deemed the presiding familial influence. We have traced the Colonel's trail through fictional generations of fathers, sons, and brothers from *Flags in the Dust* to *A Fable*. It is a given that to understand Faulkner's own apocryphal kingdom, one needs to know something about the Colonel's actual domain.
6. R. W. B. Lewis uses the term "family narrative" for the title of his current project, "The Jameses: A Family Narrative." For, as he observes, in a person's life, "it is the relationships that count. Family relations in their great variety . . . are the chief subject of my story; and to an extent, therefore, they determine the selection and handling of the abundant materials" ("The Names of the Action: Henry James in the Early 1870s," *Nineteenth-Century Fiction* 38 [1984], 467).
7. Besides familiar Faulkner primary and secondary source materials, see Anne Firor Scott, *The Southern Lady: From Pedestal to Politics, 1830–1930* (Chicago: University of Chicago Press, 1970); Catherine Clinton, "Caught in the Web of the Big House: Women and Slavery," in *The Web of Southern Social Relations: Women, Family, and Education*, ed. Walter J. Fraser, Jr., R. Frank Sauders, Jr., and Jon L. Wakelyn (New York: Pantheon, 1982; Athens: University of Georgia Press, 1985), and *The Plantation Mistress: Woman's World in the Old South* (New York: Pantheon, 1982); Bell Hooks, *"Ain't I a Woman?": Black Women and Feminism* (Boston: South End Press, 1981); Anne Goodwyn Jones, *Tomorrow Is Another Day: The Woman Writer in the South, 1859–1936* (Baton Rouge: Louisiana State University Press, 1981); Louise Wrestling, *Sacred Groves and Ravaged Gardens: The Fiction of Eudora Welty, Carson McCullers, and Flannery O'Connor* (Athens: University of Georgia Press, 1985); Minrose C. Gwin,, *Black and White Women of the Old South: The Peculiar Sisterhood in American Literature* (Knoxville: University of Tennessee Press, 1985).
8. Doreen Fowler and Ann J. Abadie, eds., *Faulkner and Women: Faulkner and Yoknapatawpha, 1985* (Jackson: University Press of Mississippi, 1986); Gwin 191–93.
9. Malcolm A. Franklin, *Bitterweeds: Life with William Faulkner at Rowan Oak* (Irving, Tex.: Society for the Study of Traditional Culture, 1977), 109–14; Jill Faulkner Summers, interview with author, 20 August 1980.

10. Clark Porteus quoting John Faulkner in "Another Talented Faulkner," *Memphis Press Scimitar,* Tues., September 14, 1954, 1, 4.

11. Interviews with author, Oxford, Mississippi, summer 1986 and summer 1987.

12. Jill Faulkner Summers, interview with author, 9 July 1986.

13. Ibid.

14. Jill Faulkner Summers, interview 18 September 1987. See also Dan Brennan's letter to the Editor in the *Los Angeles Times Book Review,* 10 January 1988, 6.

15. William Faulkner to Alabama McLean, September 1925 in Joseph Blotner, ed., *Selected Letters of William Faulkner* (New York: Random House, 1977), 20; for further discussion of the screen memory, see Sensibar, *Origins,* 52–54.

16. Describing the aesthetic legacy Willa Cather inherited from her female relatives, Sharon O'Brien questions traditional (patriarchal) definitions of art and the artist. Her insights are useful in considering the Faulkner women as well. See *Willa Cather: The Emerging Voice* (New York: Oxford University Press, 1987).

17. From early poems like "The Dancer" (1920) or "Nocturne" (1921) to novels of the 1930s like *Sanctuary,* women dance their male partners to paralysis and/or death. See *Origins,* 90–101 and 143–51.

18. For example see letter, William Faulkner to Maud Butler Faulkner, Easter 1943. Accession #10443, Alderman Library, University of Virginia.

19. The final divorce decree was issued 29 April 1929. Joseph Blotner, *Faulkner: A Biography* (New York: Random House, 1974), 1: 613. Cornell filed for divorce in both Oxford and Shanghai. See Oxford Court House Court Case Index, Book 5, p. 353, #6144 and Shanghai Archives, where final divorce decree was filed February 15 and granted February 25, 1929 (author's photocopy of document).

20. Quoted in Joseph Blotner, *Faulkner: A Biography,* rev. ed. (New York: Random House, 1984), 240. For the entire letter, see Thomas A. Dardis, *The Thirsty Muse* (New York: Doubleday, forthcoming). Dardis establishes that Faulkner wrote a series of people the same request—a fact that argues further for the letter's theatricality.

21. Stephen B. Oates, *William Faulkner: The Man and the Artist* (New York: Harper & Row, 1987), 83 and 84. See also Thomas L. McHaney's comments on "Elly," a short story Faulkner and Estelle Oldham originally coauthored. McHaney notes that "Elly" was rejected by Scribner's for being too "febrile," an adjective McHaney interprets as "*an interesting judgement about Estelle's mental condition at the time,*" [February 1929] (italics are mine) in *William Faulkner Manuscripts II, Dr. Martino and Other Stories: Holograph Manuscripts and Typescripts* (New York: Garland Publishers, Inc., 1987), x.

22. Oates, 87.

23. Leslie Aldridge Westoff, "A Faulkner Flirtation," *New York Times Sunday Magazine,* 10 May 1987, 69–78. In *Soldiers' Pay* and to the real Ms. Westoff Jones/Faulkner quotes and paraphrases from Faulkner's own love poems "Atthis," "Eros," and "Leaving Her" (poems XVII and XXV of *A Green Bough* and poem XII of *Helen: A Courtship,* respectively). For more on Jones as a self-parody, see Sensibar, *Origins,* passim, esp. 155–57.

24. For Faulkner's Pierrot persona, see Sensibar, *Origins,* passim, and, for the Cyrano persona, 250, n.27 and 268, n.25.

25. Jill Faulkner Summers, interview with author, 26 February 1986.

26. Jill Faulkner Summers, interview with author, 9 July 1986.

27. Interview with author, Oxford, Mississippi, 21 February 1986.

28. Jill Faulkner Summers, interview with author, 9 July 1986.

29. Blotner, *Faulkner: A Biography* (1974), 1: 604.

30. Estelle Oldham, unpublished short story, private collection. Her unpublished fiction is the subject of another chapter in my narrative.

31. Jill Faulkner Summers, interview with author, 23 February 1987.

32. Ibid.

33. Estelle Oldham Faulkner, interview. *Charlottesville Daily Progress*, 26 January 1969.

34. Jill Faulkner Summers, interview with author, 23 February 1987.

35. Ibid.

36. Ibid.

37. Ibid.

Carcassonne in Mississippi:
Faulkner's Geography of the Imagination

ROBERT W. HAMBLIN

Here in Oxford, where the stately courthouse looms over the town square, "tall as cloud, solid as rock, dominating all" (*RFN* 40);[1] where the Confederate statue faces exactly the way Faulkner says it does in the fiction, "not toward the north and the enemy, but toward the south, toward (if anything) his own rear" (*RFN* 240); and where even the most dedicated formalistic or mythopoeic critic slips easily into conversations about "Dilsey's cabin" or "Benjy's yard" or "Gavin Stevens's law office," it is impossible to escape or deny the local influences upon Faulkner's work. Still, as we all know, it is easy to overemphasize the regional and mimetic aspects of Faulkner's writings, and occasionally (maybe especially when we are gathered in Oxford) we need to be reminded of another point of view. In this essay I propose to examine the other side of Faulkner's art—that side represented not by Oxford and Lafayette County and Mississippi but by the fabled French city of Carcassonne.

As he made quite clear in one of his interview statements at the University of Virginia, Faulkner associated Carcassonne with the creative imagination. Asked to account for the twentieth-century renaissance among Southern writers, Faulkner observed: "I myself am inclined to think it was because of the bareness of the Southerner's life, that he had to resort to his own imagination, to create his own Carcassonne."[2] A similar use of Carcassonne as a symbol of imaginative invention is found in *Absalom, Absalom!* in the identification of Thomas Sutpen (an artist-type whose grandiose "design" [*AA* 263] is not altogether unlike Faulkner's dream of creating "a cosmos of [his] own"3) with "a madman who creates within his very coffin walls his fabulous immeasurable Camelots and Carcassonnes" (*AA* 160). In both of these quotations Carcassonne is identified not with the real world, with actuality, but with a private, inner vision that opposes and negates, respectively, the sterility of the Southerner's life and the dying dream of Sutpen. In other words, art— at least the kind of art symbolized by Carcassonne—is here presented as subjective, compensatory, and escapist, even otherworldly. This view of Carcassonne is consistent with Faulkner's definition of the artist in the Nobel Prize Acceptance Speech as one who strives "to create out of the materials of the human spirit something which did not exist before."4

Why Faulkner came to identify Carcassonne with the artistic imagination has intrigued scholars but remains very much a mystery. Neither Joseph Blotner nor Carvel Collins, the leading authorities on the details of Faulkner's biography, believes that he visited Carcassonne on his walking tour of France in 1925 or, for that matter, at any subsequent time.5 Cleanth Brooks has linked Faulkner's interest in Carcassonne to the highly popular *chanson* by the nineteenth-century French poet Gustave Nadaud—the theme of which was, according to Brooks, well-known in the South of Faulkner's youth.6 Nadaud's poem, entitled "Carcassonne," records the poignant lament of a French peasant who, sixty years old and "bent with age," is greatly disappointed that he is nearing death without ever having realized his youthful dream of seeing the "fair" and "lovely" city. While the text of the poem makes clear that Carcassonne is a symbol of perfection and thus of man's unrealized hopes and dreams—and consequently a meaningful parallel to Faulkner's notion regarding his own "magnificent failure" (*FIU* 61) as an artist—there is nothing within the poem to suggest why Faulkner chose Carcassonne and not, say, Camelot or Xanadu or Byzantium to represent his artistic ideal. For this explanation, I suspect, one must turn to the imposing physical appearance and legendary history of the actual Carcassonne.

Located in southwestern France, some sixty miles southeast of Toulouse, Carcassonne is famous as the site of the finest remains of medieval fortifications in all of Europe. Actually, there are two Carcassonnes: the *Ville Basse* (lower town), which contains the city's business district, and *La Cité*, the ancient fortifications that occupy the summit of an isolated hill on the opposite bank of the Aude River. It is, undoubtedly, the pictur- esque *Cité* that Faulkner identifies with the creative ideal. A strategic military fort dating from the fifth century B.C., this Carcassonne has played a significant role in the history of the Romans, Visigoths, Saracens, Franks, feudal lords, seneschals, and French kings who have successively ruled the city throughout its long and storied past. The most beautiful and distinctive features of the city—the massive walls punctuated by fifty rising towers and, within these ramparts, the mighty castle and cathedral—give Carcassonne an aura of enchantment and make-believe. One travel reporter of Faulkner's young manhood recorded this impression: "As you approach the city from the lower town beyond the river and lift up your eyes to the hill and behold its titanic wall with its cloud of towers and turrets sur- mounted by a citadel you will find it hard to convince yourself that what you see is not a phantom metropolis, a figment of some artist's imagination."[7]

Even if, as seems the case, Faulkner never actually visited Carcassonne, he probably had seen photographs, on postcards or in newspapers, of the town's famous skyline; and he may have read about the city in feature stories such as the one quoted above or in Baedeker's annual travel guides for tourists. He might conceivably have heard about Carcassonne in the French classes he took with Professor Calvin Brown at Ole Miss in 1919– 20. Faulkner may even have been aware of the lingering public debate concerning whether Viollet-le-Duc's restorations of the Old Town fortifications during the nineteenth century had been based on authentic history or the subjective and fanciful desires of the architect.[8] In any event, whatever the source or extent of Faulkner's knowledge of Carcassonne, the city became for him a kind of art-surrogate, embodying in its abiding presence and romantic history significant features that parallel Faulkner's characterization of his own fictional design. For example, the city's survival through centuries of war and empire-building mirrors the capacity of "saying No to death" (*FR* xi) that Faulkner identified with all great art. In addition, the city projects, in its contrast of the citadel and the lower town, a juxtaposition of the romantic past and the less-than-romantic present—an opposition that provides a dominant emphasis in several of Faulkner's major works. More pertinent to the present discussion, however, is the identification of Carcassonne with the power of the creative imagination to reshape and transcend the narrow world it inhabits. In this regard, it seems safe to assert that Faulkner would hardly have been troubled by the claim that Viollet-le-Duc may not have been entirely faithful to historical fact in his restoration efforts.

Such associations as the above may be attributed to Faulkner with some degree of confidence because the features I have just listed are precisely those that Faulkner attaches to the French city in his remarkable and revealing short story "Carcassonne."[9] Presumably written during the mid-to-late 1920s, this work is virtually without plot and consequently has been labeled "a prose poem"[10] or a piece of "romantic prose"[11] rather than a short story. In one of his few recorded comments on the story, Faulkner expressed a particular fondness for it, called it "fantasy" and not "simple realism," and defined its subject as "a young man in conflict with his environment" (*FIU* 22). The story presents, in stream-of-consciousness form, the thoughts of an aspiring poet who lives in poverty and a considerable degree of humiliation in a seaport town named Rincon. The protagonist resides in a tiny garret provided by a wealthy benefactress, Mrs. Widdrington, where he sleeps under a strip of tarred roofing paper and listens to the rats scurrying in the darkness. Notwithstanding, however, his failure as a poet and his limited material circumstances—indeed, in counteraction to these conditions—the protagonist wildly dreams of escaping his impotence and despair "to perform something bold and tragical and austere" (*CS* 899). This ambitious desire, fused in the poet's consciousness with the bold deeds of Norman warriors and steeds during the First Crusade, merges with the poet's heroic view of himself "on a buckskin pony with eyes like blue electricity and a mane like tangled fire, galloping up the hill and right off into the high heaven of the world" (895).

The principal content of "Carcassonne" is devoted to a dialogue between the poet and his skeleton. Somewhat reminiscent of a medieval debate between the body and the soul, the discussion contrasts the physical, inert, and earthbound values of the skeleton with the subjective, transcendent, and limitless fancies of the poet's imagination. In literary terms the skeleton represents realism and the poet's consciousness romance or myth. The skeleton, identified with "that steady decay which had set up within his body on the day of his birth," rests "motionless" in the "dark," under a ceiling that "slant[s] in a ruined pitch to the low eaves," knowing "that the end of life is lying still" (896–97, 899). But the imagination, which transcends the actual world and is therefore subject to "neither insects nor temperature," gallops "unflagging on the destinationless pony, up a piled silver hill of cumulae where no hoof echoed nor left print" (895). Throughout the narrative the skeleton is associated with images of immobility, confinement, and impending death, while the imagination is linked, as in the central symbol of the flying horse and rider, with connotations of activity, escape, and resurrection. Though the skeleton serves the poet by "supplying him with bits of trivial information" (899), that is, with facts (as, for example, the term *chamfron*), such information has a limited use, since in Faulkner's view facts are not to be equated with truth. Hence, despite its empirical knowledge, the skeleton "know[s] next to nothing of the world" (899). Although the story leaves unresolved the verbal debate between the poet and the skeleton, the symbolic victory of the imagination in imposing its will upon the harsh reality of the setting represents one of Faulkner's strongest statements of the necessity and power of invention. This victory, albeit an ironic one, finds expression in the evocative prose passage that serves as a refrain throughout the story. Significantly the passage opens with the factual, even the prosaic ("and me on a buckskin pony"), and then proceeds, in its employment of two similes ("eyes like blue electricity and a mane like tangled fire") and a metaphor ("the high heaven of the world"), toward the poetic and the mythic. In *Requiem for a Nun* Faulkner defines the imagination as that quality "so vast, so limitless in capacity . . . to disperse and burn away the rubble-dross of fact and probability, leaving only truth and dream" (261). "Carcassonne" dramatizes just such a conversion process.

The celebration of the transcendent and transmutable power of the imagination in "Carcassonne" invites comparison with Faulkner's remarks about the sources of a writer's material. Time and again Faulkner identified these sources as "observation, experience, and imagination" (*FIU* 123). Faulkner listed these three influences in varying orders of emphasis, and he pointed out that sometimes each can function independently of the others. "A writer," he said, "needs 3 things: experience, observation, imagination, any two of which, at times any one of which, can supply the lack of the others" (*LIG* 248). Often, Faulkner noted, it is virtually impossible to distinguish a writer's use of the separate sources. As he observed at West Point, "It's difficult to say just what part of any story comes specifically from imagination, what part from experience, what part from observation. It's like having . . . three tanks with a collector valve. And you don't know just how much comes from which tank. All you know is a stream of water runs from the valve when you open it, drawn from the three tanks—observation, experience, imagination."[12]

Although Faulkner often conceded, as in this last quotation, that the genesis of art is complex and mysterious, taken as a whole his comments reflect a bias toward imaginative invention. This bias explains his frequently expressed hostility toward "facts" and mere "reporting" of actuality. In the amusing self-portrait that appears in *Mosquitoes* Faulkner identifies himself as "a liar by profession" (145); and he told one group of students,

"I don't have much patience with facts, and any writer is a congenital liar to begin with or he wouldn't take up writing."[13] Faulkner frequently noted the writer's tendency, even compulsion, to embellish reality. "The writer is incapable of telling the truth," he said. "He couldn't take an actual human being and translate him onto paper and stick to the facts. He has got to change and embroider." (*FWP* 120). Faulkner laughingly told his students at the University of Virginia that he might conceivably use them in his fiction, but added, "You'll be changed" (*FIU* 123). Because of this insistence upon the role of the creative faculty, Faulkner was inclined to criticize those who view writing as mere reporting. "Steinbeck," Faulkner once observed, "is just a reporter, a newspaperman, not really a writer" (*LIG* 91). A writer, Faulkner insisted, does not depend upon research. "I think if he does that he is not really a fiction writer" (*FIU* 116). Of his handling of characterization Faulkner said, "I think that any writer worth his salt is convinced that he can create much better people than God can" (*FIU* 118). He told the West Point cadets: "Certainly I don't think that any writer ever wrote down or put down anything he actually saw or heard because a writer is congenitally incapable of telling the truth about anything. He has got to change it. He has got to lie. That's why they call it fiction, you see" (*FWP* 116). While it is evident that for Faulkner a work of literature is a complex alloyage of fact and fancy, history and myth, life and art—in his words, "experience, observation, and imagination"—it is equally evident that for Faulkner the principal component in this amalgam is the creative imagination of the artist.

Faulkner's ideas on the relationship of life and art become clearer upon examination of one source from which those ideas partly derived: Willard Huntington Wright's *The Creative Will: Studies in the Philosophy and the Syntax of Aesthetics*.[14] Wright, better known as the S. S. Van Dine of detective story fame, produced several works on literature and painting; and the one just named made a vivid impression on Phil Stone, who discussed its contents with his young protégé, Billy Falkner. Re-

garding the influence of *The Creative Will* on Faulkner, Stone
has written: "The aesthetic theories set forth in that book,
strained through my own mind, constitutes [*sic*] one of the most
important influences in Bill's whole literary career. If people
who read him would simply read Wright's book they would see
what he is driving at from a literary standpoint."[15] Not all of
Stone's judgments on Faulkner and his work can be trusted, but
this one seems right on target. Indeed, many of Wright's views
on art and the artist came to be those held by Faulkner.

Of particular interest are Wright's views on the relationship of
life to art. Wright contrasts Balzac, in Wright's opinion one of the
great masters of literature, with Zola and other "recorders of
nature" (23) who think that mere documentation is art. "No one
believes that a photograph of a clock will tell time," Wright
argues. "Yet there are those who assert that imitation of nature is
the life of art!" (202). This is not to say that the artist has no use for
nature. "There can be no great ascetic artist," Wright insists
(181); the artist's creativity evolves in part from contact with the
objective world. The artist stores all of his experiences, according to Wright, in his "minute filing cabinet" (23) of a mind, and
"out of his mass of data he evolves, by combinations ever new, a
microcosmos" (23–24). Wright describes this cognitive process as
follows:

> The artist's process of thought is like an arithmetical progression. He
> conceives a trivial idea from his contact with exterior nature. Some-
> thing in this trivial idea, after a period of analysis, calls up another
> idea which, in turn, develops, through volitional association, into a
> group of ideas. And this group becomes, for him, the basis of
> constructive thinking, replacing, as it were, the original basis of
> objectivity. From his segregation and arrangement of these ideas,
> which are no longer directly inspired by nature, there springs the
> great idea. (83)

Thus, Wright asserts, true art derives from "the imagination of
him who has understood and experienced life" (23); the genuine
artist "takes the *essence* of his special world of sound, colour or
document, and creates a new world of them" (24). In this en-

deavor the artist sacrifices "facts" and even distorts "because he is ever after a profounder truth than that of the accuracy of detail" (12). "Art," Wright proclaims, "has nothing to do with truth in the sense of 'verity' or 'accuracy'" (28). Wright concludes: "In all great and profound aesthetic creation the artist is an omnipotent god who moulds and fashions the destiny of a new world, and leads it to an inevitable completion where it can stand alone, self-moving, independent, and with a consistency free of all exterior help or influence. In the fabrication of this cosmos the creator finds his exaltation" (221–22). This last statement, of course, sounds remarkably similar to Faulkner's comments about his godlike creation of an independent and self-generating cosmos that could stand as a "keystone in the Universe" (LIG 255). The principal ingredient in the formation of such art, for Faulkner as for Wright, is the creative imagination of the artist.

Faulkner's preference for a fabricated literature over a representational one finds distinct, if at times amusing, expression in the record of his work on The De Gaulle Story, an unproduced movie script he wrote for Warner Bros. Pictures in 1942.[16] Between July and November of that year Faulkner wrote, in rapid succession, a story outline, a treatment, a revised treatment, a full-length screenplay, and a revised screenplay dramatizing the contemporary struggle of General Charles De Gaulle and the Free French Underground against the Nazi occupation of France. To retrace Faulkner's progress on this project, intended as a propaganda film to promote De Gaulle's image in the eyes of the American public, is to follow a debate on the fundamental conflict inherent in the techniques of documentary and imaginative filmmaking—in short, between fact and fiction. Assigned to assist Faulkner on the biographical and historical details of the story were Adrien Tixier, the Free French representative in Washington, D.C., and De Gaulle's personal agent on the project; and Henri Diamant-Berger, a French film director and producer who was the principal Gaullist spokesman in Hollywood. Opposition between Faulkner and these Free

French consultants quickly surfaced, deepened as the project continued, and eventually became a key factor in the studio's decision to cancel the proposed film.

In the initial stages of his work on *The De Gaulle Story* Faulkner relied heavily upon Philippe Barrès's book, *Charles De Gaulle,* as well as upon specific chronologies of events provided by both the Warner Bros. Research Department and the French Research Foundation, a Gaullist front organization located in West Hollywood. Demonstrating his typical disdain for facts, however, Faulkner quickly began to exercise his fertile imagination and to substitute fictional events and characters for the historical details. Given the Free French representatives' loyalty to De Gaulle and their deep commitment to the liberation of France, the results of Faulkner's alterations were predictable—and, from a detached perspective nearly a half-century later, quite comical. When Tixier read Faulkner's story treatment, he responded with a long list of "Observations on Inexact Details" challenging Faulkner's accuracy and verisimilitude.[17] For example, Tixier noted that the French army had been on alert in May 1940 and would not have been granting furloughs to soldiers as Faulkner had allowed in his narrative. Moreover, Tixier pointed out, Breton peasants would not employ a cook; the French play cards or billiards, not dominoes, in cafes; the general French public had never heard of De Gaulle's books on tank warfare; and De Gaulle's first followers were experienced, well-equipped soldiers and hardly, as Faulkner had claimed (for obvious dramatic effect), desperate crowds of beggars and refugees.

Diamant-Berger's evaluation of Faulkner's completed script echoed Tixier's call for closer adherence to the historical record.[18] According to Diamant-Berger, Faulkner had grossly misrepresented De Gaulle's military strategy, and he had placed the general in Syria at a time when he was in France. In addition, noted Diamant-Berger, Faulkner had erred in characterizing Bretons as being more loyal to their region than to their nation; in misunderstanding and misinterpreting the roles of French mayors, constables, and maids; in creating a situation involving

forced labor when in fact there had been none; and in anach-
ronistically alluding to announcements over loudspeakers in
public places. Diamant-Berger even detected an affront to
French manners in Faulkner's handling of hospitality: "The
custom of washing the dishes while the guest is still there," the
Frenchman insisted, "is typically American. [Emilie] should
never do it before [Jean] has left." What bothered Diamant-
Berger most, however, was that De Gaulle's role in the script was
being steadily diminished as Faulkner focused more and more
on two fictional brothers: Georges, a De Gaulle sympathizer,
and Jean, a Vichy collaborator. As Diamant-Berger rightly
noted, "General De Gaulle disappears practically from the story
after the first third, and the Fighting French movement with
him. This was the strongest objection made by London [the Free
French headquarters] on the first story and it should be even
more stronger [sic] in the second which has practically nothing
to do with De Gaulle nor with the movement."

For a time Faulkner sought to placate the French consultants
by making many of the changes in the script that they requested.
In fact, on one occasion Faulkner demonstrated that he could be
as much a stickler for accurate detail as anyone else. When an
objection was raised to Faulkner's having a character allude to his
task of "planting corn"—an objection based on the grounds
(expressed in an attached note) that "the French don't eat corn;
Coupe-Tête would be planting potatoes"—Faulkner inserted his
rejoinder in the margin: "Planting potatoes in May??? What does
horse eat?" But this notation was undoubtedly made as much in
spite or anger as in jest. For soon afterward, exasperated by the
unbending literal-mindedness of the Free Frenchmen and rec-
ognizing the impasse as having become insurmountable,
Faulkner petitioned producer Robert Buckner for a free hand in
structuring the screenplay. In an interoffice memorandum dated
November 19, 1942, Faulkner suggested to Buckner: "Let's
dispense with General De Gaulle as a living character in the
story." The problem, as Faulkner stated it, was that the
Frenchmen wanted to produce "a document" rather than "a

story." As a consequence, they would "insist upon an absolute adherence to time and fact, no matter how trivial the incident nor imaginary the characters acting it, and regardless of the sacrifice of dramatic values and construction or the poetic implications and overtones." The matter was further complicated by the fact that De Gaulle was a living figure. According to Faulkner, any historical hero "becomes colorful and of dramatic value only after he has been dead for years, because only then can a dramatist make him dramatic without challenge from the people who knew him in the flesh and who insist on fact."[19]

Another work that exhibits Faulkner's contempt for facts and documentation is the short story "Artist at Home," published in 1933. Primarily a satirical treatment of popular notions of artists and their behavior, the story contains an interesting detail that relates to the question of fact versus imagination as a source for the writer's materials. When Roger Howes, a novelist of limited accomplishment, is confronted with the developing love affair between his wife Anne and his friend John Blair, a poet, Howes turns immediately to his typewriter: "Now get this. This is it. He came back down to the office and put some paper into the typewriter and began to write. He didn't go very fast at first, but by daylight he was sounding like forty hens in a sheet-iron corn-crib, and the written sheets were piling up" (*CS* 638). Throughout the next several days and weeks, interrupted only by Anne's exits to meet Blair and the discussions following her returns, Howes continues to type at a frantic pace. Each new development in Anne's affair enhances this "bull market in type-writing" (639). Toward the end of the story the reader is told what it is that Howes has been working on so feverishly: "And what was it he had been writing? Him, and Anne, and the poet. Word for word, between the waiting spells to find out what to write down next, with a few changes here and there, of course, because live people do not make good copy, the most interesting copy being gossip, since it mostly is not true" (644). Given the comic tone of the story, one is inclined to view with amusement Howes's dependence upon a traumatic experience to resurrect his feeble art. "Artist at Home" provides an ironic reversal of the traditional literary plot: here the reader's haste to read the next fictional episode is transferred to a writer who must wait to see what happens in an actual situation before he can know what to write in his next scene. Faulkner's purpose appears to extend beyond a mere desire to satirize the Freudian notion (one, by the way, with which Faulkner basically agreed) that all art derives from suffering. In Howes's frantic, even futile, efforts to record the fast-developing events of his experience, one perceives the dilemma of any realist seeking to mirror a constantly changing life process. Not only, Faulkner seems to suggest, is such photographic rendering impossible; it is not even desirable. Thus it is that Howes cannot help but make "a few changes here and there" and fictionalize the actual. Even the most confirmed realist, Faulkner implies, cannot completely close off the workings of invention; besides, gossip makes better copy than fact. In this manner "Artist at Home" ridicules the notion that art is mere copying and underscores Faulkner's emphasis upon the necessity of imagination in the fictive process.

How different to the realistic, "word for word" approach of a Roger Howes is the imaginative handling of experience by Quentin Compson in *Absalom, Absalom!* Michael Millgate and others have perceived in the relationship of Quentin to the story he tells a dramatization of the problems of authorship.[20] Support for this view is found in Miss Rosa's remark that Quentin may one day utilize the Sutpen story as material for fiction: "So maybe you will enter the literary profession as so many Southern gentlemen and gentlewomen too are doing now and maybe some day you will remember this and write about it. You will be married then I expect and perhaps your wife will want a new gown or a new chair for the house and you can write this and submit it to the magazines" (*AA* 9–10). The overall structure of *Absalom, Absalom!* further supports the view of Quentin as author-surrogate. The first five chapters relate Quentin's immediate, if principally second- and third-hand, involvement in the Sutpen narrative, but the remaining four chapters present the

imaginative reconstruction of the story by Quentin and his Harvard roommate, Shreve McCannon. This shift from listening to
telling, from assimilation to invention, reflects more than the
creation of an aesthetic distance involving time and place: the
shift mirrors also the play of imagination over experience.

In this visionary realm where the imagination interfuses and
transforms fact, actual characters and events become unreal,
fictional: "the two of them creating between them, out of the rag-
tag and bob-ends of old tales and talking, people who perhaps
had never existed at all anywhere, who, shadows, were shadows
not of flesh and blood which had lived and died but shadows in
turn of what were (to one of them at least, to Shreve) shades too,
quiet as the visible murmur of their vaporizing breath" (303).
Any reader who has sought to ascertain which of the characters
in *Absalom, Absalom!* knew what, and when, recognizes the
degree to which the novel is grounded in speculation and ambiguity. Such distortion of event and action, though, is not loss but
gain.

> It seemed to Quentin that he could actually see them: the ragged
> and starving troops without shoes, the gaunt powder-blackened
> faces looking backward over tattered shoulders, the glaring eyes in
> which burned some indomitable desperation of undefeat . . . ; he
> could see it; he might even have been there. Then he thought *No. If
> I had been there I could not have seen it this plain.* (189–90)

Readers who discern in such a hypothetical recreation of the
Sutpen narrative only the negative emphasis of man's inability to
know and comprehend the past must discount Faulkner's stated
preference for invention, even for "lies"—for imaginative "truth"
over actual "facts."

In this connection Quentin's treatment of Sutpen may be
meaningfully compared to Faulkner's observation concerning his
legendary great-grandfather, Colonel W. C. Falkner:

> People at Ripley talk of him as if he were still alive, up in the hills
> some place, and might come in at any time. It's a strange thing;
> there are lots of people who knew him well, and yet no two of them

remember him alike or describe him the same way. One will say he was like me and another will swear he was six feet tall. . . . There's nothing left in the old place, the house is gone and the plantation boundaries, nothing left of his work but a statue. But he rode through that country like a living force. I like it better that way.[21]

Faulkner "like[d] it better that way," presumably, because such ambiguities and uncertainties free the imagination for the creative process. An excessive reliance upon facts would stifle originality. "Research" and similar "documentary" approaches to fiction are thus to be eschewed. The imaginative faculty is indispensable to the creation of art.

Not surprisingly for a writer who expresses such faith in imaginative invention, Faulkner's work abounds in constructs that are, or border upon, pure fantasy. This aspect of his fiction has never been held in high regard by critics who insist on viewing Faulkner as a realist, yet it is crucial to an understanding of his art. Extreme examples are four of the stories that Faulkner included in the "Beyond" section of his *Collected Stories*. One of these, "Carcassonne," has been discussed earlier and lends its name to the focus of my present remarks. Another, the title story of the section, treats the death (actual or anticipated) of an elderly Federal judge and his subsequent journey into the Hereafter. In this postmortal flight of consciousness he encounters a past acquaintance—an atheist named Mothershed—as well as his idol, agnostic Robert Ingersoll. The judge also views Christ as a baby but with crucifixion scars on his hands and feet. There is considerable conversation treating the questions of God and immortality, after which the judge is offered the opportunity to be reunited with his ten-year-old son who had been killed in a riding accident almost thirty years earlier. However, the judge declines, reluctant to sacrifice his long-held beliefs of agnosticism and humanism. In keeping with its exotic nature, Faulkner labeled "Beyond" "a tour de force in esoteria."[22]

The subject matter of another of these stories, "Black Music," is just as fabulous. This one treats the supernatural experience (again, whether real or imagined is left ambiguous) of Wilfred

Midgleston, who for one day has been transformed into a faun and thus has "done and been something outside the lot and plan for mortal human man to do and be" (CS 821). Formerly an architect's draughtsman, "a small, snuffy, nondescript man whom neither man nor woman had ever turned to look at twice" (799), Midgleston believes himself to have been used by Pan to frighten away some rich Park Avenuers who threatened to alter an idyllic mountain retreat. The newspaper account of the incident had described a half-naked maniac who attacked Mrs. Carleton Van Dyming in her garden, but Midgleston is convinced that the newspaper account is erroneous. Now, twenty-five years later, he lives in self-exile in a foreign country, impoverished but contented with the knowledge that he has been "fortune's favorite, chosen of the gods" (799).

"The Leg" is a ghost story based on the idea of reincarnation.[23] The narrative opens with a flashback to 1914 when the narrator Davy, a young American studying at Oxford, and his English friend woo a young lady named Everbe Corinthia. Then the scene shifts to 1915 and the battlefront in France, where George is killed and Davy loses his leg. In the hospital George's ghost appears to Davy, and Davy expresses the fear that his amputated leg is not dead. "I can feel it," he says. "It jeers at me" (CS 831). George promises to find the leg and make sure it is dead. Later Davy is well enough to return to action as a flyer; the ghost no longer appears, but Davy is still haunted by vague fears regarding the leg. The story next shifts forward in time to reveal that Everbe Corinthia has died as the result of an unhappy love affair, that her father has followed her in death a week later, and that her brother Jotham, who has vowed to revenge himself upon his sister's lover, has attempted to murder Davy, who is astonished by all these developments and cannot understand Jotham's hatred toward him. Jotham also dies, but in his effects is found a recently inscribed photograph showing Everbe and her lover. When Davy sees this photograph he is amazed to see his own face in the picture, since at the time the photograph was made he was lying in the hospital talking to George's ghost. The implication is that the lost leg has worked its frightful purpose. "I told him to find it and kill it," Davy concludes. "I told him to. I told him" (842).

While fantasies such as "Carcassonne," "Beyond," "Black Music," and "The Leg" are infrequent in the Faulkner canon (one could add to the list the early play *Marionettes*, certain poems in *The Marble Faun*, and the child's story entitled *The Wishing Tree*), these stories nevertheless serve to indicate the degree to which Faulkner associated creativity with fabrication. Such narratives also encourage readers to return to Faulkner's more "realistic" fiction with a heightened awareness of Faulkner's fondness for invented as opposed to representational art. In this context such experimentations as the use of clairvoyance in *As I Lay Dying*, the hypothetical exploration of a severely retarded person's consciousness in *The Sound and the Fury*, the surrealistic description of the wake in *Sanctuary*, and the startling adaptation of biblical myth in *A Fable* take on added significance. Many more instances of Faulkner's richly inventive originality might be cited; in the interest of time I shall limit myself to only three additional examples. One examines Faulkner's handling of incident, another relates to style and characterization, and the third illustrates overall structure.

The initial example is the description of Ike McCaslin's first view of the giant bear, Old Ben, in *Go Down, Moses*.

> Then he saw the bear. It did not emerge, appear: it was just there, immobile, fixed in the green and windless noon's hot dappling, not as big as he had dreamed it but as big as he had expected, bigger, dimensionless against the dappled obscurity, looking at him. Then it moved. It crossed the glade without haste, walking for an instant into the sun's full glare and out of it, and stopped again and looked back at him across one shoulder. Then it was gone. It didn't walk into the woods. It faded, sank back into the wilderness without motion as he had watched a fish, a huge old bass, sink back into the dark depths of its pool and vanish without even any movement of its fins. (209)

As much as any passage in the story, this description captures the "fairy story" quality that Malcolm Cowley perceives in "The

Bear."[24] Faulkner presents here not so much the objective, physical movements of an actual bear but rather a subjective dream-state that impresses the reader as a spiritual vision. The bear does not "emerge, appear"; it is "just there," all at once, come from nowhere, an epiphany like the mystic's view of God. Significantly, the bear is "dimensionless," and when it disappears, as suddenly and as mysteriously as it appears, it does not "walk" back into the woods but "fade[s], [sinks] back into the wilderness *without motion*" (emphasis added). Quite obviously Faulkner's interest is not in realistic, representational detail but in the subjective state of Ike's consciousness. The artistic intent is not to present a "real" bear but to communicate the idea of the bear as it exists in Ike's (and Faulkner's) imagination and as it can only be recreated in the reader's imagination through the vehicle of Faulkner's magical, evocative words. To appreciate the success of the technique, one has only to compare the film version of "The Bear" to Faulkner's marvelous prose. In the film version one sees a real bear, but it is not Old Ben; Faulkner's bear is larger than life, heroic, unreal, mythic. Faulkner clearly recognized the visionary quality of his narrative and linked the story to his overall concept of art. "There's a case," he said, "of the sorry, shabby world that don't quite please you, so you create one of your own, so . . . you make the bear a little more of a bear than he actually was" (*FIU* 59). Again, the world of fact has been infused and transformed by the creative imagination.

The next example is one of the most misunderstood and least appreciated passages in all of Faulkner's works: the description of the idiot Ike Snopes's love affair with the cow in *The Hamlet*. Many readers undoubtedly agree with Phil Stone's judgment that this episode "ruined" the novel and typifies "the complete lack of aesthetic taste which Faulkner frequently shows."[25] More sympathetic critics manage to get past the shocking bestiality of the story but still tend to view the episode as scarcely important in its own right but only as an ironic counterpoint to the lust of Labove and McCarron and the selfish materialism of Flem. However, when viewed in terms of Faulkner's interest in language as the play of imagination on experience, this section becomes a centerpiece of the novel. Consider the following passage:

> Then he would hear her, coming down the creekside in the mist. It would not be after one hour, two hours, three; the dawn would be empty, the moment and she would not be, then he would hear her and he would lie drenched in the wet grass, serene and one and indivisible in joy, listening to her approach. He would smell her; the whole mist reeked with her; the same malleate hands of mist which drew along his prone drenched flanks played her pearled barrel too and shaped them both somewhere in immediate time, already married. He would not move. He would lie amid the waking instant of earth's teeming minute life, the motionless fronds of water-heavy grasses stooping into the mist before his face in black, fixed curves, along each parabola of which the marching drops held in minute magnification the dawn's rosy miniatures, smelling and even tasting the rich, slow, warm barn-reek milk-reek, the flowing immemorial female, hearing the slow planting and the plopping suck of each deliberate cloven mud-spreading hoof, invisible still in the mist loud with its hymeneal choristers. (188–89)

Surely this is language stretched to its physical limits. As Melvin Backman recognized two decades ago, "The Keatsian poetry of the language evokes another world where reality has been suspended and the poet's imagination rules: the idiot and the cow might be lovers out of a storied past who, at one with nature and themselves, partake of a serene ineffable moment when time no longer exists."[26] At the realistic level, as other parts of the novel make clear, the idiot's story functions, literally, as an instance of "stock-diddling" (230) that provides a sordid entertainment for the debased and dehumanized inhabitants of Frenchman's Bend. Through the transforming power of the mythic imagination, however, the episode becomes, if only briefly, a joyous and moving account of a perfectly devoted lover who braves fire and beast to rescue his beloved. Burlesque though it may be, there is no better example in all of Faulkner's fiction of the power of imaginative word play to convert "the sorry, shabby world" into a place of heroism and beauty. Not coincidentally, it is Ratliff, one of Faulkner's great fabulists (and thus one who is sensitive to the opposition of actuality and invention), who defends Ike from the populace and refuses to pass moral judgment on his behavior.

The most impressive examples of the power of invention in Faulkner, though, are not to be found in his visionary handling of incident, style, and characterization but in his often brilliant and always daring experiments with form. Any one of a number of novels could be used to demonstrate this point: *The Sound and the Fury*, with its four overlapping viewpoints of the central action and its gradual unfolding of plot and meaning; *Light in August*, with its ascending and descending story lines and its frequent dislocations of chronology; *Absalom, Absalom!*, with its multiple viewpoints, its artistic interweaving of past and present, and its mythic parallels; *The Wild Palms*, with its startlingly original counterpointing of two distinct yet thematically related stories; or *Requiem for a Nun*, with its fusion of prose narrative and dramatic form. But the novel I have chosen for emphasis on this occasion is *As I Lay Dying*, principally because its simple plot (the simplest in all of Faulkner's major novels) allows the imaginative structure of the novel to stand forth in bold relief. What happens in *As I Lay Dying* can be summarized in one sentence: the Bundrens travel from their home below Frenchman's Bend to convey the corpse of Addie, the wife and mother, to Jefferson for burial. But the way Faulkner chose to narrate this basic story line placed him at the forefront of the modern experimental novelists. And even today, more than a half-century after its publication, the technique of the novel is still strikingly fresh and innovative. The kaleidoscopic shifting of viewpoint from one to another of the fifteen narrators, with their sometimes-collaborative and sometimes-contradictory perspectives, allows for a gradual, progressive illumination of both the external action and the inner thoughts and motivations of the characters. Moreover, the strategic placement of Addie's monologue two-thirds of the way through the novel, casting its light of revelation both backward and forward, further contributes to the suspensive design of the book. No novel better demonstrates the risk-taking that Faulkner expected of all writers who aspire to greatness, and no novel better illustrates the technical virtuosity that even negative critics like Clifton Fadiman[27] and Alfred Kazin must concede to Faulkner's credit. "Technically," Kazin wrote in 1942, "[Faulkner] soon proved himself almost inordinately subtle and ambitious, the one modern American novelist whose devotion to form has earned him a place among even the great experimentalists in modern poetry."[28] Where in Oxford (or in any actual place), one might ask, did Faulkner find the models for such radical experiments in form? The answer comes in Faulkner's own words. Once asked about his use of a specific historical prototype in his fiction, he replied, "I think that whenever my imagination and the bounds of that pattern conflicted, it was the pattern that bulged . . . that gave" (*FIU* 51–52). In matters of form, therefore, as in the areas of incident, style, and characterization, Faulkner resorted "to his own imagination, to create his own Carcassonne."

I have spent considerable time in documenting Faulkner's aversion to facts and "the sorry, shabby world" of actuality and his corresponding exaltation of the creative imagination because these points are crucial to understanding precisely what type of fictionist Faulkner is. It has become an accepted point of Faulkner criticism to identify his emergence as a major writer with the moment he discovered, upon the advice of Sherwood Anderson, the fictional possibilities contained within his native milieu. As he later told Jean Stein, "Beginning with *Sartoris* I discovered that my own little postage stamp of native soil was worth writing about and that I would never live long enough to exhaust it, and *by sublimating the actual into apocryphal* [emphasis added] I would have complete liberty to use whatever talent I might have to its absolute top" (*LIG* 255). A careful examination of this statement reveals that Faulkner's rediscovery of his native materials was just the initial step in his maturation as an artist. Even more crucial was his *handling* of those materials, his recognition that only "by sublimating the actual into apocryphal" could he develop his talent "to its absolute top." Those readers who view Faulkner as a realist, or, worse, a mere regionalist, make much of the first half of Faulkner's statement to Stein but usually ignore the second. Faulkner, of course, placed the emphasis exactly where it belongs. The "postage stamp of native soil," Oxford and its environs, may have supplied the raw materials he needed, but it was the imagination, Carcassonne, that produced the great art.

In studying Faulkner's fiction one quickly becomes aware that his art is quite removed from the photographic realism advocated by William Dean Howells or the scientific documentation of Frank Norris and other naturalists. Faulkner's approach to art may be more profitably compared to that of Nathaniel Hawthorne, whose *The Scarlet Letter* explores that "neutral territory, somewhere between the real world and fairy-land, where the Actual and the Imaginary may meet, and each imbue itself with the nature of the other,"[29] or of Henry James, who understood the limitations of mimetic theories of art and who celebrated in that remarkable short story, "The Real Thing," "the alchemy of art"[30] whereby imaginative invention triumphs over mere copying. When compared to his successors rather than his predecessors, Faulkner seems to belong more in the company of, for example, John Barth or Robert Coover than of, say, John Updike or Norman Mailer. For Faulkner the actual world, Oxford, was never more than "somewhere to start from" (*ESPL* 8). Like the surrealistic painters with whom he has so much in common, Faulkner sought to capture a new realism—a super-realism—that combines elements of the everyday, outer world and the inner world of the artist's creative vision. In his curious geography of the imagination both Oxford and Carcassonne are part of Yoknapatawpha. And the only map on which that fabulous land appears is the one the artist himself drew—the one signed by "William Faulkner, Sole Owner & Proprietor."[31]

NOTES

1. Faulkner works utilized in this essay are cited parenthetically within the text. In all cases quotations have been taken from the first editions. Key to abbreviations: *AA*—

Absalom, Absalom!; CS—Collected Stories; FR—The Faulkner Reader; RFN—Requiem for a Nun.

2. Frederick L. Gwynn and Joseph L. Blotner, eds., *Faulkner in the University: Class Conferences at the University of Virginia, 1957–1958* (Charlottesville: University of Virginia Press, 1959), 136. Hereafter cited in my essay as *FIU*.

3. James B. Meriwether and Michael Millgate, eds., *Lion in the Garden: Interviews with William Faulkner, 1926–1962* (New York: Random House, 1968), 255. Hereafter cited in my essay as *LIG*.

4. James B. Meriwether, ed., *Essays, Speeches, and Public Letters by William Faulkner* (New York: Random House, 1965), 119. Hereafter cited in my text as *ESPL*.

5. For Blotner's treatment of Faulkner's 1925 visit to Europe, see *Faulkner: A Biography* (New York: Random House, 1974), 444–83. Collins's opinion is expressed in a letter to me, dated August 15, 1982.

6. *William Faulkner: Toward Yoknapatawpha and Beyond* (New Haven: Yale University Press, 1978), 61.

7. T. Graydon Montague, "Citadels of the Centuries," *Travel* 39 (May 1922), 6.

8. These arguments resurfaced when additional excavations were done in 1923 and 1927.

9. Although Faulkner elected to conclude both *These 13* (New York: Cape and Smith, 1931) and *Collected Stories* with "Carcassonne," for years the story received little critical attention. Recent treatments include Richard A. Milum, "Faulkner's 'Carcassone': The Dream and the Reality," *Studies in Short Fiction*, 15 (Spring 1978), 133–38; Robert W. Hamblin, "'Carcassonne': Faulkner's Allegory of Art and the Artist," *Southern Review*, 15 (Spring 1979), 355–65; M. E. Bradford, "The Knight and the Artist: Tasso and Faulkner's 'Carcassonne,'" *South Central Bulletin*, 41 (Winter 1981), 88–90; Noel Polk, "William Faulkner's 'Carcassonne,'" *Studies in American Fiction*, 12 (Spring 1984), 29–43; and James B. Carothers, *William Faulkner's Short Stories* (Ann Arbor: UMI Research Press, 1985), 81–83.

10. Dorothy Tuck, *Apollo Handbook of Faulkner* (New York: Thomas Y. Crowell Company, 1964), 163.

11. Brooks, 60.

12. Joseph L. Fant III and Robert Ashley, eds., *Faulkner at West Point* (New York: Random House, 1964), 96–97. Hereafter cited in my text as *FWP*.

13. Blotner, 6.

14. (New York: John Lane Company, 1916).

15. See James W. Webb and A. Wigfall Green, eds., *William Faulkner of Oxford* (Baton Rouge: Louisiana State University Press, 1965), 228.

16. A detailed history of Faulkner's work on this project is recorded in Louis Daniel Brodsky and Robert W. Hamblin, eds., *Faulkner: A Comprehensive Guide to the Brodsky Collection, Volume III: The De Gaulle Story* (Jackson: University Press of Mississippi), 1984.

17. See *The De Gaulle Story*, 354–59.

18. See *The De Gaulle Story*, 376–95.

19. *The De Gaulle Story*, 395–96, 398.

20. See, for example, Michael Millgate, *The Achievement of William Faulkner* (New York: Random House, 1966), 154–55.

21. Quoted in Robert Cantwell, "The Faulkners: Recollections of a Gifted Family," in *William Faulkner: Three Decades of Criticism*, ed. Frederick J. Hoffman and Olga W. Vickery (New York: Harcourt, Brace and World, 1963), 56.

22. Quoted in Blotner, 809.

23. I have adopted the usual interpretation of the story. For an impressive argument that Faulkner's rendering of the events is highly ambiguous, and perhaps explicable in terms of psychological realism, see James B. Carothers, "Faulkner's Short Stories: 'And Now What's to Do,'" in *New Directions in Faulkner Studies: Faulkner and Yoknapatawpha, 1983*, ed. Doreen Fowler and Ann J. Abadie (Jackson: University Press of Mississippi, 1984), 219–23.

24. See A. I. Bezzerides, *William Faulkner: A Life on Paper*, ed. Ann Abadie (Jackson: University Press of Mississippi, 1980), 97.

25. Louis Daniel Brodsky and Robert W. Hamblin, eds., *Faulkner: A Comprehensive Guide to the Brodsky Collection, Volume II: The Letters* (Jackson: University Press of Mississippi, 1984), 29.

26. *Faulkner: The Major Years* (Bloomington: Indiana University Press, 1966), 151–52.

27. See, for example, Fadiman's review of *Absalom, Absalom!*, "Faulkner, Extra-Special, Double-Distilled," *New Yorker*, 12 (October 31, 1936), 62–64. Though Fadiman ridicules Faulkner's style and content, he concedes that "as a technician [Faulkner] has Joyce and Proust punch-drunk" (63).

28. *On Native Grounds: An Interpretation of Modern American Prose Literature* (New York: Harcourt, Brace and Company, 1942), 457.

29. (New York: W. W. Norton and Company, 1978), 31.

30. *The Real Thing and Other Tales* (New York: Macmillan and Company, 1893), 17.

31. The map appears as an insert at the back of *Absalom, Absalom!*

"Thinking I Was I Was Not Who Was Not Was Not Who": The Vertigo of Faulknerian Identity

PHILIP M. WEINSTEIN

The title is dizzying, and I expect during the next hour to be off-balance in a number of ways: off-balance in my moves back and forth between character, text, context, reader, and writer; off-center in my attempt to decenter our notions of identity itself; off-base in my shift from the "legitimate" scrutiny of Faulkner's work to less sanctioned considerations of ideology, psycho-analysis, and what we in this room are doing when we go to conferences like this one and listen to scholarly papers for five or six days. These are all issues of identity, I hope to show, and thinking about them, I hope also to show, can make you dizzy. I turn now to Quentin's passage in *The Sound and the Fury* from which I take my title quote:

> When it bloomed in the spring and it rained the smell was every-where you didn't notice it so much at other times but when it rained the smell began to come into the house at twilight . . . it always smelled strongest then until I would lie in bed thinking when will it stop when will it stop. The draft in the door smelled of water, a damp steady breath. Sometimes I could put myself to sleep saying that over and over until the honeysuckle got all mixed up in it the whole thing came to symbolise night and unrest I seemed to be lying neither asleep nor awake looking down a long corridor of grey halflight where all stable things had become shadowy paradoxical all I had done shadows all I had felt suffered taking visible form antic and perverse mocking without relevance inherent themselves with the denial of the significance they should have affirmed thinking I was I was not who was not was not who. (210–11)[1]

172

Spurred by the overpowering smell of honeysuckle, Quentin's thoughts go on to undermine relationships he has based his sanity on: the difference between sleep and waking, night and day; the inherent connection between things done, felt, suffered, and their significance. The smell of honeysuckle, invading him and triggering his unbearable sense of his own and of Caddy's sexuality, breaks down these "stable" connections; and Quentin's attempt to talk himself into tranquility—"saying that over and over"—ends by doing the reverse: nothing remains itself, all drifts away from its habitual moorings, becoming "shadowy paradoxical" as Quentin's very language—the script by which he knows himself—chokes on its quest for coherence, dissolving into the babble of "I was I was not who was not was not who."[2] An alien body, a wandering mind, a dizzying sense of disowned doings, feelings, and sufferings: these come together in this passage as something we call Quentin. He belongs to them, but in what sense do they belong to him?

Faulkner's most powerful strategy for representing this disunity, this incoherence that is Quentin, is, of course, the stream of consciousness technique itself. Here is Quentin early in the chapter:

Because if it were just to hell; if that were all of it. Finished. If things just finished themselves. Nobody else there but her and me. If we could just have done something so dreadful that they would have fled hell except us. *I have committed incest I said Father it was I it was not Dalton Ames* And when he put Dalton Ames. Dalton Ames. Dalton Ames. When he put the pistol in my hand I didn't. That's why I didn't. He would be there and she would and I would. Dalton Ames. Dalton Ames. Dalton Ames. If we could have just done something so dreadful and Father said That's sad too, people cannot do anything that dreadful they cannot do anything very dreadful at all they cannot even remember tomorrow what seemed dreadful today and I said, You can shirk all things and he said, Ah can you. And I will look down and see my murmuring bones and the deep water like wind, like a roof of wind, and after a long time they cannot distinguish even bones upon the lonely and inviolate sand. . . . (97–98)

If things just finished themselves: Faulknerian stream of consciousness fiendishly enacts the way in which things do *not* finish themselves. Within this rhetoric Quentin cannot finish his thought, cannot finish his identity, cannot keep Dalton Ames and Father and Caddy and honeysuckle from penetrating his being, cannot keep from quoting his mother, Dilsey, Herbert, Mrs. Bland, and others. When his desire to be with Caddy alone is denied, his only other desire is to not be, to put an end to all this uninvited company that fills his body and mind. Since he cannot finish himself he will cancel himself.

Let us generalize the model of individual identity implicit in Faulkner's stream of consciousness representation of Quentin. Unlike characters in the nineteenth-century novel (which are typically passed on to us by the narrator as coherent entities, summarized organisms existing over time), Quentin appears as a moment-by-moment involuntary recorder of others' voices, a sentient receptacle wounded by the shards of their utterances: the site on which the cacophony of the larger culture registers. Quentin is a memory-box, a porous container of others' throwaway discourse. Unable to consolidate what he has absorbed, unable to shape his own thoughts into the coherence of a temporal project, he is a figure in motley. By representing him as thus adulterate through and through, made up of what is not himself, Faulkner reveals the pathos of his fantasy of preserving Caddy's virginity.

I have spoken only of Quentin, but in a modified form this paradigm of identity shapes the other characters of the novel as well. Benjy and Jason, Caddy, Mr. and Mrs. Compson: these figures are in different ways intolerably penetrated and controlled by formulae not of their own making.3 Faulkner seems drawn to them in the measure that—fissured themselves, indebted unknowingly to unworkable scripts—they seek hopelessly to impose unity upon, to preserve identity within, their own lives and the lives around them. They seek such unity and identity through speech, and indeed *The Sound and the Fury* is full of sound, of puny humans contradictorily asserting their own authority. It is the *loud* world, we remember, that Quentin would rescue Caddy from.

What is at stake in this desire to preserve identity, this urgent need to maintain stable boundaries between the self and the world? Why is it so difficult (and for many readers painful) to read Quentin's section? What does it mean that we as readers insist on taking all novels—even Faulkner's and Joyce's novels—as "stories" about individual "characters" engaged in "plot"? Indeed, fiction is (like other forms of narrative) a privileged site for celebrating the enactment of individual identity. Fiction is one of the arenas in which the culture tells its fables of selfhood, of the successful negotiation between a self, on the one hand, and a world, on the other. And Faulkner's masterpieces come into sharpest focus as a territory in which this negotiation is both urgent and impossible, in which the need for protected boundaries is exactly as intense as the awareness that these boundaries cannot be protected. Virginity, incest, and miscegenation; Sutpen's Hundred, the McCaslin inheritance, and the wilderness—each of these phrases names a crucial Faulknerian space (psychic or material) in which boundaries have been hopelessly erected or traumatically overrun. What is it that makes these enclosed arenas simultaneously precious and beyond preserving?[4]

* * *

I suggest that identity is a privileged term within a Western vocabulary of individualism. In its primary meaning—that something is always itself—and its secondary implication—that that selfhood is different from all others—identity makes some very large promises.[5] It promises sameness over time—an unchanging essence at the core of objects (and without which it would be difficult to hypothesize about objects at all). That is, the self-sameness of objects is intrinsic (to be found within the object itself) rather than relational (to be found by way of the object's membership within a larger group: its inscription within one or several signifying networks). The term suggests, further, with respect to human identity, that we are unique creatures, essentially different from each other. To privilege individual identity

in this way is to fantasize a kind of protected sacred place—the
place of ourselves—which would be immune to the vicissitudes
of time and space. It is to allay our anxiety that we may not have
an unchanging core and therefore may take on our meanings
from our affiliations and conditions. It is to fix, enclose, and
affirm our unique difference from others, to say: "That's who I
am." By thus reifying our sense of ourselves, by charting it as a
separate essence and putting boundaries around it, we repress,
precisely, that intolerable sense of *being-helplessly-caught-up-
in-the-Other* that Faulkner represents in the plight of Quentin
Compson.

This paradigm of identity as an essentialized sacred space
commands not just how we want to think of ourselves but how
we choose to think of art objects as well. The critical position that
best enshrines it is New Criticism, the model of criticism that
has been so influential in this country during our century.[6] Most
of us in this room who are over forty and under sixty were
probably trained as New Critics. We learned that depth and
unique difference are the hallmark of the work of art. Language
is assumed, within this critical model, to be supremely manage-
able; and each work is to be studied in its precious difference
from others, each character to be probed in his rounded wholeness, each master writer to be praised for the rich inclusiveness
of his personal vision. (All along the tacit assumption was that
life, in its murk and messiness, its ideological confusions, could
not provide such fine-grained distinctions: but art could.)

"Close reading" was invented and became institutionalized as
a classroom technique for disengaging the essence, the identity,
of the aesthetic object. Through close readings the uniqueness of
the writer's vision was identified, and once the individual case
had been scrupulously delineated, it was seen to partake (para-
doxically) of the universal as well. That is, the unique vision is
simultaneously, in its wholeness, a universal or human vision. To
speak of universal or human is to be in touch with essence, with
that which is lodged so deeply within the individual that it
escapes the accidents of condition or local affiliation and reflects

instead something common to the species. In the name of en-compassing all groups, human actually disavows the power of any group to affect the essence of the unique individual.

As spectators in the presence of the human or the universal, essences freed by art for our disinterested appreciation, we are meant to praise. (How often a New Critical classroom assign-ment on a poem or a novel could be distilled to the following message: praise this object! tell me how finely, disinterestedly, inclusively it understands life in its inimitable weave of form and content!) The work, exquisitely beyond bias, stands self-com-plete before us, a microcosm of that ideal identity we would seek to posit within ourself: a sacred space. Like us, it may be embedded within other, potentially contaminating networks, but these networks are secondary. The work's aesthetic triumph, like our own fantasized identity, resides in its free-standing wholeness.

I have tried to word this in such a way that you will see the connection between how we view the identity of the work of art, how we view the writer's identity, and how we view our own. This distinction between the unique and universal, on the one hand, and the group-shaped and system-sharing, on the other, not only affects Faulkner's texts: it affects conferences on those texts. For the past two years we at this conference have chosen to discuss those texts within the "group-shaped" frames of women and race, and one of the most urgent (though unspoken) ques-tions has been: how can we still think of Faulkner as unique and universal when it becomes more and more obvious that he is also (and not just coincidentally) white and male?

For me, the most revealing moment at last year's conference occurred when a speaker eloquently reflected on potential com-plexities of motive in two of Faulkner's characters: the white deputy in "Pantaloon in Black" and the black man Jesus in "That Evening Sun." The speaker concluded that these characters, in their pain and bewilderment, should be thought of as neither white nor black, but instead as *human*. There was an immediate and audible sigh of satisfaction within a great portion of the

audience, for this conclusion spoke to our continuous anxiety
about racial difference—spoke to it by transcending all group
differences and arriving at species universality, at the human. Yet
what black reader of Faulkner will find it more illuminating to
see that white deputy as human rather than white (white here as
crucial limitation and blindness), and what woman reader will
want to see Jesus (who has beaten Nancy before and may now be
about to slit her throat) as human rather than male (male here as
crucial limitation and blindness)? The white deputy and Jesus
act deeply out of their group identity—their race and gender—
and to see them as essentially human is to obscure into secondariness the massive role played by race and gender.

I should say, in closing this anecdote, that a woman came up
after the talk to quarrel with the speaker's interpretation of
Jesus, and I (who had also come up) raised a question with him
about "human" but defended his gender reading. In the year's
interim between then and now I have been pondering this
event—it was in fact the germ of this entire paper—and the
speaker and I have, since then, discussed together as well the
elusive impress of ideology upon interpretation. For my part, I
now see that the talk and the later disagreements were all of
them instances of the legitimate shaping power of race and
gender. As a white male, the speaker could see something in
Jesus that a black reader might not see (he being focused on a
racial context that the white reader might see beyond); likewise
the woman with a quarrel *had* a quarrel: she as a woman was
more interested in reading Jesus within a gender context that
was for her primary, not secondary, though for the white male
speaker the gender context might well seem secondary to an
existentialist one. And I now realize that a Marxist might have
come up to the podium and legitimately quarreled with us all,
his focus arising from a matrix of class and economic issues that
we had all scanted.

The point is that there are no universal texts, no universal
readings of them. Each text, like each reading of the text,
achieves its power through its omissions: seeing some things is

predicated upon blindness to others. The text, like the reader, is caught up in a variety of unchosen networks; it is inextricably part of its time and its place. Its identity is inevitably adulterate and problematic, a function both of its angle of vision upon the world and of the reader's angle of vision upon it. Roland Barthes makes this point shrewdly in his essay on that "universal" bestseller entitled *The Family of Man*.7 Barthes notes that this photographic celebration of our universally shared destiny—that all over the world we are alike in being born, in growing up, in working and playing, in growing old and dying—manages systematically to repress a countertruth: that we are born into different conditions, we grow up with different possibilities, we have different work and play options (depending on what part of the world we inhabit and our class orientation), we die at different ages and of different diseases (depending on the culture we live in).8 This countertruth is attentive to the differential of history, whereas *The Family of Man* focuses upon the immutability of nature. Both points of view are valuable, but only one concedes that it *is* a point of view. *The Family of Man* passes itself off as unedited pictures of nature, of the obvious: as how things are.

The text that claims to be universal posits, then, an unchanging human truth, an essential identity uncontaminated by the accidents of time, place, and affiliation. Free of bias, it asks to be taken as a privileged portrait of how things are.9 Such a text was, I think, the object of study of New Criticism, and there is something in us that still seeks to read Faulkner in this way. I want now to posit another model of identity—this one drawing on the Marxist philosopher Althusser and the psychoanalytic theorist Lacan—and then to consider both *Absalom, Absalom!* and the activity of this conference from the perspective of this new model.

* * *

Althusser is interested in the paradox at the heart of the term *subject*.10 The subject is simultaneously the free human being and the human being subjected to another's system of beliefs and practices. Ideology is the missing term that enables this paradox, for ideological practice and the free human subject mutually constitute each other. "The category of the subject," writes Althusser, "is the constitutive category of all ideology . . . insofar as all ideology has the function (which defines it) of 'constituting' concrete individuals as subjects."[11] What this means is that we obtain our sense of uncoerced, unpredictable inwardness through our spontaneous assent to the social scripts—the ideologies—that surround us. We assent immediately, to arrangements so self-evident as to be invisible, and indeed all well-functioning ideology is invisible in this sense. It is what goes without saying, it is our daily participation in a "natural" schema of how things are, our way of wearing our name, our clothes, our unconscious convictions about the rightness of our procedures.

But we do not generate name, clothes, and convictions out of ourselves. They may be the material of our identity, but they come to us from outside, as always already established and awaiting our spontaneous participation. We join in by accepting the models thus proposed. As men or women we accept some socially proposed gender image, if we are Christians we accept Christ, if we are Americans we accept some version of the founding fathers, if we are teachers we pursue some compelling image of teaching. In each case we become ourselves by subjecting ourselves to a commanding image: we achieve our freedom by internalizing an external model. Althusser calls this model ideology, a script whose acceptance ushers us into a particular version of social reality, a version that we enact insofar as we remain faithful to the gestures, practices, and beliefs sanctioned by the script. The key to this model is noncoercion: "the individual *is interpellated as a (free) subject in order that he shall (freely) accept his subjection,* i.e. in order that he shall make the gestures and actions of his subjection 'all by himself.'"[12]

Identity on this model is decentered. We spontaneously (indeed unconsciously) subscribe to social scripts that thus empower us. They do empower us, yet they are not quite the same thing as us. Is it too much to say that Faulknerian tragedy is generated precisely by the civil war between these internalized social scripts and a something within the self more primordial than social scripts? I turn now to Jacques Lacan for a discussion of this something more primordial.

According to Lacan we come into our identity only through a series of alienations, and the earliest ones are decisive.[13] The infant, speechless (*infans* means speechless), absorbs from its first days bits and pieces of language into itself, and it absorbs as well the gaze of others. What it knows in addition is the sensation of disconnected body parts; it has as yet no totalizing image of itself. This momentous step occurs during what Lacan calls the mirror stage: that moment (Lacan sees it beginning roughly at the sixth month and continuing for another year) when the infant begins to "recognize" itself as reflected either through the eyes of its mother or in an actual mirror. The resultant external image is perceived as a totality—a completed self—and it contrasts richly, in its wholeness and mobility, with the infant's own interior sense of physical uncoordination and turbulent body parts. In other words, the infant recognizes itself only in an alien image of wholeness. Lacan writes: "the total form of the body by which the subject anticipates in a mirage the maturation of his power is given to him only . . . in an exteriority."[14] Or, as he puts it more simply, "the first synthesis of the *ego* is essentially alter ego; it is alienated."[15]

This first moment of coherent self-knowing is thus a "mirage," and it prefigures the process of unconscious identificatory merging with outer objects that will, for the rest of our lives, affect our identity as subjects. Lacan calls this dimension of identity *Imaginary*. As one of Lacan's commentators writes, "The ego is developed in a primordial discordance between natural being and identification with the forms of the oter world. In other words, *alien* images—i.e., not innate—first constitute the ego as an *object* of its own identificatory mergers."[16] The self is thus "constituted through anticipating what it will become,"[17] built upon fictions.

The second stage of identity-formation begins at about eighteen months: the time at which the child simultaneously begins to acquire language skills and to recognize the invisible presence of the father as a barrier to its desire for merger with the mother. Reconceiving Freud's Oedipal drama, Lacan sees the child's entry into language as itself a substitute satisfaction for the lost object—the mother—that the infant shall never again possess. Language appears in this argument as an alien network made up of empty differences, of signs that mean only in relation to each other; it is a system outside the self. Henceforth caught up in this system (which Lacan calls the Symbolic—the paternal field of Culture's rules and regulations, of linguistic transactions, of the Law), the child is doomed to seek in the register of language and its concepts a wholeness that language by definition cannot provide. Language keeps sending us to other language. Thus we spend our lives trying to say what we want, chasing in the channel of language for an object that never existed in that currency in the first place.

These two stages of self-formation posit an inevitable self-fissuring. The human subject is a being precariously poised between Imaginary mergers and Symbolic distinctions; he does not master either arena. Identity is therefore decentered and from the beginning adulterate; there *is* no native self. As Lacan writes, "I think where I am not, therefore I am where I do not think."[18] Or, "clarifying" himself, he writes: "I am not wherever I am the plaything of my thought; I think of what I am where I do not think to think."[19] Or, "clarifying" Lacan, we might say: "Thinking I was I was not who was not was not who." In each formulation we remain, it seems, the last ones to know exactly what we are up to, though Faulkner's wording has an urgency and a sense of the *cost* of such vertigo absent from Lacan's complacent phrasing. In any event, the social world—its language, its gestures, its images—penetrates us from the moment of our birth on: we have never been virginal. Drawing on Althusser and Lacan as formulators of a human subject inextricably and irrationally permeated by social networks—a human subject who lives his identity both through participating in ideology and through primordial Imaginary mergers with the others that surround him—I turn now to *Absalom, Absalom!*

*   *   *

Faulkner almost surely knew nothing of either Althusser or Lacan, yet *Absalom, Absalom!* uncannily responds to their enterprises. The ways in which individuals are born into alien systems of thinking, feeling, and doing—into ideology—and at the same time find themselves caught up in a primordial fusion with others in whom they see themselves mirrored: these concerns seem to lie near the heart of the book. As John Irwin has argued, individual identity in this novel is a matter not of enclosed essences but of specular relationships.[20]

The process of vicarious identification is rampant. Rosa and her identification with Judith and Charles's courtship, Henry and his shifting triangular identifications with Judith and with Bon, Sutpen's identification with the planter in the big house, Wash Jones's identification with Sutpen, Quentin and Shreve's identifications with Henry and Charles: in each of these crossings an involuntary psychic merger takes place—across "the devious intricate channels of decorous ordering" (139), the boundaries set up by Culture that tell whom we are like and whom unlike, whom we can or cannot touch, where, and when. The novel's primary image for this desire for merger is touch itself, just as the novel's primary image for the cultural prohibition against touch is the closed door.

Individual identity here remains poignantly incomplete. Even Charles Bon, in Quentin and Shreve's final version of him, finds himself moving past the cool stability of "breathing, pleasure, darkness" (300) and into the helpless state of yearning. Needing his father's recognition and not getting it he thinks, "*My God, I am young, young, and I didn't even know it; they didn't even tell me, that I was young*" (321). *Absalom, Absalom!* insists on the same kind of fluid incompleteness in its very form. Revising each finished version of its characters' identity with another version, the novel melts down whatever it has consolidated, infusing youthful instability and passion into materials gone rigid or dead. "Get on, now . . . But go on . . . Go on" (260–61)—these instigating phrases run like a leitmotif throughout the narrative, fanning the glow of its stalemated materials into the bonfire of an overpass to love, heating up painful but finished events into unbearably unfinished ones. Charles Bon enters this novel dead, is brought back to life, is shot, is resurrected, is shot again, is resurrected again, is shot again. Each time he dies it hurts a bit more, hurts Quentin and Shreve who have lent him something of themselves, hurts the reader who has lent Quentin and Shreve (and therefore Charles) something of the reader's self. The narrative keeps revisiting its most intransigent materials, rejuvenating and replaying them as a living might-be, then as a meditative might-have-been, then as a tragic was.

In this creative move to revise its own inheritance, this tormented overview of its own wasted terrain, *Absalom* goes past an Althusserian vision of ideological consent. It does so through the resurrectory energy of desire itself, the energy that psychoanalysis respects as transference and that moves through the incompleteness of individual identity—that of the doers, the tellers, the readers—and merges with the other.[21] Rather than accept the limitations of a narrative in which everything has already happened—the conventional historical novel—or accept the illusion of a narrative in which everything is yet to happen— the conventional novel of today, Faulkner combines these two frames into a narrative of tragic desire. Events come to us in the double perspective of having already happened, and yet—such is the desire of the teller—they are rekindled, still happening, being reimagined, reframed, compelling yet hopeless. This is the narrative of desire entrapped—can't matter—and desire released—must matter, of *"they mought have kilt us but they aint whupped us yit"* (184).

Such involuntary mergers recall the Lacanian field of the Imaginary—the movement of "the immortal brief recent intransient blood" (295)—in defiance of the boundaries put forth by the Symbolic order. Those boundaries, though, are beyond dismantling, and not because the authorities dispense enough police to protect them. They are beyond dismantling because internalized, bred into the very fabric of the individual's unconscious feeling and thinking. Henry Sutpen polices himself. His West Virginia father may touch blacks with impunity but, born and bred in the South, Henry cannot. He screams and vomits when his father does it, he murders at the intolerable prospect of his sister doing it. As Althusser claims, ideology is inseparable from subjecthood itself, and Faulkner tirelessly shows us—in Quentin Compson, in Joe Christmas, in Charles Etienne Saint-Valery Bon—the dissolution of the subject that follows upon the clash within of incompatible ideological scripts.

All great novels involve the clash of ideological scripts, but most do not represent that clash as beyond individual resolution. Indeed, as I suggested earlier, fiction is a privileged terrain for the successful negotiation of self and society, for the persuasive imagining of individual identity working its way through conflicts both Imaginary and ideological. I would hazard that every best-seller, one way or another, affirms a dominant ideology even as it points to its rupture or blind spots. Let us consider, for example, the ways in which two masterpieces written in 1936— *Absalom, Absalom!* and *Gone with the Wind*—play out this issue of ideological rupture and containment in terms of individual identity.[22]

Narrative voice is the novel's most potent instrument for containment—for conveying the sense of an individual speaker in control of the conflicts that arise—and *Gone with the Wind* comes to us in an uninterrupted and exquisitely satisfying narrative voice, a voice everywhere equal to its task, a voice that knows. *Absalom, Absalom!* comes to us, by contrast, in a variety of voices, and the fact that they all sound alike doesn't help us out. Each of these voices either knowingly or unknowingly calls into question its own authority. This is a case in which more is less.

If we move to the handling of time and theme, we find a comparable stability in the best-seller, instability in the experimental novel. All of *Gone with the Wind* is written as though the past history it is unfolding took place just a few days ago: the novel never acknowledges its own seventy-five-year vantage point on the events it records—the pastness of the past. (It doesn't acknowledge it but it everywhere exploits it in the unified vision afforded by retrospect.) Mitchell renders the defeat of the South as tragic, deserved, and—more to the point—secondary. She does this by focusing the reader less upon the issues of the war itself than upon two larger-than-life figures (Rhett and Scarlet) who stand neither simply for nor against the lost cause. The trauma of the war, the ways in which it called into question (still calls into question) our nation's deepest communal identity, is thus contained within Scarlet and Rhett's "immortal" love story, ending on the note of the unvanquished human will, the staying power of individual identity. (A comparison of the place of Tara and of Sutpen's Hundred within the economy of each novel's ending makes the same point.)

Absalom, Absalom! by contrast, lives uneasily on both sides of Mitchell's satisfying time frame. In *Absalom* the pastness of the past—its unrecoverability—is foregrounded. Yet the past has refused, precisely, to pass: it is still present, still unfinished, still beyond managing. 1808, 1833, 1859, 1865, 1909–10: the narrative moves bewilderingly back and forth among these times, suggesting that the racial issues over which the war was fought retain their power to haunt and confuse: who is black in *Absalom?* how much black blood does it take to be black? In place of *Gone with the Wind*'s easy separation between black blacks and white whites, *Absalom* finds black and white to be inextricable parts of each other's identity.

Gone with the Wind "masters" the trauma of the Civil War, then, by containing it within a love story of two strong individuals, narrated by a coherent and capable narrative voice, one which keeps intact key distinctions between white and black, self and system, past and present, energy and weakness: distinctions upon which twentieth-century American culture's most confident images of itself are founded. In *Absalom* all these distinctions have become problematic. No narrator can deliver this material because none has mastered it. None can speak from a later cultural vantage point of superior hindsight and sort it all out. And this means literally that the culture since 1865 has been unable to provide the narrators with a perspective—a consoling ideology—that will make that cataclysmic war go down. It sticks in the craw, and in so doing it shatters the conventional fictional contract between self and society. *Absalom* is an experimental novel, precisely, in its refusal of these blandishments, these conventions of retrospective mastery. Its frustrations are passed on to us as our own; we do not feel wise reading it, we do not feel sure of ourselves—of who we are—while reading it.[23]

In fact, Faulkner's novel (as opposed to Mitchell's) seems designed to frustrate our answer to the simple question that inaugurates all queries about identity: who is——? who is Thomas Sutpen? who is Charles Bon? who is Quentin Compson? It is not that the question cannot be answered but that the novel keeps on answering it in different ways. Thomas Sutpen is a demon, a tragic hero, a successful planter; he is also a psychically arrested child, a mountain man, white trash. Who he is depends on when and where you look at him, and who is doing the looking. He looks one way to a woman, another to a man, another to a disowned son, another to a disillusioned classicist, another to his quietly desperate son, another to a Canadian. These competing views of Sutpen's identity do not embarrass the novel; they enable it. Character in *Absalom* lives openly in someone else's *talk;* there is no illusion here of unmediated identity, of identity as enclosed essence.[24] A different narrator, a different issue (miscegenation, say, rather than incest) produces a different identity.

What indeed is *Absalom, Absalom!* "itself"? Is it the material

378 pages within the Modern Library covers that most of us know? John Irwin has shown its astonishing intertextually shared life with *The Sound and the Fury*. Less spectacularly, Noel Polk's new edition of *The Sound and the Fury* indicates the difficulty of containing any text within its material bounds. Consider the history of *The Sound and the Fury*'s Appendix.[25] To do so, we should first go forward to *Absalom, Absalom!*, for in concluding that novel in the mid-1930s Faulkner composed a chronology, a genealogy, and a map. Charmed, perhaps, by the illusion of containment that such instruments convey, Faulkner went on to write—some ten years later—an Appendix to *The Sound and the Fury*, liking it so much that he argued for its appearance at the beginning of the novel. (Probably half of you in this room first encountered the novel, as I did, in this format, joined with *As I Lay Dying*.) For sixteen years this text held sway; then, at the time of Faulkner's death, a new edition appeared with the Appendix placed more discreetly at the end of the novel proper. Some twenty-two years later, in 1984, under the supervision of Noel Polk, the most recent edition of *The Sound and the Fury* appeared, this time altogether without the Appendix. Which is *The Sound and the Fury*? If I have told the story properly, you will find the question sounding now a bit naive. The amount of critical exigesis dependent upon the originally absent and now discarded Appendix is weighty indeed, and it is not limited to undergraduates who don't know better. There are, I conclude, several *Sound and Furys* afloat (not that they are all of equal value), and whichever we prefer changes in yet other ways when we try to calculate its interaction with *Absalom, Absalom!*

*   *   *

Character and text not only exhibit changing identities; literary history is founded upon such changes. We all know relevant examples: the Romantics' Milton (of the Devil's party without knowing it) is not the Milton of the seventeenth century; T. S. Eliot's inauguration of John Donne as a major poet removes him from his Elizabethan context and places him in Eliot's ongoing battle with Wordsworth and Tennyson; *Jane Eyre* as reconceived by contemporary feminists is a text of the 1970s as much as of the 1840s; *Uncle Tom's Cabin* goes from best-sellerdom in the 1850s to obscurity for a hundred years and back into acclaim once again, now being enlisted in the contemporary battle against Modernist canons of race, gender, form, and theme; D. H. Lawrence, once one of the four or five twentieth-century darlings of survey courses of English literature, is at present disappearing silently from our syllabi.

These are not capricious changes. They testify to the fact that we do not so much receive literary masterpieces, intact, as produce them, adulterate.[26] The identity of texts is not essential but contextual; their value is inescapably conditioned by current canons of assessment. No writer comes to us "as he is," not even Faulkner. How can we see him except through the interpretive eyes of Sartre and Malraux, or Olga Vickery, or Cleanth Brooks, or John Irwin, or John Matthews—which is to say through the concomitant lenses of Sartre and Malraux's existentialism, Vickery's New Criticism, Brooks's sympathy with Southern culture, Irwin's Nietzsche and Freud, Matthews's Derrida? I have in this sentence immersed Faulkner within a fog of names, yet this is, whether we are conscious of it or not, the only access we have to him. "Faulkner" is misleading shorthand for a complex and many-voiced enterprise that operates under the cover of his name.

Individual identity is likewise misleading shorthand for a complex and many-voiced enterprise that operates under the cover of that phrase. So long as we are physically separate from each other, demonstrably lodged in separate bodies, we shall probably never concede the degree to which we depend upon the other and upon system in order to constitute the self. Equally, so long as we look solid, we shall deny the terrifying extent of our liquidity. Yet it is, so to speak, the liquid in us—what Faulkner calls the blood—that engages incessantly in acts of transference, of identificatory merger. Because our identity is perpetually unfinished, because we are never coincident with ourselves, we read books, teach students, and attend Faulkner conferences.

I have been using the pronoun "we" with abandon, but the "we" in this room is no common entity. Our orientations are here as well, invisibly differentiating us from some and joining us to others. Indeed, many of us are wearing a badge conspicuously placed upon our person, and this badge tells an interesting story. It says that we are here in our discrete bodies but not only here; we are also there, lodged in our former affiliations (and if the badge says Berkeley it suggests something different from Buffalo, something different again from Swarthmore or Ole Miss). We speak out of those affiliations, and are heard in terms of them, as we speak out of and are heard in terms of our race and gender.

Yet we do come together under a common umbrella that is appropriately named "Faulkner." It is the site less of our individual than of our transpersonal professional activity. Many of us are rewarded—either figuratively or literally—for coming to these conferences and attending thus to our place in the Symbolic field of reputations and responsibilities. Prestige and power, in however small a degree, are at stake. In addition, and more agreeably, "Faulkner" serves as a sort of absent father who enables fleeting sibling relations among erstwhile strangers spending a week together in each other's company. Not kin, we do, because of him, for moments feel like kin. I'll close by suggesting, however, that this conference is the site as well, and perhaps more profoundly, of our common acts of imaginary transference, the locus of our hopeless desire to merge our incompleteness with Faulkner's beckoning authority. Dead, he lives. Continually re-invented, he speaks to us. "Freed . . . of time and flesh,"[27] like old Colonel Sartoris or Colonel Sutpen, he broods over us all in the form of our impassioned and incompatible inventions of him.

NOTES

1. I cite from the 1962 Vintage edition of *The Sound and the Fury* and from the 1951 Modern Library edition of *Absalom, Absalom!*

2. The best full-length study of Faulknerian psychic structures menaced by pressures they cannot control is Gail L. Mortimer's phenomonological *Faulkner's Rhetoric of Loss* (Austin: University of Texas Press, 1983). André Bleikasten's *The Most Splendid Failure* (Bloomington: Indiana University Press, 1976) recurs frequently to this concern. See especially the chapters on Quentin, 90–143. For a reading of this vertigo in terms of the play of difference and deferral inherent in the system of language itself, see John Matthews, *The Play of Faulkner's Language* (Ithaca: Cornell University Press, 1982).

3. Bleikasten is acute on Jason's enclosure within the social stereotypes of his region: "His ideas are all second-hand, and . . . they all come from the threadbare ideology of his cultural environment" (164).

4. For further discussion of the idea of "sanctuary," see my "Precarious Sanctuaries: Protection and Exposure in Faulkner's Fiction," *Studies in American Fiction*, 6 (1978), 173–91.

5. Judith Egan Gardiner's "On Female Identity and Writing by Women" in Elizabeth Abel, ed., *Writing and Sexual Difference* (Chicago: University of Chicago Press, 1983) provides an excellent overview of psychoanalytic models of identity from Freud through Erikson and Chodorow. The problematic of individual identity is, of course, a common theme of post-structuralist, psychoanalytic, and Marxist criticism.

6. The preeminent spokesmen of New Criticism—Allen Tate, John Crowe Ransom, Cleanth Brooks, and William Wimsatt, to name four—have decisively shaped the institutional study of literature in this country since the 1930s; their major texts are sufficiently well-known not to require identification here. For critical assessments of their enterprise, see Frank Lentricchia, *After The New Criticism* (Chicago: University of Chicago Press, 1980), Terry Eagleton, *Literary Theory: An Introduction* (Oxford, Eng.: Blackwell, 1983), and William E. Cain, *The Crisis in Criticism* (Baltimore: The Johns Hopkins University Press, 1984).

7. *Mythologies* (Paris: Seuil, 1957), trans. Annette Levers (New York: Hill and Wang, 1972), 100–102.

8. Barthes writes: "Any classic humanism postulates that in scratching the history of men a little, the relativity of their institutions or the superficial diversity of their skins (but why not ask the parents of Emmet Till, the young Negro assassinated by the Whites what *they* think of *The Great Family of Man?*), one very quickly reaches the solid rock of a universal human nature" (101).

9. Survey courses of English literature find it difficult to avoid the same idealist perspective. The "pageantry" of masterpieces from *Beowulf* to Virginia Woolf emerges as a sequence of works that resemble nothing so much as each other in their fine-grained and unbiased universality. The differential history that occasions the production and reception of all these works is marginalized in such courses, if not repressed.

10. The central Althusser text for my purposes is "Ideology and Ideological State Apparatuses," in his *Lenin and Philosophy, and Other Essays* (London: New Left Books, 1971). The major attempt to produce an Althusserian model of literary theory is Pierre Macherey's *Pour une Théorie de la production littéraire* (Paris: François Maspero, 1966). The work of Terry Eagleton and of Fredric Jameson is considerably indebted to both Althusser and Macherey. See especially Eagleton's *Criticism and Ideology* (London: New Left Books, 1976) and Jameson's *The Political Unconscious* (Ithaca: Cornell University Press, 1981), 9–102. Other useful commentary on Althusser includes Tony Bennett's *Formalism and Marxism* (London: Methuen, 1979); James Kavanaugh's "Marxism's Althusser: Toward a Politics of Literary Theory," in *diacritics*, 12 (1982), 25–45; and William Dowling's *Jameson, Althusser, Marx* (Ithaca: Cornell University Press, 1984).

11. Althusser, 171.

12. Ibid., 182.

13. The most useful collection of Lacan's major essays in translation remains *Ecrits: A Selection*, trans. Alan Sheridan (New York: Norton, 1977). The essay most relevant to this portion of my argument is "The Mirror Stage as Formative of the Function of the I," 1–7. Lacan's

work is notoriously difficult, and I have benefited greatly by the following discussions: Anika Lemaire, *Jacques Lacan*, trans. David Macey (London: Routledge & Kegan Paul, 1977); Fredric Jameson, "Imaginary and Symbolic in Lacan," in Shoshana Felman, ed., *Literature and Psychoanalysis* (Baltimore: The Johns Hopkins University Press, 1982), 338–95; Luce Irigaray, *Ce Sexe qui n'en est pas un* (Paris: Minuit, 1977); Jane Gallop, *The Daughter's Seduction* (Ithaca: Cornell University Press, 1982), and her *Reading Lacan* (Ithaca: Cornell University Press, 1985); and Ellie Ragland-Sullivan, *Jacques Lacan and the Philosophy of Psychoanalysis* (Urbana: University of Illinois Press, 1986).

14. Lacan, 2.

15. Lacan, Seminaire 3, as quoted by Ragland-Sullivan, 275.

16. Ragland-Sullivan, 2.

17. Gallop, *Reading Lacan*, 81.

18. Lacan, 166.

19. Ibid.

20. Irwin, *Doubling and Incest/Repetition and Revenge* (Baltimore: The Johns Hopkins University Press, 1975).

21. The best work I know of on the role of desire in the production of literary texts is that of Peter Brooks, *Reading for the Plot* (New York: Knopf, 1984), and of Charles Bernheimer, "Toward a Psychopoetics of the Text," in his *Flaubert and Kafka* (New Haven: Yale University Press, 1984), 1–44.

22. Eric Sundquist touches briefly on this comparison in his *Faulkner: The House Divided* (Baltimore: The Johns Hopkins University Press, 1983). Peter Brooks brilliantly explores the logic of the intertwined failure of narrative and genealogical authority in his "Incredulous Narration: *Absalom, Absalom!*" in *Comparative Literature*, 34 (1982), 247–68.

23. Not enough critical attention is generally paid to the sense of readerly empowerment or incapacity wrought by a given text's "narrative contract." Insofar as a narrative invokes (in its forms even more than its themes) the comforts of the already-known, it consolidates the ideological bonding between reader and culture: it makes one feel rich in common wisdom. Virginia Woolf's commentary in *A Room of One's Own* (New York: Harcourt, Brace & World, 1957) on this aspect of reading is unsurpassable:

> But the effect [of an unconventional text that the narrator is reading] was somehow baffling; one could not see a wave heaping itself, a crisis coming round the next corner. Therefore I could not plume myself either upon the depths of my feelings and my profound knowledge of the human heart. For whenever I was about to feel the usual things in the usual places, about love, about death, the annoying creature twitched me away, as if the important thing were just a little further on. And thus she made it impossible for me to roll out my sonorous phrases about "elemental feelings," the "common stuff of humanity," "depths of the human heart," and all those other phrases which support us in our belief that, however clever we may be on top, we are very serious, very profound and very humane underneath. She made me feel, on the contrary, that instead of being serious and profound and humane, one might be—and the thought was far less seductive—merely lazy minded and conventional into the bargain. (95)

24. John Matthews richly opens up this dimension of characterization in his chapter on *Absalom, Absalom!* in *The Play of Faulkner's Language*. For a study of the ways in which the novel's entire representational project is dependent upon voice, see also Stephen M. Ross, "The Evocation of Voice in *Absalom, Absalom!*," in *Essays in Literature*, 8 (1981), 135–49.

25. Noel Polk discusses these issues at length in his *Editorial Handbook on The Sound and the Fury*. In a telephone discussion of 3 July 1987 Noel Polk spoke to me of some of Faulkner's reasons in the mid-forties for wanting to give a privileged position to the Appendix, yet without "pandering" to those who would refuse to struggle with the body of the text itself.

26. To Marx's question, "Where does the eternal charm of Greek art come from?" Etienne Balibar and Pierre Macherey respond as follows:

> There is no good answer to this question, quite simply because there is no eternal charm in Greek art: for the *Iliad*, a fragment of universal literature, used in this instance as a vehicle for memory, is not the *Iliad* produced by the material life of the Greeks, which was not a 'book' nor even a 'myth' in our sense of the word, which we would like to apply retrospectively. Homer's *Iliad*, the 'work' of an 'author' exists only for us, and in relation to new material

conditions into which it has been reinscribed and reinvested with a new significance. . . . To go further: it is as if we ourselves had written it (or at least composed it anew). Works of art are processes and not objects, for they are never produced once and for all, but are continually susceptible to 'reproduction': in fact, they only find an identity and a content in this continual process of transformation. There is no eternal art, there are no fixed and immutable works. (Quoted in Bennett, *Formalism and Marxism*, 68)

27. William Faulkner, *Sartoris* (New York: Signet, 1964), 19.

Word without a Word: How the French Translations of Faulkner's Texts Don't Always Fit What They're Trying to Say At

BETH DYER BIRON

The French literary world has long been proud to note that it recognized William Faulkner as a major talent nearly ten years before his work began to receive critical acclaim in the United States. As early as 1930, a student at Princeton University, James Burnham, called to the attention of his French professor, Maurice-Edgar Coindreau, the works of a little-known novelist from Mississippi. As Coindreau relates, *"As I Lay Dying* had just been published. I had not read fifty pages of this admirable book before my mind was made up. The French nation had to become acquainted with an artist of such pronounced originality."[1] Coindreau published the first article in French on the American's work in the *Nouvelle Revue Française* in June 1931. In the ensuing years, he translated into French several of Faulkner's short stories and six of his novels, among them *The Sound and the Fury* and *As I Lay Dying*. He also wrote numerous critical essays about the works as well as several explanatory prefaces to his translations.

The other major translator of Faulkner's works into French was René-Noël Raimbault; he did eight of the novels published by Gallimard, including *Sanctuary* and *Absalom, Absalom!* He also collaborated with Coindreau and Charles Vorce on the translation of the stories in *These Thirteen*. Although Raimbault wrote only one slim volume on Faulkner and his work for a university series, there is evidence that Raimbault was the translator who best understood what Faulkner was about. However, since Coindreau's opinions were more widely circulated, his interpretations carried the most weight in shaping the perception in France of Faulkner's work.

The enthusiastic reception accorded Faulkner's work in France came, says Roger Asselineau, because "for all his Southern trappings . . . the French immediately recognized him as one of their own," finding in his work elements with which they were already acquainted.[2] The saga of Yoknapatawpha County with its realistic, sometimes naturalistic descriptions reminded the French of Balzac and the tradition of the "roman fleuve" in their literature, and of course there were his "impressionistic" techniques reminiscent of Mallarmé. Having described such affinities of Faulkner's work with the French tradition, Asselineau then makes the somewhat exaggerated claim that Faulkner "started to exist when he was perceived by French critics and readers," concluding that in a way Faulkner can therefore be regarded as "a French invention."[3]

In an ironic way, Asselineau's claim is true. The French did "invent" a Faulkner, one whose texts were passed through a screen of translation and interpretation that often filtered out important elements essential to a full understanding of his work. From the very first, concern for the meaning in Faulkner's work took second place as French interest focused on the "art," the technique of its realization. That tendency is evident even in Coindreau's 1931 essay: "In the works of William Faulkner the subject is only a pretext for the display of a technique which, in this instance [in *Sanctuary*] approaches perfection. To be fair to Faulkner one must forget his themes and consider only the way he deals with them. Then he ceases to be the Satanic creator of nightmares and becomes the virtuoso, the master of a new technique based on the power of the unexpressed."[4] In his explanation of why Faulkner was immediately successful in France, Coindreau once observed that the aspects of Faulkner's work which he admired were the ones that appealed to his countrymen as well: "A psychological acuteness which digs down into the most concealed folds of the subconscious, a technique entirely new although based on elements already known (stream of consciousness, for example). Nothing else was necessary to conquer the esteem of the French intellectuals."5

To see Faulkner primarily as either a stylist or as a psychologist, however, is to distort the very essence of his work whose most distinctive characteristic is its fusion of content and form, of consciousness and the language of its expression, of idea and image, of spirit and flesh. To try to separate those interpenetating elements is to violate the texts. One French critic, even, has spoken a similar word of caution. Michel Gresset once suggested that Faulkner's reputation in France, created by the work of his "heralds," might be seen "in much the same light as one can see the relationship between Poe and France through the uniquely powerful filter of Baudelaire's enthusiastic reading. In both cases, one might go as far as finding a rather remarkable case of misunderstanding as communication, or of communication through misunderstanding—depending on whether we are pessimists or optimists."6

Many scholars consider the translations of Coindreau and Raimbault outstanding. In many respects they are. Both translators have taken great care to reproduce the syntactical convolutions of Faulkner's style as scrupulously as the French language will allow. They also have been generally successful with psychological portraiture and with the reproduction of some narrative voices. Coindreau has done a remarkable job at times in sorting out the tortured language and telescoped syntax in the interior monologues of *The Sound and the Fury,* and he has accurately preserved the poetic imagery of Darl's speech in *As I Lay Dying*. Raimbault has done fine work in capturing just the right dreamy, elegaic tone in his translation of Miss Rosa Coldfield's overblown prose in *Absalom, Absalom!*

Major weaknesses of the translations, however, include their failure to reflect how Faulkner's shaping of language is related to the message it bears, their failure to reproduce accurately many aspects of Southern culture so richly described in the original, and most serious of all, their failure to capture the symbolic and metaphysical implications of much of the language. Those problems become evident at the most basic level of translation, in the choice of vocabulary.

To be fair, one must acknowledge that a certain skewing of information is unavoidable in any translation since no two languages have precisely equivalent systems of symbols and referents. One of the linguistic problems pertinent to the French translations of the Faulkner texts, then, arises from a basic difference in the vocabularies of French and English. French, like Latin, tends to be a more analytical, abstract language than English. Julien Green, the twentieth-century author who wrote with equal ease in French and English, has discussed that very problem of vocabulary in his work *Le Langage et son double*. In translating, says Green, the choice of words is always of primary importance because it is in the names of things that any language first puts "son empreinte obscure et profonde," shaping thought itself in that primary process of *naming*. He offers this example: "French could never furnish us with such an emotionally disturbing word as *doom*; it would say 'final judgement,' with a direct appeal to the intellect. 'Jugement dernier' makes me think whereas 'the Crack of Doom' makes me feel like running for shelter under a mountain. And there lies the difference."[7]

Faulkner, of course, makes full use of the suggestive, implicative qualities of English words like *doom*. One of the hallmarks of his style is his ability to choose concrete words which provide vivid, exact descriptions yet which are also laden with rich connotations, bearing both emotional and mythic overtones. Raimbault called Faulkner "l'un des plus magnifiques musiciens de la prose américaine," and noted after working on the translations that "chez Faulkner . . . le souci de la phrase a toujours dominé celui de la composition." Faulkner, said the translator, was a creature possessed by "le démon du verbe."[8] The French language does not always contain a suitable equivalent for the words of this author dominated by the "daemon of the word," however. For example, there is no word in French that means *home*, with all of the associative richness that has made that word highly evocative for speakers of English. In *Light in August* the foundling Joe Christmas is taken from the orphanage, where he has always lived, by McEachern, his new foster father. Nearing the end of a long journey, the stern man points to a light shining through the dusk and says to the child, "Home."

> The child said nothing. The man looked down at him . . . "I said, 'There is your home.'" Still the child didn't answer him. He had never seen a home, so there was nothing for him to say about it.9 (135)

In Coindreau's translation, *home* becomes first "chez nous" and then "de chez lui."

> L'enfant ne dit rien. L'homme abaissa les yeux vers lui. "J'ai dit que nous voilà chez nous." L'enfant ne répondit pas davantage. N'ayant jamais eu de chez lui, il ne pouvait pas en parler. (187)

To say that one has never *had* a place of his own is not as strong a message as to say that he has never even *seen* a home. The concept of "dwelling" is expressed in French as particularized and specific, signifying either place with "foyer" or ownership with the proposition "chez." It does not in either case suggest those intangible qualities of comfort and belonging that the word *home* conveys in English. The difference is important in this novel that emphasizes Joe's existential isolation, his utter rootlessness.

Coindreau also had to translate the word *home* in *As I Lay Dying*, and there he was even less successful. At the end of a monologue in which Darl tries to determine what he is, *if* he is, after the death of his mother, he says this:

> In a strange room you must empty yourself for sleep. And before you are emptied for sleep, what are you . . . I don't know what I am. I don't know if I am or not. . . . And Jewel *is*, so Addie Bundren must be. And then I must be, or I could not empty myself for sleep in a strange room. And so if I am not emptied yet, I am *is*.
> How often have I lain beneath rain on a strange room, thinking of home. (396)

Coindreau translates that last sentence as "Combien de fois ai-je dormi sous la pluie sur un toit étranger, pensant au foyer pa- ternel?" (81). There is a problem in his sentence with both vocabulary and context. Darl is obviously thinking of "home" as an essential connection with his mother, and thus as a state of being, certainly not as a "foyer paternel" presided over by the unfortunate and ineffectual Anse Bundren. Yet there really is no good way to reproduce the message of the original in French.

Beyond the unavoidable problems arising from differences in the vocabularies of French and English, however, there are discrepancies in the translations that could have been avoided by a more judicious choice of words or by a more sensitive under- standing of Faulkner's intentions. Since Faulkner is in one sense the most regional of novelists, his texts are full of specific re- gional terms and expressions that reflect Southern culture in an almost palpable way. American readers generally regard his descriptions as reflections of the "real" South, whereas, accord- ing to Michel Gresset and Patrick Samway, Europeans have usually regarded Yoknapatawpha as a more "mythic," more "ab- stract" place.[10] Perhaps for that reason, or perhaps because of their scant acquaintance with Southern culture (Coindreau, for example, apparently had not visited the South until the 1950s when he stayed for a time at the home of Flannery O'Conner in Georgia), the translators are often careless about reproducing cultural details exactly. Two examples will suffice to illustrate the problem.

In the final section of *The Sound and the Fury*, Faulkner describes Dilsey in the Compson kitchen making biscuit for breakfast. Since the word *biscuit* in French refers to a wafer-like cookie, just as it does in British usage, Coindreau did not bother to include an explanatory footnote, as he might have done; he simply changed "biscuit" to "pains de maïs" in his translation, evidently thinking that the use of "cornbreads" would make his translation seem appropriately Southern. It was a regrettable mistake. In the first place, anyone familiar with the culture would know that Southerners of the Compsons' station would not be likely to have cornbread for breakfast. Furthermore, "cornbread" is never used in the plural. One might speak of "corn cakes," or "corn muffins," but one would never say "cornbreads." Also, as Faulkner writes the scene, Dilsey is making not just ordinary biscuit, but beaten biscuit, a specialty of good Southern cooks from Charleston to New Orleans. He goes into detail about how she sifts flour onto the breadboard, and he describes the special mallet she uses to beat the dough. Coindreau changes none of those details in his translation; thus the section is hopelessly confused. It is also funny, for as anyone with even a rudimentary knowledge of cooking will realize, to make cornbread batter on a bread board and then beat it with a mallet would result in a considerable mess in the kitchen.

Turnip greens, another Southern dish, also caused a problem for the translator. In *As I Lay Dying* the Bundrens ask Peabody to stay for supper, even though the menu consists of bread, buttermilk, and turnip greens. Peabody complains that "plain turnip greens is mighty spindling eating for a man my size" (381). To translate the sentence, Coindreau uses the generic term for "green vegetables," "des légumes verts," instead of preserving the specific term as he certainly could have done. The French don't eat "les fanes de navets," but French readers would have understood the term since turnips are a staple item of the diet of farm folk in nearly all countries. Furthermore, use of the exact term would have made the meal seem more interesting and exotic to French readers.

The translator's use of the general term for "green vegetables" instead of a more specific one points toward his general tendency to give in to the intellectual, abstract quality of French already described rather than to mirror the rougher, coarse-textured language that Faulkner typically uses with great dramatic effect. A similar instance in *The Sound and the Fury* weakens the symbolism in that book. Throughout the novel, Faulkner refers frequently to Benjy's pasture that has been made into a golf course. Coindreau translates the word *pasture* first as "prairie" ("meadow") and later as "pré" ("mead"). In the original, however, Faulkner never uses a synonym for the word; he always writes "pasture," the most specific term available. The word is culturally exact. Rural Southerners would never use the word *meadow* to describe a field where animals are kept. The word is thematically important. The land now a golf course *was* formerly a cow pasture, Benjy's inheritance sold so Quentin might go to college, and Benjy always thinks of the grassy land as "the pasture," even when he is watching some golfers "hitting."

In addition to its contextual appropriateness, the word *pasture* is important to an understanding of two aspects of the novel, one social and the other symbolic. The fact that the pasture has become a golf course dramatizes the fact that the rural, agricultural South is rapidly changing. The very word *pasture*, derived from Latin through Old French into Middle English, recalls an agricultural tradition common to both cultures, and its French equivalent, "le pâturage," is thus a richly connotative word, meaning both the field where animals are kept and the food they eat. Furthermore, since the word is used in the pastoral imagery of the Psalms, it has acquired a symbolic dimension: "He maketh me to lie down in green pastures" (Psalm 23:2). All those resonances are appropriate to the role of Benjy who is animalistic in actions and appearance, and who becomes the scapegoat of his family practically in the tradition of ancient Hebrew ritual. Although his brothers and sister commit sexual sins, he is the one who is castrated. However, Dilsey sees him as "de Lawd's child," as a lamb. To preserve all of those levels of meaning and symbolism, Coindreau should have chosen "le pâturage" the first time he translated the word *pasture* instead of the more elegant "prairie," and he should have used "pâturage" consistently throughout the rest of the novel.

The Biblical allusion inherent in Faulkner's use of the word *pasture* is typical of how elements of the Christian gospel are woven into his texts and are part of the lives and consciousness of his fictional characters. Religion is always taken quite seriously, even by those who rebel against it. Even the vivid, rolling oratory of the Reverend Shegog has a genuine effect on the

members of his congregation. Faulkner's presentation of this
sermon and of another black preacher's sermon at the end of
Soldiers' Pay may have a humorous edge, but it still acknowledges with respect the powerful communication that takes place.
Furthermore, for all his elaborate style of delivery, the Reverend
Shegog's message is quite orthodox. Coindreau seems to have
missed that point, for his translation makes the preacher's sermon seem mostly a fanciful, garbled parody of "real" preaching.
For instance, at one point the preacher tells his flock that there
will come a time when Jesus will confront each sinner to ask, "O
bredden? O sistuhn? Is you got de ricklickshun en de blood of de
Lamb?" (311). Now, earlier in the novel Coindreau has correctly
translated the verb *ricklick* as "remember": Luster's remark to a
stranger, "I don't ricklick seeing you around here before" (68)
became "Je m'rapelle pas vous avoir vu par ici" (69). But in
translating the sermon, Coindreau casts the preacher's question
as "Avez-vous recueilli le sang de l'Agneau?" (344). The word
recueillir means "to gather," "to collect," not "to remember," as
"ricklick" signifies. The preacher is evoking the mystery of the
eucharist in which the sinner receives forgiveness by partaking
of the body and blood of Christ "in remembrance" of his sacrificial death. "Souvenez-vous . . ." the ritual begins in French.
Therefore, Coindreau should have translated the sentence "Vous
souvenez-vous . . ." to indicate a genuine relationship to a more
formal ecclesiastical language and to give proper weight to the
Reverend Shegog's words.

A more complex problem with vocabulary can be found in the
Quentin section of *The Sound and the Fury* in a poignant passage
dramatizing the young man's troubled thoughts the night before
he commits suicide. Unable to sleep, Quentin goes to the dor-
mitory bathroom to get a glass of water. That ordinary action
takes on high symbolism for the young man who longs for
cleansing, life-giving water but who is soon to die by drowning.
In his musings there are references to Moses who found water by
striking a rock in the desert. Then there is this sentence, related
to Quentin's anguish over his mother's lack of understanding, his

father's cynicism, and his own spiritual crisis: "She couldn't see that Father was teaching us that all men are just accumulations dolls stuffed with sawdust swept up from the trash heaps where all previous dolls had been thrown away the sawdust flowing from that wound in what side that not for me died not" (194). So powerful is this entire section that English-speaking readers usually respond to Quentin's stream-of-consciousness associations by entering themselves into an emotional, impressionistic involvement with the text, adding their own associations, so that the communication reaches into the depths of memory and experience. Reading the short passage cited, for example, evokes images of T. S. Eliot's hollow men, their "headpieces filled with straw," as well as echoes of an old Protestant hymn, "Rock of Ages," with its plea that "the water and the blood" which flowed from Christ's side might purify the repentant sinner.[11] Clearly it would not be possible for any translator to preserve the more oblique allusions in the passage, but the obvious reference to Christ in the phrase "what wound in what side" could certainly have been retained with proper word choice. Although the word used to describe Christ's pierced side in both Catholic and Protestant translations of the Bible in French is "le côté," Coindreau chose the word "flancs," ("flanks"), and he made it plural, thus obliterating the intended allusion.

Another important aspect of this short passage that disappears in translation is Faulkner's curious use of the double negative in the last clause—"that not for me died not." In the original, the indecisive ambiguity of the syntax mirrors the anguish in Quentin's soul. His thoughts can be unraveled into three separate parts: Christ died. He did not die for me. He did not die. The garbling of those ideas, however, represents Quentin's profound despair over what he perceives as his moral failure and over his inability to find the "living water" which Christ represents. In discussing Faulkner's use of unusual negative expressions in other texts, André Bleikasten has explained how the kind of redoubled negation used here tends to preserve the very idea that is ostensibly being denied, thereby succeeding in reinforcing it.[12] Coindreau's use of standard negation—"qui n'avaient pas souffert la mort pour moi"—greatly dilutes the powerful, complex message of the original. Even though the purists among French rhetoricians might have shuddered, he could have written of the wound "dans le côté qui non pas pour moi n'avait pas souffert la mort."

When Faulkner's language is not enriched by allusion or made more vivid by innovative syntactical patterns, it is often intensified through accumulation and repetition. In *Light in August* Faulkner uses the latter method to develop one of the major themes of that novel, quietness. He dramatizes the quality of quietness as it is manifest in the natural world, in people, in time. Quietness is an inherent characteristic of Lena Grove; she moves in slow, patient rhythms, certain that people will be kind, sure that she will find a father for her child before its birth, almost as an embodiment of that Old Testament promise, "In quietness and in confidence shall be your strength" (Isaiah 30:15).

Faulkner describes the various sensory aspects of quietness, but he also uses repetition of the adjective *quiet* in a series of phrases and passages to elevate the temporal condition of "quietness" to a metaphysical state of being that encompasses both primal innocence and restored peace. He uses the strong, simple word *quiet* over and over until it somehow opens up to shimmer with transcendent meaning.

Quietness is what the ill-fated Joe Christmas seeks down all the long corridors and endless streets of his restless life, and it is what the disillusioned Reverend Hightower longs for but does not know how to attain. Joe Christmas knew quietness once. As a five-year-old living in an orphanage, he found solace and solitude in a deserted corridor in a time of stillness, a time of innocence before his theft of the dietitian's pink toothpaste set in motion an inexorable chain of events that culminated in his execution. Describing that early time, Faulkner uses the word *quiet* three times in one sentence, melding time, place, and mood into a single experience, dramatizing the moment's intensity, and inviting the reader to participate in an exploration of it:

> In the quiet empty corridor, during the quiet hour of early afternoon, he was like a shadow, small even for five years, sober and quiet as a shadow. (111)

In translating the passage, Coindreau follows those standards of French style that encourage "elegant variation." He explores the "quiet" *for* his readers by using a series of synonyms. Consequently, the passage in French becomes a discussion of the various aspects of calmness and tranquility rather than a dramatization of an essential state encompassing all of experience:

> Dans le corridor tranquille et vide, à l'heure calme du début de l'après-midi, il avait l'air d'une ombre, petit même pour ses cinq ans, discret et silencieux comme une ombre. (157–58)

While the general mood of the original is maintained, the intensified unity that created the effect of a timeless moment is broken up. It was in that unity alone that the child was isolated and protected from all the harsh voices and loud clamoring that were to pursue him for the rest of his life. Joe searched always to regain that state of quietness which he lost:

> He thought that it was loneliness which he was trying to escape and not himself. But the street ran on: catlike, one place was the same as another to him. But in none of them could he be quiet. (213)

In French, the last sentence of the above passage reads, "Mais nulle part il ne trouvait la paix" (286). The meaning has been distorted. Faulkner wrote of Joe's need to *be* quiet; he was again explaining quietness as a state of being, not as an external situation that one might "find."

Although Joe never finds quietness, Lena's baby, also named Joe, is born "in peace and quiet" (394), thanks to the support of Byron Bunch, who epitomizes kindness just as Lena embodies quietness. In describing the birth, Coindreau writes that Byron Bunch "a veillé à ce que le bâtard du type naisse en paix et

tranquillement, et à ses frais" (519). Substitution of the adverb
"tranquillement" for the prepositional phrase "in quiet" makes
the sentence indicate the nature of the actual birth rather than
the existential state in which the child is born. The matter
obviously had symbolic importance for Faulkner, however, because as the child Joey is born "in quiet," Joe Christmas dies in a
moment of terrible, unbearable noise: "Again from the town,
deadened a little by the walls, the scream of the siren mounted
toward its unbelievable crescendo, passing out of the realm of
hearing" (440).

Although there is no adjective in French that means both
"calm" and "silent" as "quiet" does in English, "tranquille" is a
close equivalent.[13] Furthermore, unlike many French words,
"tranquille" converts smoothly into noun and adverb forms.
Coindreau could have used the adjective in all three phrases
describing Joe in the orphanage corridor, and he could have said
that Lena's baby was born "en tranquilité." His fragmentation of
Faulkner's original word through the use of synonyms prevents
clear understanding of its metamorphosis from the sign of a
particular quality to the symbol of a universal state of being.

Even as Faulkner uses single words and the order of words in a
sentence to indicate various levels of meaning, he also explores
the connotations of the word *word* itself. The very existence of
the term raises the whole epistemological question of the relationship between idea and thing, symbol and referent, that has
become one of the major concerns of modern literature. But in
Faulkner's work, questioning of the validity of words *per se* is
done in full awareness of the Christian tradition that interprets
"word" as the *logos* by which all things were "spoken" into
existence and as the Word that became flesh, according to the
Gospel of John: "In the beginning was the Word, and the Word
was with God, and the Word was God" (John 1:1). The semantic
question, then, is posed at a metaphysical level. Faulkner makes
full use of all the connotations that *word* has acquired. In *Light
in August* he uses it as an allusion in a cleverly organized scene
showing that he does not consider the harsh religious attitudes of

McEachern as representative of true Christianity. McEachern
has tried to make Joe Christmas learn the Presbyterian cate-
chism, but Joe stubbornly refuses even to open the book. Intend-
ing to beat Joe until he obeys, McEachern takes him to the
barn, but Joe still will not open the book. He puts it on the floor:

> The boy laid the book on the floor. "Not there," McEachern said,
> without heat. "You would believe that a stable floor, the stamping
> place of beasts, is the proper place for the word of God. But I'll learn
> you that, too." (140)

McEachern's statement is marvelously ironic, of course, since
when the "Word became flesh," it was indeed in a stable. There
is no problem in translating the passage into French almost
literally. Coindreau uses "la parole de Dieu" for "the Word of
God," but one cannot be sure that the allusion is as strong in
French as it is in English since the *logos* in John I is not always
translated as "la parole" in French Bibles; sometimes it is "le
verbe."[14]

The problem of words and the Word comes up again in *As I
Lay Dying*. Addie does not have much use for words in general:
"I would think how words go straight up in a thin line, quick and
harmless, and how terribly doing goes along the earth, clinging
to it, so that after a while the two lines are too far apart for the
same person to straddle from one to the other" (465).

The words she talks about here are the ones spoken by human
beings trying without success to *name* essential experiences like
love and fear. Later, however, Addie talks about hearing the
"voiceless speech" of the dark land "talking of God's love and His
beauty and His sin" (466). She then says she has thought of the
sin she and the Reverend Whitfield committed as "garments
which we would remove in order to shape and coerce the terrible
blood to the forlorn echo of the dead word high in the air" (466).
It is important to notice that Faulkner has used "word" in the
singular here; the last phrase invites multiple interpretations.
Addie has already talked of the word *love* as being "just a shape
to fill a lack" (464); she also has obviously seen a great gap open

between human words and human experience. She has realized, too, a void lying between the promise of transcendent love and any manifestation of it. (The Reverend Whitfield, "ordained by God . . . to sanctify that sin He had created," has committed adultery with her instead of revealing God's love to her). Her description of "the dead word high in the air," then, must be understood in the light of all those experiences.

For a reason not quite clear, perhaps by analogy to an earlier passage about human speech where he used the French word *mots* appropriately, Coindreau translates the last phrase of the passage cited as "l'écho des mots sans vie, perdus là-haut dans les airs" (168). Once again, the term he has used is too literal, too flatly specific—"mot" instead of "parole" or "verbe." Also, he has made it plural, thereby eliminating any possible evocation of the Word, an allusion implied in the original.

Moreover, the translator's description of "mots sans vie" does not imply that the "words" were ever alive, whereas the phrase "the dead word" clearly shows Addie's perception that something once living is now dead. Coindreau also adds the participle "perdus" ("lost") so that in French it seems as if words spoken by people simply became lost in the air. But Faulkner's text points to a broader meaning. With all the discussion of sin and beauty and God's love as well as of human language that precedes this passage, he has expanded the context in which Addie's remarks can be understood. "The dead word high in the air" can be interpreted as the meaningless human language that cannot say "love," or as the incomprehensible *logos* now far removed from the world it supposedly created, or as the dead Christ now "high in the air" whom the Bible has described as love incarnate. In the French translation, only one of those interpretations, the least suggestive one, is possible because of Coindreau's limiting language. He could have retained the allusions inherent in the original sentence by translating "the dead word high in the air" as "la parole morte, en haut dans les airs."

To analyze the skill and subtlety with which Faulkner uses highly connotative language, implicative word orders, and evocative allusion to develop his themes is to understand his "mythic thinking" as it has been so well explained by Florence Leaver in "Faulkner: The Word as Principle and Power." In that essay she illustrates, as this paper has also attempted to do, just how the author's use of words bearing powerful associations in evocative patterns makes language "transcend itself by hypersuggestion."[15] While one can appreciate the difficulties that interpreting such language poses for any translator, one can also see that more careful or more insightful translations could more faithfully reflect the power of Faulkner's work. The present French translations do not reflect the culture of the South as accurately or as vividly as Faulkner described it, and they do not have as compelling a mythic dimension as do the original texts. Furthermore, in the French, allusion usually remains at an intellectual, rational level so that French readers would not always experience the same kind of communication through the unexpressed, the implied, that draws an English-speaking reader into an impressionistic involvement with the novels.

NOTES

1. Maurice-Edgar Coindreau, *The Time of William Faulkner*, ed. and trans. George McMillan Reeves (Columbia: University Press of South Carolina, 1971), 64.

2. Roger Asselineau, "The French Face of William Faulkner," *Tulane Studies in English*, 23 (1978), 163.

3. Ibid., 172–73.

4. Coindreau, *The Time of William Faulkner*, 27.

5. Ibid., 11.

6. Michel Gresset, "From Vignette to Vision," in *Faulkner: International Perspectives*, ed. Doreen Fowler and Ann J. Abadie (Jackson: University Press of Mississippi, 1984), 100.

7. Julien Green, *Le Langage et son double* (Paris: Editions de la Différence, 1985), 209–10.

8. René-Noël Raimbault, *Faulkner* (Paris: Editions Universitaires, 1963), 81, 91.

9. Faulkner works cited parenthetically in the text are from Random House editions of *Light in August* (1959) and *The Sound and the Fury and As I Lay Dying* (1946) and from Gallimard editions translated by Coindreau: *Le Bruit et la fureur* (1938), *Lumière d'août* (1935), and *Tandis que j'agonise* (1934).

10. Michel Gresset and Patrick Samway, eds., *Faulkner and Idealism: Perspectives from Paris* (Jackson: University Press of Mississippi, 1983), 6.

11. Rock of Ages, cleft for me, let me hide myself in thee;
   Let the water and the blood from thy wounded side which flowed,
   Be of sin the double cure, save from wrath and make me pure.
                                                    (*The Book of Hymns* 120)

12. André Bleikasten, "*As I Lay Dying*," in *William Faulkner*, ed. Michel Gresset (Paris: Librairie Armand Colin, 1970), 382.

13. In Old French there was an adjective *quiete* like the one now used in English; it, too, was derived from the Latin past participle *quietus*, but in modern French, the root is retained only in the noun *quiétude*, in the negative adjective *inquiète*, and in the verb *inquiéter*.

14. A translation of the Bible directed by A. Em. Le Cardinal Lienart for La Bible pour Tous in Paris, 1956, uses "le verbe" in John 1:1. A translation published in 1980 by the Association Biblique Internationale uses "la parole."

15. Florence Leaver, "Faulkner: The Word as Principle and Power," in *William Faulkner: Three Decades of Criticism*, ed. Frederick J. Hoffman and Olga W. Vickery (East Lansing: Michigan State University Press, 1960), 201.

Appendix

Program
First Day of Issue
William Faulkner Stamp
Oxford, Mississippi
August 3, 1987

Presiding   James L. Hammons
                        Postmaster
                        Oxford

Good morning. Distinguished guests, ladies and gentle-
ment—welcome to the first day of issue ceremony for the 22-
cent William Faulkner stamp.

Presentation of Colors   University of Mississippi
                             Air Force ROTC Color Guard

National Anthem   Nancy Carsten, Soloist
                             Jerri Lamar Bradley, Accompanist
                             University of Mississippi

Invocation   Reverand Duncan M. Gray
                            St. Peter's Episcopal Church
                            Oxford

Almighty God, whom saints and angels delight to worship in
heaven. You have been present with your servants who seek
through art and literature to perfect the praises offered by your
people on earth. You have given them glimpses of your beauty
and splendor, and they have been the often unknowing bearers
of your grace.

We give you thanks this day for your servant, William; for his
gift of insight that saw into our hearts and souls and for his
courage to write of what he found. We give you thanks for his

211

prophetic witness and for the hope that he affirmed in the midst of human tragedy.

May the stamps that we here dedicate be witness of the achievements of this magnificent artist who through the common and ordinary gave us a glimpse into the eternal nature of the human spirit.

Amen.

Hammons   Thank you, Reverend Gray, the Misses Carsten and Bradley, and the Color Guard.

On behalf of the United States Postal Service, I wish to express my appreciation to all of you for attending the ceremony this morning. All of Oxford and Mississippi are proud and pleased that a native son is being honored for his abundant contributions to literature. And, the Postal Service is particularly pleased to be able to share this occasion with attendees at the Faulkner and Yoknapatawpha Conference here at the University.

At this time I am pleased to introduce the Honorable John O. Leslie, Mayor of the City of Oxford.

John Leslie   The consensus of American scholarship is that Mr. Bill was a better writer than he was a postmaster. Although he relinquished the postmastership, he never surrendered this deep emotional fidelity to the place, to its old immemorial human heart in conflict with itself.

It is an honor to welcome you to Oxford. We are celebrating our sesquicentennial. Faulkner's words chronicled the town from what it was—to what it has become. My own fictional predecessors as mayor include the De Spains, the Compsons, the Sartorises, and the Stevenses. Every inch of earth here resonates with Faulkner's presence.

I believe he would be proud of the strides his town has made since his death a quarter of a century ago—the integrated public schools, the absence of slums, the recreational complex, the new city hall, the public swimming pool, the completely renovated county courthouse—not to mention legal sales of beer, wine, and spirits!

In his forthcoming article on William Faulkner in *National Geographic* Willie Morris writes: "The courthouse chimes rever-

berate through the town—pervading his landmarks and his people with an almost palpable transcience; they suffuse me with
the bravery and timeless majesty of his genius."

On behalf of the citizens of Oxford, which some call Jefferson,
I wish you a most pleasant and fruitful visit.

Hammons   Thank you, Mayor Leslie.

It is now my pleasure to introduce Dr. R. Gerald Turner,
Chancellor of the University of Mississippi, who will introduce
some of the distinguished guests who are with us today.

Chancellor Turner   The heritage of the Faulkner family is a
treasure that is enjoyed by the Oxford and University community, Mississippi, and scholars of literature around the world.

We are especially honored to have with us today the daughter
of William Faulkner, Jill Faulkner Summers, of Charlottesville,
Virginia. Mrs. Summers, would you please stand and allow those
present to show their appreciation of your being with us today?

We are pleased to have two nephews of Mr. Faulkner with us
today also. At this time I would like to recognize Chooky
Faulkner and Jimmy Faulkner.

Although time will not permit individual introductions, I
would like to ask that all other Faulkner relatives please stand
and be recognized.

The presence of members of the Board of Trustees of Institutions of Higher Learning always adds distinction to any activity
on our campus. We are honored today to have two members of
the Board of Trustees with us: Oxford's own Will Hickman and
Ms. Diane Miller of Gulfport. Mr. Hickman and Ms. Miller, will
you please stand.

There is a large group of honored guests that I would like to
introduce at this time. They have come here from all over the
United States and around the world, and they do *us* honor by
attending and contributing to the Faulkner and Yoknapatawpha
Conference. Would all conference attendees please stand and be
recognized?

Many scholars have devoted themselves to studying and ana-
lyzing the complex, brilliant work of William Faulkner. We have
with us today two gentlemen whose critical and literary exploration of Faulkner's fiction is known and respected the world over.

Please greet Dr. Cleanth Brooks of Yale University and Dr. Evans Harrington of the University of Mississippi.

The next person I am to introduce has a variety of vested interests in today's event. Born in Enid County to a pioneer family there, he is a devoted admirer of William Faulkner and, indeed, studied under Dr. Cleanth Brooks at Yale. For the past twenty years he has been curator of sculpture and decorative arts at the National Gallery of Arts in Washington—but more to the point, he is the vice chairman and nine-year member of the Citizens' Stamp Advisory Committee, which recommended William Faulkner as a stamp subject and approved the final design. Ladies and gentlemen, Dr. Douglas Lewis.

For many years, the study of William Faulkner's work, the collection of Faulkner materials, and indeed the Faulkner and Yoknapatawpha Conference itself, received tremendous encouragement and support from the gentleman I am about to introduce. Ladies and gentlemen, the Chancellor *Emeritus* of the University of Mississippi, Dr. Porter L. Fortune, Jr.

In a state with such rich tradition, historical preservation is highly important. But the task of restoring and maintaining a landmark often requires great determination and inspiration. With that in mind, I would like to recognize Mrs. Lynn Crosby Gammill, whose mother, Mrs. Dorothy Crosby, has played a leading role in the development of Rowan Oak and the preservation of the home as a national historic landmark.

We know who painted the portrait that was the basis for the William Faulkner stamp design. But the man whose photograph served as the artist's guide for the aforementioned portrait is with us today. Please greet Oxford's own Jack Cofield.

We are also indebted to Mr. Guy Turnbow, Jr., who graciously allowed the University to reproduce a unique drawing entitled *Post Office Blues* as the cachet for first-day covers and as the illustrations for postcards to support Faulkner programs on campus. Please recognize Mr. Turnbow.

Dr. Ed Meek served with Postmaster Hammons as cochairman of the Faulkner Stamp Committee and performed a myriad of related services as director of Public Relations for the University. Dr. Meek, will you please stand?

Also with us today is Mr. R. Dean Buchanan, who is General

Manager/Postmaster of the Memphis Division of the U.S. Postal Service. His Division's responsibilities include the Oxford area. Mr. Buchanan.

The Postal Service's only regret is that it could not use *two* post offices for its first-day concellations of the Faulkner stamp, for the University Post Office has key ties to Mr. Faulkner. But we are happy to have with us and to recognize the University Postmaster, Mr. Vernon Maples. Postmaster Maples.

Thank you.

Hammons Thank you very much, Chancellor Turner.

When we commemorate the achievements of such an outstanding author as William Faulkner, I think it is most appropriate and beneficial to recall his contributions to literature and to our lives. Our next speaker does us considerable honor by being here today to give us a personal view of Faulkner, the man and his career. I might note that her own career is not dissimilar from Faulkner's in terms of her subject matter and her following.

For Eudora Welty has achieved great critical and popular acclaim by focusing with precision on the regional manners of people living in a small town similar to her birthplace. The accuracy of her portrayals of local speech, the subtlety of her plot developments, and the extraordinary occurrences that her characters encounter brought Miss Welty well-deserved attention from the beginning of her career.

A Curtain of Green, a collection of short stories published in 1941, earned her major national attention, and she followed with such fine efforts as *Delta Wedding* in 1946, *The Ponder Heart* in 1954, *The Bride of the Innisfallen* in 1955, and *Losing Battles* in 1970. In 1973 she won a Pulitzer Prize for *The Optimist's Daughter*. She was awarded the Presidential Medal of Freedom in 1979, the National Medal for Literature in 1980, and the National Medal of Arts in 1986.

Ladies and gentlemen, from Jackson, a Mississippi and national treasure, Miss Eudora Welty.

Eudora Welty I'm thrilled with being counted part of this group today and thrilled with having lived in the same time as our great man we're honoring today.

Let us imagine that here and now we're all in the old University Post Office and living in the twenties. We've come up to the stamp window to buy a 2-cent stamp, but we see nobody there. We knock and then we pound, and we pound again and there's not a sound back there. So we holler his name, and at last here he is. William Faulkner. We have interrupted him. Postmaster Faulkner's treatment of the mail could be described as offhand, with a strong local tradition and some soul who still can personally remember that during post office hours when he should have been putting up the mail and selling stamps at the window up front, he was out of sight in the back—writing lyric poems. He was a postmaster who made it hard for you in general to buy a stamp and send a letter or to get your hands on any of that mail that might have come for you. Faulkner the Postmaster called it quits here in 1924. Faulkner the Poet was able to move on with his pen into his vast prose world of Yoknapatawpha County.

So here we are today, and it might have tickled the future great master of comedy if he could know that the real tale of his post office career came to its close not in 1924 but today. Sixty-three years later the tale ends with a postage stamp. The occasion is the issue of a stamp named in his honor with his portrait on it. It's as if the United States Postal Service had forgiven him for the mail he had lost in the trash barrel in light of his proven deserts in other fields, beginning with what he was doing there in the back room.

Once portraits of our presidents of the United States seemed obligatory to make postage stamps the real authentic thing. It took George Washington or Thomas Jefferson in the upper right-hand corner of your letter to make the letter go. But a more imaginative tradition has happily grown up in the designing of our postage stamps today. William Faulkner will be in good literary company—T. S. Eliot, Emily Dickinson, Nathaniel Hawthorne, Herman Melville, Willa Cather, Edith Wharton.

Of course here in Oxford and at the Faulkner Conference going on at the University, we keep hearing people asking one another "What would *Faulkner* have thought of the Faulkner stamp?" If the man himself were here, and available for questioning, he would be asked the inevitable question of our times: "Mr. Faulkner, sir, how do you *feel* about having a stamp named in your honor?"

Well, who knows what the great man might have said? He might have suggested that the portrait painted by his mother might have possibly improved it. He might simply have observed that stamps have gone up since he had anything to do with the postal system from 2 cents to 22. Again, he might have just gone on puffing at his pipe, meditating, as we see him on the stamp. My only guess today is that William Faulkner would have accepted his stamp because he knew what an honor was.

For all of us—scholars, teachers, writers, and collectors brought here today for the value of the rarity of the stamp itself—it's unavoidable that we should be reminded of a key statement Faulkner once came to write: "I discovered my own little postage stamp of native soil was worth writing about and that I would never live long enough to exhaust it and that by sublimating the actual into the apocryphal, I would have complete liberty to use whatever talent I might have to its absolute top." As we celebrate the first day of the issue of the William Faulkner stamp, we do so in this awareness that this writer remains himself a bringer of the written word, that he is himself that rare thing—the rarest—a genius. He exists, as he always did, in the world at large for anyone to whom the written word travels. The stamp can stand for that, too. It serves as a symbol of communication.

Thank you very much.

Hammons   Thank you, Miss Welty.

Now I am honored to introduce our next speaker. Harry C. Penttala is the Regional Postmaster General for the Postal Service's eleven-state Southern Region, which includes Mississippi and Oxford. Prior to his appointment in March 1985, he served more than four years as Assistant Postmaster General, Mail Processing Department, at our headquarters in Washington, D.C.

Mr. Penttala began his career as a letter carrier in 1958 in Girard, Ohio, and it did not take him long to rise in the ranks. Along the way, he earned a number of honors which pay tribute to his concern for people and for his employees.

While in the Central Region, he received the Handicapped Employer of the Year Award in 1979, the Distinguished Service

Award in the Hispanic Community, also in 1979, and the Outstanding Contribution Award of the Management Sectional Center Women's Committee in 1980. In 1983 he was the recipient of the Defense Department's Outstanding Civilian Service Awrd for his initiative in improving military mail service in the European and Pacific theaters.

Ladies and gentlemen, Regional Postmaster General Harry C. Penttala.

Harry C. Penttala Chancellor Turner, Mayor Leslie, distinguished guests, members of the Faulkner family, ladies and gentlemen.

I am honored to share with you the dedication of this beautiful stamp commemorating William Faulkner. While I am a Southerner only by residence, and only for two years, I confess it did not take me long to start name-dropping when I spoke to colleagues and friends in other parts of the country. All it would take would be mention of Mississippi or Memphis—and sometimes not even that—for me to say, "yeah, I'm only about 60 miles from where William Faulkner lived and wrote. It's a really interesting area."

I'm still not entirely sure what possesses me on those occasions, although I imagine that many of you can relate to that urge. But I can tell you that I have never lived anywhere that an individual in any field has had such an impact on people and continues to maintain such a presence as does William Faulkner.

It has been twenty-four years since his death and twenty-five years since his last novel was published. And yet the power of his work, and his depiction of a region and a people and the experiences that molded them have solidified the man in the consciences of several generations of readers both here and abroad.

It would be easy to classify Faulkner as a regional writer, and some have. Certainly, a region has proudly claimed him as its own for some sixty years. But while the settings for his stories were largely Southern, his truths were universal. The thoughts and ideas he expressed deeply affected readers in Meridian, Moscow, and Munich, in Pascagoula and Paris, in Tupelo and Tokyo.

What other authors, aside from a Shakespeare or a Tolstoy, attract the attention of so many dedicated scholars as does

William Faulkner? The attendance here today and this week of hundreds of experts and enthusiasts from all over the world for the annual Faulkner and Yoknapatawpha Conference is ample proof of his craft and his staying power.

Perhaps one of the most significant signs that William Faulkner is a standard unto himself lies in reading what literary critics and literary historians have to say about him. Almost always, when they characterize an outstanding writer, they will qualify their praise: "*among* the finest," "one of the best *living* authors," in the top ranks of *nineteenth-century* writers." Among numerous appraisals of William Faulkner, the most lukewarm to be found was "he is one of the most important literary figures of the twentieth century." Several others in so many words said simply, "he is generally considered to be the finest American writer to date."

In short, William Faulkner is in very select company. In some ways, to some observers, he *is* the company, by himself. But I would like to tell you about some of the company he is joining when it comes to stamps issued by the Postal Service. In the last forty-seven years we have issued many stamps commemorating writers of all types. In fact, William Faulkner is the forty-first person to be so honored.

We began in 1940 with a Famous Americans Series of stamps that had seven categories, such as Scientists, Educators, Artists, etc. And Authors and Poets.

The authors were indeed an illustrious group. They included Washington Irving, James Fenimore Cooper, Ralph Waldo Emerson, Louisa May Alcott, and one Samuel L. Clemens, known to the world as Mark Twain.

The poets in that Famous American Series of 1940 were of equal stature. They were Henry Wadsworth Longfellow, James Greenleaf Whittier, James Russell Lowell, Walt Whitman, and James Whitcomb Riley.

From that time on, the list of literary individuals who have appeared on stamps includes such masters of the written word as Edgar Allen Poe, Henry David Thoreau, Robert Frost. Emily Dickinson, Edna St. Vincent Millay, Paul Laurence Dunbar, Carl Sandburg, Ernie Pyle, Carter Woodson, Willa Cather, Jack London, Pearl Buck, and many more.

That partial list sounds like it came from a veritable Who's

Who of American Literature, doesn't it? Well, I'm not through yet. The William Faulkner stamp is the sixth to be issued in our Literary Arts Series. He joins such luminaries as Nathaniel Hawthorne, Herman Melville, Edith Wharton, John Steinbeck, and T. S. Eliot.

Those forty-odd stamps, and the persons they commemorate, form an awesome collection. It literally is mind-boggling to consider their total contribution to the richness of our culture and thought.

But even if I were tempted to praise William Faulkner further, I would hesitate to say that he—or any one of those other brilliant individuals—contributed the most. At the same time, I think it is fair to declare that no other literary figure has enriched our lives more than William Faulkner.

With that in mind, I think it is highly appropriate and thoroughly fitting that we issue the William Faulkner stamp here today.

The man and his work belong, not just to his neighbors and his native state and region, but to all Americans everywhere. And beginning tomorrow, approximately 130 million images of this modest genius will be available in post offices across the nation.

That might—just *might*—be enough to provide one stamp for each life he has touched with his work.

Thank you.

Contributors

Beth Dyer Biron studied comparative literature and romance languages at Emory University, where she earned an M.A. degree, and at the University of Georgia, where she earned B.A. and Ph.D. degrees. Her doctoral dissertation was entitled "Faulkner in French: A Study of the Translations of His Major Novels and Their Influence in French Literature." She teaches English, French, and Spanish at Dalton College and has served on advisory committees on foreign languages and on fine and applied arts for the University of Georgia System.

Cleanth Brooks is coauthor with Robert Penn Warren of the epoch-making *Understanding Poetry* and its successors *Understanding Fiction* and *Modern Rhetoric*. He is the author of other celebrated works, including *Modern Poetry and the Tradition, The Well-Wrought Urn, William Faulkner: The Yoknapatawpha Country,* and *William Faulkner: Toward Yoknapatawpha and Beyond.* A founding editor of *The Southern Review* at Louisiana State University, he has taught and lectured at colleges and universities in America and abroad.

Robert W. Hamblin earned M.A. and Ph.D. degrees from the University of Mississippi and is now Professor of English at Southeast Missouri State University. In addition to writing his master's thesis and doctoral dissertation on William Faulkner and publishing Faulkner articles in various books and journals, he is coeditor of *Faulkner: A Comprehensive Guide to the Brodsky Collection,* a multivolume work being published by the University Press of Mississippi. He has directed three National Endowment for the Humanities Summer Seminars for Secondary School Teachers on "William Faulkner: The Regional and the Mythic."

221

Donald M. Kartiganer was educated at Brown University and teaches at the University of Washington, Seattle. He has held Fulbright lectureships in Yugoslavia and Poland, and was a visiting professor at Tel-Aviv University in the spring of 1988. He is the author of *The Fragile Thread: The Meaning of Form in Faulkner's Novels* and is coeditor of *Theories of American Literature*. Professor Kartiganer has in progress a book on *As I Lay Dying* and another on the use of repetition in the works of Wordsworth, Kierkegaard, Freud, Conrad, Kafka, Mann, Faulkner, and Hawkes.

Chris LaLonde completed an undergraduate degree at Cornell College and then studied at the State University of New York at Buffalo. While earning M.A. and Ph.D. degrees, he won a Graduate Student Excellence in Teaching Award; was editorial assistant to Bruce Jackson, editor of *Teaching Folklore;* presented papers at National Popular Culture Conventions; and wrote a dissertation on "Faulkner's Frontier: Rites of Passage in Five Novels." Now on the English faculty of North Carolina Wesleyan College, he participated in the National Endowment for the Humanities Summer Seminar for College Teachers held at the University of California, Irvine, in 1986 and has published an essay on Faulkner's *Mosquitoes* in *The Faulkner Journal*.

John T. Matthews studied at the University of Pennsylvania and Johns Hopkins. He is an associate professor of English at Boston University and coeditor of *The Faulkner Journal*. Among his works on Faulkner are *The Play of Faulkner's Language;* "Intertextuality and Originality: Hawthorne, Faulkner, and Updike," in *Intertextuality in Faulkner;* and "The Elliptical Nature of *Sanctuary*," in *Novel*.

William E. H. Meyer, Jr., was educated at Concordia Teachers College, the University of Arkansas, and the University of Chicago. He has taught at the University of Houston and Houston Community College. He now lives in Beaumont, Texas, where he writes and does art work full time. His essays have appeared in *Western Humanities Review, Arizona Quarterly, Ball State University Forum, The Thomas Wolfe Review,* and many other journals. His poetry has been published in nearly fifty journals, including *The Chicago Review, Modern Poetry Studies, Amherst Review,* and Berkley Poetry Review.

Richard C. Moreland earned a B.A. degree *cum laude* from Harvard University, an M.A. from Louisiana State University, and a Ph.D. degree from the University of California, Berkeley. He is the author of *Faulkner's Modernism under Revision,* essays in *The Southern Review* and *The Faulkner Journal,* and a number of book reviews. Professor Moreland now teaches at Louisiana State University.

Judith L. Sensibar, an associate professor at Arizona State University, earned a B.A. degree at Vassar College and M.A. and Ph.D. degrees at the University of Chicago. Her many publications on Faulkner include essays in *Mississippi Quarterly, William Faulkner: Modern Critical Views,* and *Psychoanalytic Studies of Biography;* an introduction to *Vision in Spring,* which she edited; *The Origins of Faulkner's Art;* and *Faulkner's Poetry: A Bibliographical Guide to Texts and Criticism.* Among her works in progress are a critical biography of Faulkner and a complete edition of his published and unpublished poems.

Philip M. Weinstein was educated at Princeton University, the Sorbonne, and Harvard University, where he taught for three years after receiving his Ph.D. in 1968. He has been a member of the faculty at Swarthmore College since 1971 and served as Chairman of English Literature from 1980 until 1985. In the fall of 1987 he was Visiting Distinguished Professor at Rhodes College in Memphis. His publications include *Henry James and the Requirements of the Imagination, The Semantics of Desire: Changing Modes of Identity,* and numerous essays on Faulkner and other authors. Professor Weinstein has received two NEH grants and, most recently, an ACLS fellowship in order to complete a book-length study of Faulkner.

Index